The Straits of Messina

Major Steinhoff (*left*) and his aide, at the time of the battle for the Straits of Messina

Johannes Steinhoff

THE STRAITS
OF MESSINA

Diary of a Fighter Commander

Translated by Peter and Betty Ross
With a foreword by Peter Townsend

 ANDRE DEUTSCH

First published 1971 by
André Deutsch Limited
105 Great Russell Street London WC1

Copyright © 1969 by Paul List Verlag KG
Translation Copyright   1971
by André Deutsch Limited

Originally published in Munich under the title
Die Strasse von Messina: Tagebuch des Kommodore
by Paul List Verlag
All Rights Reserved

Printed in Great Britain by
Ebenezer Baylis & Son Ltd
The Trinity Press, Worcester, and London

ISBN 0 233 96313 8

Contents

Translators' Note

The German words *Geschwader* and *Gruppe* have been translated as group and wing respectively but they are not synonymous with the terms as used either in the RAF or the USAF. At full strength a *Geschwader* normally consisted of some 100 to 120 aircraft made up of three *Gruppen* and a headquarters formation – in the present case a headquarters flight (*Stabsschwarm*). Thus Steinhoff's *Jagdgeschwader* 77 appears as the 77th Fighter Group. In the German Air Force it was not unusual for a unit of this size to be commanded by a major although the appointment conferred a higher status than the rank suggests.

We have included a few explanatory footnotes.

Foreword

General Johannes Steinhoff tells us that the purpose of his book is to demonstrate 'from the point of view of the fighting soldier' that the crucial mistakes of the German High Command (in the Second World War) lay in their mismanagement of both technology and men.

Let me reassure anyone who picks up *The Straits of Messina* that they will not find it a prosaic essay. Quite the contrary – it is a finely drawn, sensitive story of young men who, while fighting for their lives in the face of certain defeat, are showered with insults and contempt from their commander-in-chief, Hermann Göring.

Johannes Steinhoff and myself were on opposite sides during the Battle of Britain. I cannot (any more than he) resist contrasting our plight in 1940 with his in Sicily exactly three years later: the Battle of Britain began on July 10, 1940, and on the same date in 1943 the American Seventh Army was reported firmly established in Sicily.

'Fortress Europe' had been breached. It was the beginning of the end for Hitler – and the young Steinhoff, *Kommodore* of the 77th Fighter Group, and his comrades knew it. The war had brought Steinhoff 'years of wandering'. He had been with the Luftwaffe (then 'invincible') when it blasted Europe into submission. He had subsequently tasted defeat in the Battle of Britain, when German fighters suffered losses 'which could not be made good'. Having survived the inferno of Stalingrad, he had campaigned in North Africa. When the German Army capitulated in Tunisia, Steinhoff's group had repaired to Sicily (the little Messerschmitt 109 fighters carried two extra men wedged into the fuselage). And there, as Allied bombers 'softened up' the island's defences before invasion, his group was harried from one dusty airstrip to another, short of equipment, spares, fuel and ammunition, its landline communications hanging by a thread. In those conditions the 77th Fighter Group was ordered to defend the island against the massive and incessant bomber assault.

If the odds weighed heavily against British fighter pilots in 1940, they were still heavier against the German *Jaeger* in the blazing heat of that Sicilian summer of 1943. We believed in victory, they in defeat. We were inspired – by our leaders, by the resistance of a brave people and by the knowledge that our own liberty and that of the civilized world lay in the balance. There were no such benign influences to stir and uplift the hearts of Johannes Steinhoff and his pilots. Despite that, their submission to orders and to their fate was total. (It was not until after the war, Steinhoff tells us, that the German soldier was for the first time granted legal rights.)

First, the Führer's orders, disobeyed on pain of death. Then Göring's. Living in the glorious past of his 'Circus' days, Göring was quite unable to grasp what Dowding, the British fighter C-in-C, had defined as 'the application of science to operations'. Göring, the author of a series of imperial blunders since well before the war. 'Unser Hermann', a monster who tried to pass as a jovial *bonhomme* with his airmen, yet who could order 'one pilot from each wing [in Sicily] to be tried by court martial for cowardice ...' (How many times did he scream 'cowards' at the British fighter pilots in the Battle of Britain?) Then Göring's older commanders: most of them were ex-soldiers without the 'professional' understanding of air warfare that our own commanders possessed.

Johannes Steinhoff supports his thesis – the High Command's mismanagement of technology and men – with vivid and often moving narrative. This is where I like him best. He has all the fighter pilot's keen awareness and *joie de vivre*, and he can breathe romance – the hell of it is, there is some – into the vile business of war. While the big-talk *communiqués* from somewhere safely behind the lines announce that targets have been pounded, battered, smashed or wiped out, Steinhoff, with more realism, notes: 'It was harvest time . . . but most people had fled in a panic . . . For wherever we appeared in the land, death and destruction followed.' Of a youthful, fair-haired pilot, a boy barely out of his 'teens: 'The flames had made ghastly work of his head . . . His hair had melted . . . His face was a featureless, liquefied mass.'

'Yet,' he says of his pilots (the oldest was twenty-six), 'in spite of all this frightfulness . . . their youthful high spirits . . . kept on breaking through' – not with the help of booze or pot, but through the sheer will to live. Life was certainly worth living, too; oppressed as Steinhoff was by a sense of waste and futility, his senses continued to register 'the aromatic smell of new wood', 'the ribbon of white foam' which girdled the bay, 'the snow-capped summit of Etna, glowing like a torch', or 'the smell of oil and dope, the reek peculiar to a Messerschmitt 109'.

Flying was a sensual thing, a passion common to friend and foe. How paradoxical that it should have led us to kill one another. As he contemplates two Allied airmen, prisoners whom he had invited to dinner, Steinhoff muses, 'Heaven knows what stories they'd been told about us Huns; now perhaps they were discovering to their surprise that the enemy was made of just the same stuff as any other human being.'

The tragedy of war is that the young have to pay so dearly for the failings or the evil of their elders. The old ones send the young ones forth with orders to kill and destroy. In Steinhoff's time German airmen and soldiers were required to act in blind obedience to their superiors' orders, however wrong or inhuman they believed them to be. Today in Vietnam soldiers kill their superiors or desert in protest. Whichever way you look at it, war imposes dilemmas too hard and cruel for the young to solve. Johannes Steinhoff, a seasoned veteran, reminds us of 'that pathetic, unknown quantity, sacrifice and heroism, which has played so disastrous a role in German military history'. It added up to over ten million German dead in the Second World War – with about three times that number on the other side.

No one in his senses would disagree with the author when he says 'War can only be regarded with abhorrence.' But in a world still made horribly unsafe – mostly by fear and mistrust – nations must defend themselves and all that they hold dear. In a humane, constructive conclusion to his excellent book General Johannes Steinhoff argues that, since effective defence depends on a lead in technology, Germany, now a powerful element in Western European defence, should possess the latest technological means. Further, that the technicians who work the delicate equipment involved should enjoy commensurate training, pay and status.

The argument is a logical one, backed as it is by the bitter experience of a young commander who, on the scorching, dusty soil of Sicily over a quarter of a century ago, was witness to the chaos and despair of certain defeat.

PETER TOWNSEND
15 March 1971

'At the Casablanca conference in mid-January, 1943, it was decided by the Prime Minister and President Roosevelt . . . that the island of Sicily should be assaulted and captured as a base for operations against Southern Europe and to open the Mediterranean to the shipping of the United Nations . . . The operation was to be given the code name "Husky".'

FIELD MARSHAL SIR HAROLD ALEXANDER
THE SURRENDER OF SICILY

'[Although the landings in Sicily started on 10 July] . . . Operation Husky properly begins on 13 May, when the Tunisian campaign ended . . . As soon as Axis forces in Tunisia surrendered, Northwest African Air Force was able to turn its entire attention to softening up Sicily . . .'

HISTORY OF THE UNITED STATES NAVAL OPERATIONS IN
WORLD WAR II
SICILY–PALERMO–ANZIO

'The Allied air forces, estimated at 5000 first-line aircraft, were opposed by no more than 1250 Axis machines, of which roughly half were German and half Italian. Of this number 320 German aircraft were available for operations, among them 130 fighters of the Messerschmitt 109 type.'

FRANZ KUROWSKI
DAS TOR ZUR FESTUNG EUROPA

'On transfer from North Africa to the mainland via Sicily, the Group (Nos 1 and 2 Wings) moved to Sicily and was reported operational on 20 June 1943.'

WAR DIARY, 77TH FIGHTER GROUP, GERMAN AIR FORCE

Trapani, 21 June 1943

We took the car through the narrow streets in the direction of the harbour. The vehicle bounced over the rough surface, its engine filling the air with noise. Behind us a wake of dust billowed up to the rooftops. Over everything – street, houses, doors and shutters – lay a fine layer of white powder. Here and there a bomb had torn a hole in a house front.

Not a soul was to be seen. It was air raid time and the town of Trapani had been abandoned by its inhabitants.

We turned off down an alleyway just wide enough to let the vehicle through and emerged almost at once into glaring sunlight beside the quay. To our right was the semicircle of the bay ringed by white houses, windows shuttered. One door only stood open, its gaudy fly curtains hanging motionless in the sun. Two men in tattered black suits, caps pushed on to the back of their heads, squatted in the shade of the wall shelling mussels from a tin bucket. They ignored us completely.

We climbed out of the car. Straden cocked his machine pistol and we made our way over the soft sand down to the water's edge.

The little port was shaped like a horseshoe. To the west we could see the Mediterranean, its leaden surface apparently motionless under the blazing midday sun, merging imperceptibly with the dazzling vault of the sky.

To our left two rusting, abandoned lighters lay alongside the quay. The harbour was small and shallow. Oil slicks streaked the surface of the stagnant water. Seaweed and mussels grew thickly on rotting timbers.

'It can't be far away,' I said, pointing. 'I saw it yesterday from the air. There's a white sandy beach over there.'

Returning to the quay wall, we walked past the houses and across a neglected garden. In a few moments we were again beside the sea.

Here the air was somewhat fresher, and there was a warm gentle breeze blowing. The sandy beach stretched northwards as far as the eye could see. In the other direction lay Trapani, its white houses shimmering in the sunlight, while to the east Mount Erice rose up in the blue distance. Not a sound was to be heard. We undressed and lay down on the white sand.

'How dead and empty it all seems now,' said Straden. 'When we left North Africa for Sicily it was pretty obvious where we'd end up, sir, though we didn't want to admit it at the time.'

I let the sand trickle through my fingers and remarked, 'A fine place to fight a losing battle in! Sicily's all rock and no cover.'

'They'll finish us off here,' he said morosely.

'But these past six weeks have given us a bit of time to recover. You've got to admit that.'

'Yes,' said Straden, 'compared with the two last months in North Africa this is like a convalescent home.'

'Come on. We'd better bathe if we don't want to get badly sunburnt.' The water was lukewarm and we had to wade a hundred yards out before it even came up to our hips. Then we started swimming.

Suddenly and for no particular reason a feeling of apprehension came over me, impelling me to turn round at once and make quickly for dry land. I raced back to the dunes and threw myself down on the sand. A breathless Straden arrived soon after. At that moment we heard the air raid warning signal – three rounds from an anti-aircraft gun. High above the town three pale yellow flak bursts floated in the sky.

'They're on their way,' Straden said.

As we hastily got dressed there came the sound of engines, rising and falling.

'Mitchells or Marauders. I wonder if they're after our airfield?' Just as we were about to start back we heard the dull thud of explosions. Far away on the side of Mount Erice dirty brown dustclouds rose into the air. When we got to the car the harbour was empty and lifeless as before. Every door was closed. Even the men with the mussels had disappeared. We saw no one as we raced through the streets, our engine screaming.

Straden parked the car in front of No 2 Fighter Wing's hut. Captain Freiberg, the commanding officer, rose from the entrance steps as we arrived. 'About sixty Mitchells,' he said. 'I don't know yet what damage they've done. No 1 Squadron seems to have been on the receiving end. The telephone line's been cut.'

Several pilots, sheltering in the shade of the olive trees, now stood up. Dust from the slit trenches still clung to their life-jackets and to the knees of their trousers.

Freiberg looked tired and overwrought; his sweat-stained fore-head was almost concealed by a shock of fair hair. Like his pilots he wore a yellow life-jacket which covered the upper part of his body and encircled his hips. Secured to it by a small snap hook was a yellow dye pouch. Straps round each calf held Very cartridges. On his feet he wore sandals. His khaki shirt was stained with sweat on the back and under the arms.

How many times, I thought to myself, have I told him not to wear sandals when flying. One of these days he'll have to bale out and if he's lucky enough to come down on dry land, he's going to break his ankles.

Freiberg was twenty-six, a born pilot, but nervous as a thoroughbred. Everyone in the squadron knew that he drank, indeed that he was drunk almost every night. He had a panicky fear of bombing raids. Anyone could send him racing headlong for the slit trenches simply by hammering on the wall of the hut and yelling 'Air raid!' But he had never shirked a mission. During the air battles over Malta and in the course of the North African campaign he had shot down ninety-nine aircraft. He wore the Knight's Cross. For months now his hundredth victory had been eluding him.

The telephone rang in the hut. No 1 Squadron reported casu-alties among the ground staff but added that the anti-aircraft fire from the eighty-eights had been effective.

'We mustn't lose our heads, Freiberg,' I said. 'We're going to need a lot of serviceable aircraft for what lies ahead. Within the next few days the General of Fighters[1] will be flying here to take charge of fighter operations with his HQ in the group operations room. He's coming from Reich Air Defence and has the experience of the heavies we still lack.'

'Quite, quite,' answered Freiberg moodily, 'we've seen the marvellous reports about operations in the Reich. At breakfast they're told politely that a gaggle of bandits is on its way from eastern England so they ought to take off round about ten. And if they have to bale out or force land, they're back home by lunchtime . . . But we down here have to fly over the lousy Mediterranean – always provided we get into the air – and if we have to bale out not a soul's going to fish us out of the drink.'

'All right,' I said soothingly, for I knew his ways. 'But this is a theatre peculiar to itself. In any case, things are going to get better very soon. Some big direction-finding equipment is going up near Marsala which will be able to pick up the heavies as soon as they're on the way; in future we'll be able to get into the air in good time whenever they attack Rome, Naples or the Straits of Messina.'

'There's a direction finder on Mount Erice now,' put in Straden, 'which pinpoints our exact position over the Mediterranean the moment we come on the radio-telephone. So they'll be able to pull us out of the water after all.'

'Who will?' asked Freiberg without looking at him.

To get to the group operations room one had to drive up a steep dusty road full of hairpin bends and then turn left, below the high saddle and the village of Erice, along a bumpy track leading to a small piece of level ground immediately below the summit. From there the view was magnificent; to the southwest stretched the great expanse of the island while at one's feet, almost, it seemed, within touching distance, lay the port and the white

[1] Galland

buildings of Trapani beside the bay. Adjoining the town was the airfield with its new concrete runway and further to the south the shimmer of the salt workings. Marsala could only be guessed at in the haze. In the distance the olive groves were no more than a blur of greyish green from which houses, villages and small towns stood out like white smudges. Only the neighbouring airfield at Chinisia was readily identifiable by reason of its light-coloured runway.

Behind the hut the rock face of Mount Erice rose steeply. For weeks now workmen had been busy excavating a cave in its side. Ever since our return to Sicily, their picks and pneumatic hammers had been battering away at the brown rock while the excavated material had piled up at the yawning entrance and was now as high as a house. The cave was to form a horseshoe round one of the immense natural pillars supporting the table of Mount Erice, and would thus have two exits. Although the work had not yet been half completed, the cave was already serving as an air raid shelter.

No sooner had the vehicle come to a halt on the level ground than three flak bursts appeared above our heads – the air raid warning signal. The noon breeze, which had just risen, carried up to us the roar of engines as the squadron at readiness prepared to take off from the airfield below.

'Which squadron?' I asked.

'No 2.'

'Who's leading?'

'Zöhler.'

There must have been some fifteen machines about to become airborne. We could see the swirl of dust in the blast pens as the engines started up, the hurried taxiing to the runway, the turning into the wind and the rapid take-off. In the meantime the cool breeze off the sea had dispersed the haze. Below, the plain of Trapani was clearly visible. On the roads round the airfield we could see people running. Alerted by the warning anti-aircraft shots, everyone who could do so was getting under cover. Up here, too, men were hurrying for the shelter of Mount Erice.

Lieutenant Bachmann, my adjutant, was on duty in the operations room. In contrast to Straden, who was one of Germany's leading athletes and who possessed a physique to match, Bachmann tended to corpulence and was averse to sport. His sallow manly features, framed by a shock of unruly hair, were the more expressive for his eyes which were large and dark. He laughed often, revealing fine, regular white teeth. Whenever I took the group into the air these two officers, so dissimilar to each other, flew in my HQ flight.

'Twin engines, sir,' Bachmann reported. 'Making for Sciacca.'

The group's No 1 Wing was in Sciacca.

'Has No 1 been warned?'

'They have one squadron in the air. Godert's leading.'

Always Godert, I thought. A former sergeant, his face disfigured as a result of a crash, he had been the mainstay of his wing ever since the outbreak of war; steady and reliable, he had never missed a sortie. He did not possess the tracker's instinct of the great fighter pilots, nor had he ever been able to acquire their skill in marksmanship. But he had trained generations of fighter pilots and taught them flying tactics. When, as a young second lieutenant, I had joined the Maritime Fighter Squadron in order to learn to fly fighters, I had been placed in the care of a flight sergeant who thereupon became my instructor. His name was Godert. From him I had learnt how to keep station – as if glued in position – with my section leader when flying in close formation, how to attack and shoot, how to begin and break off a dogfight.

One year later I was promoted and exchanged my rabbit's role for that of section leader. All at once Godert became my wing man, following my manœuvres as if 'glued in position' and carrying out my orders.

Often, in the whirl of flying fighters in close formation, when the aircraft appeared to become weightless, when clouds, sun and horizon described circles through the windscreens and bracing wires of our biplanes, a grin would spread over Godert's face and he would nod approvingly as if to say: 'That's the way. You're doing fine.'

'They've overflown Sciacca and are approaching Palermo. Zöhler has made contact with the enemy.' From the loudspeaker came the staccato sounds of exclamations, reports and orders, sounds capable of interpretation only by those who have repeatedly experienced that moment when interception is made and the enemy engaged. 'Look out!' 'Keep there!' 'Angels ten!' 'I'm attacking . . .'

'They've turned round and are coming back over Mount Erice,' Bachmann said. Fresh position reports were reaching him all the time from our Aircraft Report Centre. 'Apparently there are Spitfires along with them. Palermo harbour has been attacked and they're now at about ten thousand feet.'

All at once the heavy flak went into action. Then the sound of engines became audible, the whistle of falling bombs. Tumbling out of the hut we saw that the western edge of the airfield was obscured by a cloud of dust. Dust plumes were rising from the olive groves surrounding the field. The flak was firing continuously at the sound of engines in the west, but the enemy formation itself was invisible to the naked eye. Shortly afterwards No 1 Wing reported that their squadron had landed. One pilot was missing; one bomber had been shot down over Palermo. Sergeant Reinhold had baled out of his Messerschmitt but had landed safely.

At dusk I drove with Straden to our billet. The roads were crowded with carts drawn by donkeys or horses, for the heat of the day – and with it the time for mass bombing attacks – was over. When we turned off the main road and took the narrow track along the ridge, a view of the sickle-shaped Bay of Bonagia opened up in front of us.

We, the HQ officers, lived and ate in a small inconspicuous villa. It stood in a vineyard, its front colour-washed in pink. This was the domain of Corporal Rieber, my batman, mess cook and orderly – in short, my maid-of-all-work. He was a glass-blower by trade and there was not a man in the whole group whose weight or chest measurement exceeded his. For this reason he needed neither name nor rank and everyone addressed him simply as 'Tubby'.

Four months previously, following the arduous defensive battles in the Caucasus, when a brief spell of home leave from my fighter wing had been cut short by my unexpected posting to North Africa, I had asked for my kit to be sent on after me as soon as possible. Two months later – we were in Sicily by then – Tubby had reported to me with my baggage. He had been my batman for a number of years and wanted to stay with me.

I climbed the narrow stairs to my room. My camp-bed stood against the wall by the door. Under the chair lay the small brown suitcase scarred by its travels through the various battle zones in which the armed forces of the Greater German Reich were or had been involved. Wherever my Messerschmitt might take me, this case was my constant companion. The ingenious Rieber was expert at filling it with the things I needed until the heavy baggage caught up with us. The French windows giving onto the balcony stood wide open. Beyond, the waters of the bay were illuminated by the last of the evening light while houses, slopes and rocks glowed deep yellow. It was a scene of such classical beauty that it hurt when one remembered the gravity of our situation.

I dropped on to the bed to relax for a little. Smells of Rieber's cooking wafted through the house. It was a comforting, peaceful atmosphere, the silence broken only by friendly, familiar sounds – the scraping of a chair, water hissing in the pipes. And then, all at once, came the low roar of aircraft engines.

The Wellingtons are starting early today! I thought. Every night they came over immediately after dark. Like the old biplanes used by the Russians, theirs was a nuisance role, the object being to create anxiety and spoil our rest. They would drop their bombs at regular intervals round about our airfield, on the HQs and on the billets. And we loathed them, for the nights were short and we were overtired and wanted to sleep.

Waking with a start from the deep sleep into which I had involuntarily fallen, I saw Tubby standing at the foot of my bed.

'The meal is ready, sir,' he announced.

It was dark by now. The wooden shutters of the dining-room were closed, for otherwise swarms of insects would have found their way inside. The evening had brought no relief from the heat.

The HQ officers were assembled at the table – Straden, Bachmann and Bernhard, the last a young second lieutenant whom we called 'the Imp'. Although he had been with us for only two months, no one could remember why he had been given the nickname. He had left school at seventeen, normal regulations having been modified to allow him to matriculate, and had been awarded his 'wings' as a fighter pilot after a shortened officers' training course. He would soon be celebrating his twentieth birthday. The old hands at HQ looked after him and were getting him ready for operations. But since our arrival in Sicily Bernhard had been quiet and withdrawn. The boy looked anxious and worried as though aware that a new chapter in the air war was about to begin; no doubt the others' flippant tone was rather beyond him. When spoken to he would emerge as if from a different world, at pains to be impeccably polite. It was my impression that he had had little or no sleep during the past nights.

In addition to the officers, Sergeant Zahn also sat with us at table. He flew in my HQ flight. A motor mechanic by trade, he was a gifted pilot and reacted dependably, courageously and with precision whenever he flew as my wing man. Tall and very fair, he came from northern Germany and he would jump at every opportunity of a sortie.

While we were sitting at the table the electricity failed. Tubby, ever prepared for such an event, calmly placed a pot-bellied carbide lamp among the dishes. It cast a hard, bluish light, at the same time emitting an inordinately loud hiss. Straden turned to me. I knew that he really wanted to say something other than 'This heat gets me down' or 'Bloody Mediterranean' or 'I feel absolutely clobbered.' But there seemed to be no point; we all of us used the same debased wartime vocabulary which betrayed nothing of our true selves.

In the half light their faces showed up like flat, bluish green discs. How tired and worn out everyone was! Two months had now passed since the hurried evacuation of North Africa. At this particular moment the wan faces revealed what no one wanted to admit: We've been beaten. All of them – Bernhard excepted – had reached Sicily at the eleventh hour, mentally and physically exhausted. And there was little hope that circumstances would change.

It had been only by the skin of my teeth that I had managed to persuade the field marshal[1] that my group needed rest, that it was no longer a useful and effective fighting unit and that it should be taken off operations.

The order to withdraw had come at the very last minute. The tragedy of Tunis was over and the German and Italian troops, together with the remnants of my group, were crowding into the narrow tongue of land that was Cape Bon on their way to captivity. During that night, when anarchy had begun to spread among the forlorn multitude, we received the signal: '77th Fighter Group will move to Sicily forthwith.' Fortunately, as it happened, my earlier experience at Stalingrad and the Kuban bridge-head had led me to arrange beforehand, and without my superiors' knowledge, the transfer of almost all our ground personnel and equipment to the island.

It had been more like a hasty retreat than a move. The group's Messerschmitts landed at Trapani on 8 May; they were riddled with bullets and had not been serviced for days. Inside the fuselage of each aircraft knelt a mechanic, peering over the pilot's shoulder, a position he had reached with some difficulty by squeezing through the wireless hatch. Without a parachute and with no hope of escaping from his prison in an emergency, he was at the mercy of his fate and his pilot's skill.

The remnants of the group had taken off in dramatic circumstances. The air above Cape Bon, the final bridge-head, was controlled by Allied fighters. We had spent the night beside

[1] Kesselring, Commander-in-Chief, South

a small meadow, then, in the short North African spring, an uninterrupted sea of flowers. Our aircraft were able to depart only during the intervals when the Spitfires and Kittyhawks were relieving each other. Once airborne we sought to escape by flying at treetop height. There were dogfights and losses, and columns of smoke from shot down aircraft marked our course.

As soon as the blue contours of Mount Erice rose up out of the sea, the exchanges on the R/T had recovered their old liveliness. Now that the worst was over, the possibility of crashing into the sea before reaching land or of having to abandon a badly damaged aircraft seemed so insignificant as to be absurd. We were all of us subject to this euphoria after an engagement. Filled with happiness, we would enjoy the few hours or days of life granted us until the next operation.

Having landed on the runway at Trapani I had been on the point of finding out how things were with the remainder of my group when there was a surprise attack by a formation of British bombers. Hardly had the clouds of dust from the bomb bursts dispersed than the impending arrival of the field marshal was reported. Everything was in utter confusion. Somewhere, among the chaos of ambulances racing hither and thither and the burning aircraft on the edge of the runway, I had come upon Rottberg, who commanded the 'destroyer' group then about to move to the mainland. 'Delighted to see you,' he said, 'and a happy birthday!' There was something comforting about his friendly grin.

'Thank you. If I only knew how I could round up the remains of my poor old group. We can hardly prize our eyelids open – haven't slept for days.'

'I've got everything ready for you. So far twenty-four Mes from your HQ flight and your second wing have landed. Now, of all disastrous things, we've just had a report that the field marshal is on his way. We'll have to get him away from the airfield as quickly as possible in case a second wave comes along. He'll be landing any minute now.'

'That's all we need . . .' As I was speaking, green Very lights, the signal for permission to land, rose up in front of flying control. The Dornier 217 lumbered awkwardly along the runway before coming to a halt on burst tires in the middle of the airfield.

'Right,' Rottberg growled, 'now we can drive over to receive him and play at being heroes. God forbid that a second wave should arrive!'

We watched the Commander-in-Chief, South, emerge from a hatch in the belly of the aircraft. First there had appeared a pair of legs, the trousers adorned with a broad white stripe. Then the burly figure started to crawl out from under the fuselage. Behind him an aide-de-camp hastily unzipped a leather case, took out the field marshal's baton and handed it to him.

The field marshal's face had radiated confidence and optimism. He bared his powerful teeth as he advanced towards Rottberg who, once the welcoming formalities had been concluded, advised him in urgent terms to leave the airfield as quickly as possible. But instead the field marshal turned to me to hear my report.

'How are things going – what's the state of your group?'

'Rotten, sir. The group's just a fragment of what it used to be. We now have only forty aircraft, none of them serviceable.'

Here Rottberg intervened:

'Don't you think we should move away from the airfield? The next wave of bombers may be here at any moment.'

The field marshal seemed imperturbable. 'Why are you so nervous, gentlemen?' he asked. On the way to the car, he wanted to know all details of the raid.

Once at Rottberg's HQ, I tried to impress upon him the hopeless state of the group, adding that we needed a short rest from operations. But I failed.

'We must lose no time in building up the defence of Sicily. You'll have to try and give your people some rest here. I shall arrange for the allocation of aircraft, equipment and personnel, but from today your task is this: the defence of Sicily.'

I made yet another effort:

'Sir, the group is no longer a battleworthy unit. Its combat value is precisely nil. Do, please, believe me when I say that after coming through the murderous defensive battles in North Africa and Tunisia my pilots are absolutely all in. The heavy casualties have utterly demoralized them. May I therefore request that they have a few weeks off operations?'

My entreaties met with blank refusal.

'The overall situation demands that your group remain operational.' With that he had got into his car to drive to Marsala, where the remnants of the army in Tunis, those who had survived the sea crossing, were disembarking.

The following morning we had seen the field marshal off from the airfield. His heavily built figure was bowed as he came towards us and his hands, bandaged with white gauze, were supported by slings. The house beside the harbour, on whose upper floor he had been conferring with the naval commanders, had been hit during an air raid. His young A D C had been killed. The staircase had been destroyed and the field marshal had had to slide down a rope to reach the street. In doing so he had been unable to check the descent of his heavy body and had burned his palms.

Before climbing into his aircraft he had turned to me with the words: 'You may move to Bari in Apulia for a few weeks. But be quick about it. I shall want the group back in Sicily soon, fit for action.'

In the light of the carbide lamp, the local wine glowed like amber in the bottles. Tubby had roasted some Italian tinned meat and had placed fresh local cheese on the table.

A desultory conversation started up, but most of us preferred to pursue our own thoughts. The half light and the sultry atmosphere had made us drowsy. I do not know whether anyone heard the whistle of the falling bomb before an explosion, close by the house, shattered the evening's deceptive calm. The blast, bursting open the shutters, produced a stabbing pain in our ears.

Chairs rocked, glasses shattered on the tiled floor. Cursing and laughing, we crowded down the narrow staircase in our disorderly flight towards the door that led into the garden. 'Tubby,'

27

I called, 'fetch my sleeping-bag. I'm spending the rest of the night in the grotto.'

To get to the grotto one had to squeeze through an opening in the wall behind the house and then crawl under some grape-laden vines before arriving in front of the entrance, dark but for a faint gleam of light. The grotto had been hewn out of the rock on which the villa stood and combined the functions of wine cellar and air raid shelter. The space was dimly lit by a paraffin lantern; in the gloom the vault seemed bigger than it really was.

The stable lantern stood on a table among an array of wine bottles. Round the table sat the pilots and a fair-haired girl called Teresa. On the far side, almost invisible in the shadows, we could just make out the sallow features of her *nonna* – her grandmother – who had taken up station against the rocky wall, her back straight as a ramrod.

The usual company was there, those who each evening sought out this cool spot, bombs or no bombs: Straden, Bachmann, Freiberg, Bernhard, Zahn and the commander of I Squadron, Zöhler.

Zöhler came from a circus family and as a boy had, so he told us, performed with the Rivels. He was extremely interesting and amusing when he talked about circuses and circus performers, his stories gaining in effect by being told in a broad Saxon accent. He had a sallow complexion and for some considerable time had been plagued with malaria. He also had trouble with his stomach – indeed everyone suffered from nervous stomach trouble after a certain period on operations. The one exception was Bachmann who, even when we were at readiness in our cockpits, would often call for a helping of soup within minutes of take-off. This he would lap up with an enjoyment that was almost sadistic, since his pleasure was obviously enhanced by the other pilots' expressions of disgust at such unnatural composure.

Freiberg was resting his feet on a crate. His white sandals were made from the chrome leather used to protect the aeroplanes' petrol tanks; he wore spotless white stockings. In striking contrast to his otherwise unconventional manner, his dress was always clean and immaculate.

'Well, Armin,' he said, turning lazily towards Zöhler, 'you didn't make much impression on those Marauders today.'

Zöhler looked at him in surprise. 'What can you do to those chaps when you only have eight machines? They're the same ones who used to bomb us daily in North Africa. Although their bombing may not be all that accurate, their formation flying couldn't be better. When you go for them the tracer comes back at you like out of a watering can.'

'I'm not sure that isn't a foretaste of what the Boeings and Liberators are going to do,' Freiberg said soberly.

He had put into words something that had been exercising everyone's minds. I knew what was in their thoughts – how, during the attack, the bombers loomed large in their illuminated sights. I also knew that when that happened they would open fire too soon, would want to turn away and break off because the chances of coming out unscathed were so small, because this form of concerted attack was going to become everyday routine – and also because each one of them, conscious of the law of averages, would be asking himself: 'How much longer . . .?'

Bachmann was one of those who seemed to have no nerves. Lying on a camp-bed, he was carrying on a whispered conversation with Straden who was relaxing in an old deck-chair beside him.

'Bachmann, tell me what's the matter with Reinhold,' Freiberg called over to him.

'Oh, Reinhold isn't quite all there at the moment. This afternoon he was parading along the village street in his white tunic. And he had his ceremonial dagger dangling at his side.'

'Reinhold needs a woman,' Freiberg said.

'The troops laughed like drains when they saw him swanning up and down.'

'None of the women here ever takes any notice of us. All they want is to see us go.'

'You mustn't be too hard on Reinhold,' Freiberg said, 'he

hasn't been home since last summer. He had a girl in Bari – fairly chucked his money about. She worked in the kitchen at the *Oriente* and wore a black dress with a little white collar fastened with press-studs. Her seat shone like a mirror. He was always going down to the kitchen on cleanliness inspections and he took Italian lessons from her. You know – you touch her nose and ask "What's that called?" then you repeat the performance with her chin, and so you carry on, working slowly downwards.'

'But why does he cart his white tunic round with him?' Zöhler asked.

Freiberg poured himself another glass. 'Because he doesn't want to look as scruffy as you do,' he said.

It was past midnight but no one had any inclination to return to the house. Freiberg put an arm round the fair girl's waist. Her grandmother stared fixedly at his hand while the girl remained silent and motionless.

The conversation started up again when Straden suddenly wanted to know the code name for the day's operation. 'Odysseus,' I said, 'it's an appropriate name, Odysseus.'

'It might happen all over again,' mused someone in the darkness. 'Scylla and Charybdis separate us from the mainland and up north we shall be flying over Circe's mountain – and in the end we may even be cast up on shore after long journeyings on a raft. But I don't imagine that ball-playing virgins will be there to welcome us . . .'

'Enemy air raid on Messina (200 aircraft). Heavy damage to private dwellings, public buildings, barracks and other military objectives. Fuel store in flames, ammunition dump blown up. Rail link between Palermo and Catania cut. Casualties reported to date: 62 dead, 75 injured.'

WAR DIARY OF THE OBERKOMMANDO DER WEHRMACHT
25 JUNE 1943

'We located the heavies 100 miles off Trapani. They were right down on the water, skimming the crests of the waves and heading for North Africa. By the time we had expended all our ammunition we found ourselves running low in fuel. This was something that alarmed old hands and new boys alike. Above us the sky was greyish blue. I could hear despairing cries: "My tank's nearly dry — I'm going to drown!"'

DIARY OF CAPTAIN KÖHLER OF
NO 1 WING, 77TH FIGHTER GROUP
25 JUNE 1943

'During the defensive action against the bombing attack on the Straits of Messina the fighter element failed in its task. One pilot from each of the fighter wings taking part will be tried by court martial for cowardice in the face of the enemy.   *Göring, Reichsmarschall.*'

DIARY OF CAPTAIN KÖHLER OF
NO. 1 WING, 77TH FIGHTER GROUP
25 JUNE 1943

Trapani, 25 June 1943

The general had arrived on 24 June and driven at once to the operations room on Mount Erice. In his customary laconic manner he had asked to be briefed on our recent operations and had then expressed the wish to speak to the commanders of the two fighter wings and their squadron leaders.

They had sat on stools and in deck-chairs in front of the hut, their eyes fixed on his face as he began to speak. He had talked about the Air Defence of the Reich, about measures against the four-engined bombers and about tactics. And when he had finished not one of them asked a question. Their expressions, which had grown increasingly wooden as he went on, were brooding and sceptical.

With the words: 'Very well then – until tomorrow,' the general had risen and departed.

Tubby woke me in the grey light of dawn. I felt exhausted, for I had slept little and the general's words had kept ringing in my ears: 'Get in close', 'Don't fire too soon', 'Lead them in head-on in close formation . . .'

Very early, we were at readiness. 'Kuddel' Abben's fighter wing, the third wing in my group, had flown over from Sardinia the previous evening, their arrival coinciding with that of Meyers and one wing from the Ace of Spades group. Trapani airfield was now crowded with Messerschmitt fighters as if for an air display and we were very well aware of the disastrous consequences a surprise attack might bring.

We sat in front of the hut under the olive trees no more than a few paces from our aircraft – and the slit trenches – indulging

B

in the sort of inconsequential small talk that is wholly unconnected with what one is really thinking. But all the time we kept our ears cocked in case the morning breeze should drown the threatening rumble of engines.

The night had brought no relief from the heat and the day was going to be oppressively hot. 'Well, my lads, the general's going to show us how to fight an air battle,' Freiberg said, 'and it'll be just like a parade for a party rally.'

'Ever seen a Flying Fortress close to, Kuddel?'

'No,' replied Kuddel Abben, 'I'll be careful not to. They don't seem to like it very much.'

'But the general made it all so beautifully plain yesterday evening,' said Freiberg in schoolmasterly tones. 'Are you still in any doubt about how we should attack them head-on and from below and astern, or about the fantastic things the blue-eyed boys in Reich Air Defence are doing? He forgot to ask how many of us were non-swimmers.'

'You'll drown even if you can swim. If you have to bale out and you're out of sight of land, nobody's going to pick you up.'

Abben knew something of the sea. He had served as a rating in destroyers before transferring to the aviation branch where he had risen rapidly. Like Godert, he was one of the mainstays of the group.

Freiberg swatted an invisible fly with his hand. 'It's something you just don't think about,' he said.

'Funny thing,' said Abben, 'as soon as I cross the coast and head out to sea, my engine always seems to sound twice as noisy.'

Listening to these young captains it was difficult to imagine that they held important military commands. But such was the professional style, a style that had evolved out of this particular war. The commander of a fighter unit was, without exception, the first to engage the enemy, but when the fighting had begun and no one could be leader, he was simply a pilot, dependent on his own resources in single combat with another pilot – one who swore in English.

Meyers was young, bright and not unlike Freiberg in his studied nonchalance. Both belonged to a certain type of flyer, the type produced by the successful years of the war in the air.

A gentle morning breeze stirred the olive grove but it brought no coolness, for the atmosphere was damp and sticky. It was weather typical of the Sicilian summer.

I had lost count of the number of times I had debated with myself how I should lead and mount the attack. My experience was somewhat meagre. Over the Channel during the Battle of Britain I had commanded nothing larger than a squadron. I was aware of the problems when manœuvring with a large formation of fighters, but I myself had never led on such occasions. Either the leader flies too fast so that the formation opens out astern, concertina fashion, to the accompaniment of repeated calls over the R/T from somebody at the back for less speed, or else he flies too slowly, which means that during turns – and these must in any case be executed as gentle, skid turns – the inside man is forced to lose height through lack of flying speed.

Shall I, I wondered, succeed in bringing my formation intact to the point of interception with the heavies? Shall I, perhaps, have to attack head-on? And then, of course, the usual thoughts – the ones you could never suppress – kept cropping up: the murderous return fire from the Fortresses, the parachute descent, the rubber dinghy . . .

'Sir,' I heard someone say, 'Colonel Larsen, the Inspector, South, has just landed.'

The last time I had seen Larsen had been in southern Russia. My wing had been attached to his group when the attack against Stalingrad began in the summer of 1942. We had been friends ever since. As he got out of his car, he shouted to me: 'I want to be here for your first big defensive battle!'

The deck-chairs were set out in a semicircle under the olive trees beside the hut. There we sat down and told each other what had happened to us since our last meeting. Fighter pilots at readiness, deprived of these items of furniture, would be altogether inconceivable. How many hours had I spent in a deck-chair since the outbreak of war? It had started in the west during the 'sitzkrieg' against France when we would occasionally chase away a reconnaissance aircraft – a harmless occupation compared with what we were doing now. But since that time we had been in an almost constant state of readiness, either 'cockpit readiness', sitting in our aircraft, or else in deck-chairs close by our machines. A day seems very long when it is spent in waiting, with nothing to occupy one's imagination except the war in the air.

Today, for the first time since the Battle of Britain, I was conscious of the same oppressive atmosphere that used to afflict us then. In August and September 1940 we were normally at readiness by first light. After breakfast – a meal that stuck in most of their throats – the group's pilots assembled in front of the operations room, a Nissen hut on the edge of the airfield. Pale and short of sleep, and all of them young, almost boys, they leaned silently against the wall of the hut or propped their elbows on the bonnet of a Kübelwagen.[1] Occasionally someone made a brief remark about the weather or the next operation. Cigarettes glowed in the grey half light. Our trousers of heavy cloth, liberally supplied with pockets, were known as 'Channel pants'. Over our leather waistcoats we wore yellow life-jackets to which were secured the various items of equipment designed to give us a better chance of survival in the event of our having to abandon our aircraft: a dye pouch to stain the water round us bright yellow, a clumsy Very pistol, cartridges, a signalling lamp and emergency rations. And we each had a yellow scarf which was worn, as often as not, with some panache and yet was indispensable when one was in the sea and wanted to attract the attention either of one of our own air-sea rescue aeroplanes, or of a British high-speed motor launch—with captivity the inevitable condition of rescue.

Then came the decisions about the operation, about timings, about the order in which the squadrons were to take off, about the formation they were to adopt. If weather conditions above the British Isles were such as to cause the postponement of our

[1] Kübelwagen or Kübel – military version of the Volkswagen

departure, we were subjected to the ordeal of waiting in deck-chairs in the gloom of the Nissen huts beside the squadron dispersal point. Conversation very soon died away altogether or became nothing more than an indistinct murmur. Most of the pilots would doze, their eyes closed, or else would pretend to sleep while conjuring up an endless sequence of horrors. The ringing of the field telephone acted on us like an electric shock: now, at last, this was it! But if the call was nothing more than a weather report or a routine inquiry about the aircraft-state, many would curse the telephone as an instrument of torture, prolonging as it did the agony of passive waiting perhaps for minutes, perhaps for hours. And they would settle back again into their comfortable deck-chairs where, physically at least, they were able to relax.

It was to these same deck-chairs in the shade of the olive trees that I led Larsen. Veterans with a colourful past, they were the most important articles in our baggage. Their cheerful, striped covers from the days of peace had long since disintegrated and been removed by the riggers. Now their wooden frames, shiny from contact with human skin, were clad in sturdy, grey tent canvas. 'Today's your big chance,' Larsen said. 'You must keep close together when you attack and dismiss from your mind any thought of mixing it with the Spitfires. The Fortresses are like a fleet of battleships and you can only get in among them if you break through their defensive fire in a compact phalanx.'

'For God's sake, Franzl,' I interjected, 'spare me that awful patter! For days now, advice and instructions have been raining down on our heads from on high. The general keeps dangling the gallant pilots of the Reich Air Defence as a shining example before our eyes. He's also let us know that the Reichsmarschall[1] takes an exceedingly dim view of the fighter pilots down here in the south. In fact our sense of inferiority has got to such a stage that the boys' only reaction is one of biting sarcasm and they simply won't listen any more. You must remember that they're no longer a bunch of young heroes who risk their lives without

[1] Göring

37

a second thought. But equally they don't want for guts. A handful of them survived the Battle of Britain and since then they've been on operations non-stop, and they've been doing it bravely and well. Every so often someone's number comes up and a younger man takes his place. But the new ones haven't much hope of coming through. They've not been thoroughly trained and few of them survive the critical first phase.

'You people don't know this horrible theatre yet. It's mostly water and in the long run it gets us all. We're exposed to the enemy and we've no protection. They'll wear us down by keeping us grounded and destroying our parks and workshops. You don't, by any chance, do you, believe in the Teutonic superhero who, after a bombing raid, rises from his slit trench, shakes the dust from his feet and ascends on steely pinions into the icy heavens, there to wreak havoc among the Flying Fortresses . . . ?'

At this point I realized that I was falling into Freiberg's irreverent manner of speech. Larsen seemed to have got much the same impression for he gave me a long, penetrating look. He remained silent for a time before saying suddenly, as though all at once the scales had fallen from his eyes: 'Yes, but how's it all going to end here?'

'That's what I wanted to ask you!'

Another silence. Something seemed to be holding him back before he went on: 'Before leaving Rome today I was at the C-in-C South's situation conference. Last night the British bombed Wuppertal. Over ten thousand incendiaries started continuous fires between two and three miles long. Düsseldorf, Neuss, Mönchen-Gladbach and Solingen were attacked at the same time . . .'

'And d'you believe we can stop this systematic destruction of everything at home?'

'The general has been asking vainly and all too long for more fighter groups. But they can't just be produced from thin air. Ever since it's been appreciated that these four-engined bombers are in fact real fortresses which can only be taken on individually, some ludicrous proposals have been put forward about how to deal with them. You'll soon be getting some rockets from the army – they call them *Nebelwerfer*. They're large-calibre missiles and one of them is mounted beneath each wing. They're fired so that they explode in the middle of the bombers and cause them to scatter. Once flushed from their defensive hedgehog the Fortresses can be destroyed without difficulty. Others are trying to drop large bombs above the formations in such a way that they explode at the same height as the enemy. Here the intention is to destroy the whole formation in one go, or at least to make it disperse. But it's extraordinarily difficult to position yourself correctly above the Fortresses. Your altitude must be calculated with absolute accuracy since the bomb has a time fuse and is quite ineffective if it goes off at the wrong height.'

'And no doubt the escorting fighters have long been aware of this trick and make sure the air above the bomber stream is clear.'

'Exactly. Another thing is winged bombs suspended from steel wires and trailed through the air by fighters. They're meant to cut the Fortresses to pieces, or at any rate to spread alarm and despondency. One can never say for sure beforehand whether these inventions are going to be any good or whether they're just pieces of nonsense. But a head-on attack – a closely knit assault carried out on a collision course – that's what spreads panic among the bomber crews and reduces the fight to single engagements. Today it's the classical opening to the battle.'

'Provided the fighters let you get there . . .'

'Provided the fighters let you get there. And provided you manage to lead your formation, well closed up, to where you have enough space and height to come down on them from in front and above. Often there are only seconds between the moment of your dive and a collision. And, of course, in this crazy manœuvre you're closing at the sum of both your speeds. The heavies' silhouettes loom up in your windscreen as though in a speeded-up cine-film. You've only a few seconds in which to fire your cannons. You have to aim at the Fortress's glass cockpit and all your chaps must fire like mad at the same time. Then you pull up at once, hard, or alternatively you dive away underneath. After that you're on your own, for your formation will be all over the place. Then is the time to attack single-handed and knock off the lame ducks who've turned tail with an engine stopped or a white trail of petrol streaming out behind them.'

'But it'll all be different here, Franzl. This island's like an aircraft carrier without engines. They can approach it from any direction and fly home at any height they want. The only places where we have any flak are round the ports and the airfields and on either side of the Straits of Messina.'

'That's so. It's a short flight and the whole island's within range of the fighters on Pantelleria and Malta.'

'Since they took Pantelleria, their fighters have been arriving at breakfast time. Fine show *that* surrender was. Makes you wonder what fate's in store for Sicily. I was there in Pantelleria in April and after I'd landed at Marghana, their only airfield, the commandant pretty well tied himself in knots in an effort to convey the impression of stubborn determination. We walked round the rock dug-outs and the emplacements and drank coffee together in his wood-panelled room while he spoke with splendid conviction about the impregnability of the island. He was a willowy sort of chap with a sallow complexion and dark rings under his eyes. I still remember vividly the nervous movements of his hands and the way I kept glancing at the nicotine stains on his fingers. He gave me a terrific buttering-up, holding forth about courage, bravery and comradeship in arms. While I was climbing into my aircraft he saluted, standing stiff as a bronze statue between two carabinieri with red plumes in their helmets. And then he goes and surrenders the island without firing a shot.'

Larsen listened quietly to my tirade and then came straight back to the matter in hand:

'It's going to be a tough time for you all. The general's a realist. You may be certain that he's the last one to think you're not giving of your best . . .'

We were silenced by three rounds of anti-aircraft fire. From the east, over Mount Erice, came the steadily increasing roar of engines. Even as we raced for the slit trenches we could hear the whistle of bombs – a vile noise. I dived into the trench head first, landing on the back of an airman who had got there sooner than I. For a few seconds all was quite still. Then the carpet of bombs came thundering towards us with appalling crashes and explosions. The formations were releasing their bomb loads one after the other so that the carpet kept rumbling closer, unrolling to the rhythm of successive bursts. In the trenches everyone held his breath, hoping that the next stick would fall on the far side.

Close by me I saw Larsen. The fine dust had coated his forehead as though with a layer of white face powder through which the sweat had trickled, forming dark runnels. We pressed our faces to the ground as an explosion close by us nearly burst our eardrums and sent a cloud of dust sweeping through the trench. Presently the sound of engines died away and for a moment or two there was complete silence, a silence that was broken almost at once by the cries of the wounded, shouted commands and calls for stretcher bearers.

'Bloody nice for the general,' Larsen cursed, 'sitting up there on his mountain among his telephones and wireless sets watching us going through the mincer . . .'

'There's absolutely no comparison, Franzl. The second wave may be along at any moment, so we might as well stay quietly where we are in this delightful spot and continue our discussion about offensive tactics with special reference to the Flying Fortress.'

The only answer elicited by my sarcastic remarks was a good-natured 'Shut up!' By now the dust had settled. Looking up, I saw the deep blue of the sky and the branches of the olive trees with leaves the colour of verdigris. From somewhere came the 'pop-pop' of ammunition going off in a burning aircraft.

'Come on, let's get the general on the telephone and ask him if he has any more surprises like this in store for us.'

'Yes,' Larsen said, 'let's do that.'

We rose, hauled ourselves up to ground level and sat for a moment, our legs dangling in the trench, ready at any moment to

B*

dive in again. The troops were already moving about between the trees and the hut as though nothing had happened. Splinters of glass from the blast-shattered windows glinted in the sunlight. Not far away two of the ground crew, their hands on their hips, stood silently contemplating the sorry spectacle of a Messerschmitt 109 standing atilt with one tire cut to ribbons. The bomb had burst close beside it, riddling fuselage and cockpit with innumerable splinters. From the perforated fuel tanks a steady drip of petrol was soaking away into the ground.

For days now we had been on the receiving end of the bombers' work of destruction and the general apathy towards the elimination of our fighting potential had begun to take on certain alarming aspects.

The ground crew removed the parachute from the seat and started dividing up the spoils. The pilot of the aircraft would get a new machine – provided the supply branch had kept pace with requisitions. After flying it he would say to the others: 'She's very fast' or 'She's got a nice engine', but there had long since ceased to be any personal relationship between man and machine.

At the outbreak of war we had used to give our aircraft names – usually girls' names – which we painted elaborately on the fuselage. During the Battle of Britain there had been a sudden craze for getting the outer skin of one's machine smoother than anyone else's. We wanted to cut down wind resistance and fly faster because we had found out that we were not the only people with good aeroplanes. The practice continued until some ingenious individual calculated that no advantage was being gained since the additional weight of filler offset any improvement in speed. Until quite recently the more successful of our veterans had been marking up their victories on their rudder units. But since we had returned to Sicily the advanced workshops, which were housed in a large tent beside the airfield, had been able to do no more than spray the tactical numbers on to the fuselages in figures three feet high, perhaps adding the group's badge – a red heart – as well. That was all, for there was no longer any time for frivolities. During the preceding days we had been collecting the few aircraft allotted to us from the supply depot in Bari and putting them into service. Like short-lived insects, many of them had failed to survive this flight while others had expired on the ground before they could even take the air.

'That was my aeroplane,' I said. 'She's barely a couple of months old. She had a nice smooth engine and all in all she was a fine machine. I was rather fond of her . . .'

'What should we do, sir?' my chief mechanic asked.

'The engineer officer had better get a machine from one of the squadrons. Repack my parachute and be quick about it.'

The group clerk reported that the line to the operations room had been cut. A short while later a Kübelwagen stopped in front of the hut, its driver bearing instructions from the general that I should telephone him immediately from No 1 Squadron's operations room, the line from there being still in order.

At No 1 Squadron a dismal scene met my eyes. Ground personnel, who had been hit by bomb fragments while sheltering in the trenches, lay in rows in the shade of the hut attended by medical orderlies. The group MO was bending over one of the wounded. He straightened up at my approach and looked at me without saying a word. Bombs had churned up the slope which rose immediately behind the dispersal point.

'Sorry I couldn't warn you earlier,' the general said. 'We didn't know the Marauders were on their way. They were so close to sea level that our direction finders didn't pick them up. Have you any idea yet of the damage they've done?'

'No, sir.'

'You must get ready to take off as soon as possible. The radio monitoring service is reporting a great deal of test transmission from the bombers in Tunisia. I'm expecting a major attack.'

'Can't we be warned as soon as they set out, sir?'

'Our radio operators do, of course, try to pick them up straight away, Steinhoff, but without much prospect of success. Once the bombers have tuned in, they keep wireless silence. A repair squad is on the way to patch up the line to your operations room.'

I returned to the group hut and flopped into my deck-chair

once again. More waiting. Before long the line to the general was repaired. All conversation had ceased for the heat was soporific. Every so often, when the telephone sounded in the hut, we would tense our muscles and hold our breath.

At last, the general came on the line and told me that our direction finders had picked up a formation of bombers well to the north of the island and proceeding in the direction of Naples. It was too late to intercept them now but he was going to order my group into the air so that it could attack them on their way back. He said we had one hour to go.

One hour! I called my commanders, Abben, Freiberg and Meyers, and briefed them on the new situation.

'You have a good chance,' said Larsen. 'They don't expect to be attacked on the homeward flight; their formation isn't so close then, so they're easier to deal with.'

I wasn't really listening, for my thoughts were already busy with the operation. I wanted to show them that we were neither tired nor finished . . . Hence the operation must be mounted with great care. First I intended to assemble my people above the airfield in a deliberate, orderly fashion before turning onto the course ordered.

The final preparations were under way. Everywhere damaged aircraft were being worked on, refuelled and rearmed. Suddenly in the midst of all this came the general's order to start: 'Take off straight away, Steinhoff. The bombers have turned south and attacked the port of Messina. You must hurry if you're going to catch them . . .'

'Scramble!' I shouted to the operations room clerk. 'Give them a green!'

Once again we swung automatically into the routine of combat drill. Some engines had already started. My ground crew had parked my new aircraft in a blast pen and were now helping me in the usual ways. I taxied out and waited for my HQ flight.

Taxi, run up engine, check magnetos. A glance astern. The life-jacket with its heavy kapok collar made head movements difficult; the oxygen mask swung to and fro at the level of my chin. Clouds of dust wherever I looked. Straden and Bachmann in position now. A hand signal from me – acknowledged: ready for take-off.

Once I had released the brakes and pushed the throttle right forward I felt an overwhelming sense of liberation, of delight in going for the umpteenth time through the same, familiar routine, a routine that in due course would bring us into contact with the enemy and so resolve our tension. With the engine vibrating at maximum revolutions, my wheels came clear of the ground. The next task facing me was the careful execution of the plan designed to assemble this train of one hundred fighters above the airfield. It was a plan that needed to be carried out deliberately, yet speed was vital for we did not want to waste fuel. My intention was to meet the heavies in a broad phalanx flying at several different heights. I throttled back and, with undercarriage up and flaps up, brought the fighters in a gentle climbing turn round and above Mount Erice where they took up their appointed formation.

Next I established R/T communication with the fighter control room. 'Odysseus One to Eagle, receiving you loud and clear. Over.'

Now the general himself took over the microphone: 'Pantechnicons withdrawing. Grid reference two Able two-two King. Steer zero-two-five.'

Making a wide left-hand turn, I brought No 2 Wing into position behind me. During the climb I had made one circuit of Mount Erice and we were now crossing the north coast of the island at 10,000 feet. Above and astern of me my command had formed up in battle formation. Like some enormous dragon, the triangular pattern of over one hundred aircraft headed northwards. The hiss in our earphones was interrupted only by orders and information about the enemy's latest position, for I had ordered radio silence until such time as we should intercept.

Back at the control room the general was speaking into the microphone again. His voice was unmistakable, his speech measured and almost impassive. His calmness communicated itself to the hundred men who, in a condition of acute nervous tension, were flying into battle. Success could well depend on the orderly and disciplined use of the R/T prior to the moment of interception. But if this was difficult enough to achieve even with a small unit that flew and fought together almost daily, how much harder was it going to be with a massed formation assembled at random? One uncontrolled shout of warning, a single report blurted out prematurely, could upset the whole pattern of the attack, for panicky nervousness would then result and our wave length be inundated with uncontrollable chatter.

The general was speaking again: 'Odysseus, turn onto three-zero-zero, pantechnicons at 20,000 feet heading west.'

'Message received.'

The sea was visible only when one looked vertically downwards. I loathed this sort of weather – associated by meteorologists with a high-pressure situation – which is characterized by an appreciable thickening of haze. In such conditions it is still just possible at high altitudes to discern the contours of the landscape, but aside from these there is nothing to indicate one's position, no fixed reference point, for earth, sky and sea all merge together in a dark blue haze. One's eyes strain to see through the nothingness, returning at frequent intervals to the instruments, the only reliable source of information. In a 'soup' of this description it was virtually impossible to lead a large formation of fighters.

'Odysseus, vector two-nine-zero, angels sixteen.'

Very gently I adjusted the course. When I threw my head back I saw behind me the silhouettes of the aeroplanes crossing over each other and changing position in apparent disorder as the pilots endeavoured to keep formation without using up too much fuel.

Air bubbles began rising in the glass tube beside my left knee, an indication that the drop tank below the fuselage was now empty. Still a good hour's flying time left!

Again the calm words of command sounded in the headphones: 'Odysseus, steer two-eight-zero. Pantechnicons presumably now at low level since the Freya[1] has lost contact.'

Immediately all eyes looked downwards, seeking to penetrate

[1] A radar device

the haze, but all that could be seen between wings and fuselage was a little patch of sea, patterned with white wave crests.

By now we must have been more than half way between Sicily and the southern tip of Sardinia. The aircraft behind me were showing an increasing tendency to rise and fall – a sure sign of growing uneasiness among the pilots as each one of them became more and more aware of his isolation in his single-engined fighter.

As if foreseeing that there was now virtually no prospect of a successful battle so far as we were concerned, I began to hope that we might miss the bombers. I did not intend to remain on this course for more than ten minutes, by which time shortage of fuel would force us to turn back. The aircraft on the outer flanks of the formation were particularly at risk; in order to keep station they had to cover a greater distance whenever I altered course, which meant that they were frequently flying at full boost and maximum revolutions, consuming in the process their precious combat reserve of fuel.

The formation was already widely strung out. At 10,000 feet the haze was exceptionally dense and when I looked back I could see only Freiberg's unit against the sky. The others had been swallowed up in the murk.

'Odysseus calling, close up! Close up!'

'Throttle back a bit please, we're using too much fuel – got to turn back . . .'

Already the R/T was coming to life as though the pilots felt less oppressed by their isolation when they were able to communicate with each other and hear the sound of their own voices. For the most part the tone was highly phlegmatic, having been adopted, of course, to disguise the state of extreme tension engendered in each of them as they waited for the first report of a sighting, the cry of 'Look out!' or 'There they are!' The crackle of the R/T, each time it came to life before the actual sound of the words, made everybody jump.

'Pantechnicons right beneath us – right beneath us, lots of them, heading west!'

It was Zöhler's voice – his accent was unmistakable. So loud

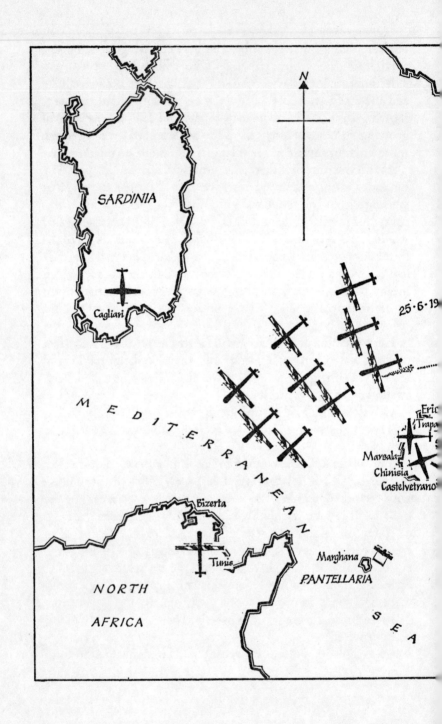

Foggia Manfredonia Bay

ADRIATIC

Bari SEA

ITALY Taranto

Cosenza
Sila Crotone

Stromboli Vibo Valentia

Cefalù Reggio
Calabria

Mt. Enna Mt. Etna

Sciacca

SICILY Gerbini Catania

Agrigento
Licata Comiso Augusta
Gela Syracuse

Cape Passero

'43

Gozo
MALTA Valetta harbour

had been his shout that he must have intended to alert every single man by sheer volume of noise. Electrified, I looked down at the grey sea below. And then I saw them too: the surface had suddenly become speckled with a curious pattern of light brown smudges. With their upper parts painted desert yellow the Flying Fortresses stood out clearly against the silver grey of sea. They were flying very low and fast, racing over the waves almost wing tip to wing tip. I could only see them in the angle between my main plane and engine cowling; elsewhere they were invisible in the haze. They were making for North Africa on a reciprocal course to our own. There were intervals between the individual squadrons of nine or perhaps twelve aircraft. Beneath the formation the wave crests of the Mediterranean were like a patterned carpet, slowly unrolling.

I knew that there was no time for a carefully calculated tactical manœuvre. I was compelled to start the attack from this unfavourable position without a moment's delay, whether my formation followed me or not. Small hope now of giving any orders over the radio! As I dived in the direction of the bombers' left flank, the screech and uproar in the earphones had reached such proportions that I could only catch a few random words or phrases.

'Pantechnicons – look, very low, crowds of them!'

'Got to turn back . . .'

'Stay there, stay there!'

6000 feet. The Messerschmitt 109's speed had built up tremendously. The more height I lost, the faster the bombers seemed to be moving. Straden, Bachmann and Bernhard followed me down, keeping correct station. 3000 feet!

Suddenly a gap appeared between the enemy squadrons. I had to get low enough to be at the same height as the bombers when I met them. The rolling waves were now a few feet below me and the extended line of huge aircraft was approaching at an incredible speed. I fixed my gaze through the front windscreen, keeping the illuminated reflector sight on the aircraft at the centre of the formation. 'You have to aim at the Fortress's glass cockpit . . .' Exactly when I opened fire I do not know – the moment to do so must have been conveyed automatically to my thumb on the stick. In that last brief phase of the attack it was all suddenly like the sequence of a familiar exercise. I pulled my Me up to the same height as the bombers as though I had done it a hundred times before. My task was to spray the gleaming cockpit with a hail of shot. In a curving trajectory the incendiary tracer streaked away from the machine guns towards the giant bomber, crossing the blue smears of smoke tracer. The luminous cross-wires of my sights shook to the 'pop-pop-pop' of the cannons. The flashing panels of glass were plainly visible, and then I had to wrench the machine upwards, the 'g' force pressing me hard down into my seat. The impetus from this burst of speed took me high above the bombers. My mouth felt as though it had dried up and my saliva tasted bitter. The cockpit was full of the smell of cordite. As I banked I noticed that I was on my own; my HQ flight had broken. Looking back I saw a column of white water rising as high as a house at the point where the bomber had crashed.

The radio was inundated with the hubbub of battle. Mixed with orders and encouraging shouts was the hysterical shrieking of incipient panic.

'. . . course for Trapani, please – I'm on my own . . .'

'My fuel's running out!'

'Trapani, a fix, please.'

Freiberg and his wing must have followed me down into the attack on the bombers, for I could hear shouted scraps from the battle: 'Get closer, get closer . . .'

'Release your drop tank!'

'Flatten out!'

But at the same time increasing numbers were reporting a shortage of petrol and the need to withdraw. My own fuel gauge indicated a reserve equivalent to twenty minutes' flying time. I climbed through the haze to 10,000 feet and, now quite alone, turned on to the compass course which I estimated must lead me back to the island.

Already I was beginning to assess just what had happened. It was a disaster that we should have come upon the bombers at the last minute. And there were no instructions about the tactics to adopt when attacking low-flying Boeings. Nothing, absolutely nothing, had favoured our attack.

The bombers had been swallowed up in the haze. All at once I relapsed into the state of anxiety that assails those who fly solo over the sea. I listened uneasily to the sound of the engine, calculated course and flying time yet again, and stared at the greyish blue wall ahead out of which Mount Erice must soon appear.

By now the tumult on the R/T wave length had reached such hysterical proportions that I was suddenly overcome with rage. 'Odysseus One to all Odysseus pilots,' I called, 'keep your mouths shut. Your course is one-three-zero.'

As the pale blue tapering cone of Mount Erice rose up like a beacon from the haze, I was able to make out isolated Messerschmitts which, like mine, were struggling to reach the island. The panic had subsided and only rarely did anyone now request a course to bring him home.

The returning aircraft circled Trapani airfield in quick succession. I watched them land and taxi, and observed the swirls of dust they raised when turning round in the dispersal pens.

No sooner had I switched off the engine than there came the realization that we had been beaten. Up till that moment I had suppressed this knowledge and even then, against my better judgement, I went on hoping that we might have shot down a few Fortresses, although it seemed highly improbable. There had been no indication on the R/T of any successes and not one of the aeroplanes landing after me had rocked its wings – the traditional manner in which a victory in the air is announced.

Bachmann and Straden were standing beside my machine when I opened the cockpit hood. I pulled off my helmet and wiped the sweat from my forehead. Here on the ground I was again assailed by the unbearable heat. Beneath my life-jacket my shirt clung to my body.

Straden seized my hand in congratulation as I jumped down from the wing. 'You bust that Boeing's cockpit into smithereens, sir,' he said. 'It was only by the skin of my teeth I didn't fly into the waterspout. She hit the water with a hell of a smack and bits of her were flying hundreds of feet into the air.'

'Were any more shot down, did you see?'

'No, the withdrawal had already started and a set attack wasn't possible any more.'

'Did Freiberg and his wing get to the shooting stage?'

'They intercepted – I heard that on the radio, but whether they got anything . . .'

'Bachmann, I'd like to see the wing leaders as soon as they've all landed.'

'Very well, sir.'

As I approached the hut, Freiberg rose from the steps.

'That was a gorgeous balls-up, sir,' he said.

'Didn't your wing get any?'

'Not a single one. I lost sight of you in the haze and it was only then I saw the bombers. So we had to attack from astern. And we botched it, really botched it. Evidently the other two wings never found the bombers.'

'Have all your pilots landed?'

'All but two corporals. I heard a distress call shortly after we attacked. The defensive fire was really rough. We were flying at the same height as the heavies and an absolute hail of tracer was coming back at us as we closed to get within range.'

Abben telephoned to report his wing's return. He said that he had seen the Fortresses when he had already turned back; to pursue them would have made a return to Trapani impossible.

Shortly afterwards Meyers, too, reported an unsuccessful battle: they had attacked from an unfavourable position and had come back on their last reserves of fuel. Two of his pilots were missing.

A moment later I heard someone saying: 'The general would like to speak to you, sir.'

I took the telephone: 'I have to report the group's return from the operation, sir,' I said. 'We sighted the heavies at the last minute; it must have been at least a hundred miles northwest of Trapani. It was too late to carry out a set attack and a number of pilots had already turned back because of fuel shortage. So far I can only report the destruction of one Fortress . . .'

There was a long silence at the other end of the line. Finally: 'But I told you in good time that they'd gone down low. It really isn't possible – a hundred fighters and only one enemy shot down . . .'

A crack from the muzzle of an eighty-eight millimetre anti-aircraft gun shook the thin wooden walls of the hut and unleashed a stampede for the protection of the trenches. The telephone crash-ed on to the wooden floor and even as I sprang towards the door and ran for cover, I could hear the drone of engines mingled with the noise of the flak. And, just as though he had been waiting in the trench all the time, there was Larsen, crouching down, his head hunched between his shoulders. He peered up at me and jumped out of the way as I let myself drop.

Huddled side by side we cowered silently against the ground while the whistle and whine of falling bombs continued to mingle with the bursts of the anti-aircraft shells.

When things began to quieten down I stood up and glanced over the edge of the trench. Although I felt depressed and ex-hausted, I could not help asking him sarcastically: 'Have you been sitting here all the time, Franzl, while we've been fighting our big battle?'

'Don't be an ass. I was following the whole thing on the radio at operations – it's bad, very bad. He's seething with rage. Was there really absolutely nothing to be done?'

'No,' I said, 'absolutely nothing.'

'But you found the bombers and there wasn't even a fighter escort . . .'

I detected a faint note of reproach and even though I had come to the end of my strength, I turned towards him abruptly and said with intense exasperation: 'I'll be accountable to the general for everything – but what I do insist is that you finally get it into your heads that we're trying to do the impossible here!'

I had deliberately associated him with the general in this last remark, but then I said something that I would gladly have taken back the moment the words had passed my lips: 'If you want a taste of what air fighting is like here, you'd better come along the next time the heavies turn up.'

'I'm sorry,' Larsen answered, 'I'm truly sorry. I honestly wasn't reproaching you. But, my God, how's it going to end, how's it all going to end?'

At this hour there was a great deal of traffic on the road to Mount Erice. Donkey carts, mule carts and women with bundles on their heads were hurrying back to Trapani, for the local people had acquired the habit of spending the hours of daylight away from the danger areas of the town and the airfield. At night all they had to contend with were isolated attacks by Wellingtons and so they were streaming back to their houses in the town to attend to essential tasks.

The sun was already low by the time I arrived at the group's operations room where the General of Fighters was now in personal control.

The general was sitting on a camp-chair with his back to the wall of the hut; at his feet lay the magnificent panorama of the Sicilian landscape. Peaceful and innocent, the vine-clad slopes of Mount Erice fell away to meet the outskirts of the town whose buildings, in the pale evening sunlight, were bathed in a rich yellow glow. Up here the tall pines and cypresses looked dark blue against the sky.

But just then the general did not seem to appreciate the melancholy beauty of the scene. As I saluted, he rose to his feet with the words:

'I'm about to fly back to Comiso.'

'I'm sorry, sir,' I said, 'that everything went wrong.'

'We can't go on like this. The answer to the heavies is the massed attack. So long as we commit ourselves in penny packets and try to fight off every intruder, we'll never be successful. It's time you learnt how to tackle the bombers, how to approach them in tight formation and attack them head-on. You're hesitating and you're failing to get close enough . . .'

As he spoke, he transferred his black cigar from one corner of his mouth to the other and looked at me in an unfriendly manner.

Soon, I thought, I would be able to recite the thing backwards. It was what they all kept telling us and by now we knew by heart the combat reports from the fighter pilots in the Reich. I understood his disappointment and would have liked to have told him that everything was different here – weather, tactical circumstances, sighting conditions – and that there were contributory factors of which those in the Reich knew nothing . . . But partly because I felt ashamed that we should have disappointed him so much, and partly because I believed that a soldier should not make excuses if he thinks he has done his best, I just looked at him and said nothing.

No doubt the general himself realized that we were unlikely to agree that evening for he brought the conversation to an end with a gesture that was half conciliatory, half despairing.

'I shall telephone you later today. We must consider different tactics.' With that he got into his car.

The shrilling of the telephone snatched me rudely from a brief sleep so blissfully deep and so far removed from the reality of the present that it was several seconds before I could give my name or realize that I was speaking to the general, who by now had arrived at Comiso. Looking back today, the conversation still seems unreal to me and even at the time I could not help hoping, at least for a few minutes, that it had all been a bad dream.

'Steinhoff,' he said, 'I've just had a teleprint from the Reichsmarschall. Don't, please, get agitated when I read it out to you. Take no action for the moment. But I've got to inform you. Listen:

"To the Fighter Leader, Sicily. During the defensive action against the bombing attack on the Straits of Messina the fighter element failed in its task. One pilot from each of the fighter wings taking part will be tried by court martial for cowardice in the face of the enemy.

(signed) *Göring, Reichsmarschall*."

I repeat: take no action. I've told Air Corps in the most forceful terms that the thing's impossible.'

I remained silent as though confronted by an imputation too outrageous to be refuted. I struggled to think clearly so as to grasp the enormity of it.

'Cowardice in the face of the enemy.' The voice at the other end of the line had had an unfamiliar ring about it – 'One pilot from each wing . . .' It couldn't, it mustn't be true!

'Are you still there?'

'Yes, sir.'

'I'll call you tomorrow. He always gets furious when his fighters don't measure up.'

'Didn't we measure up, sir?'

'It's not me that said it. I'll call you tomorrow morning. And don't worry!'

Don't worry about what? Could I, as an officer, fail to worry when something like this had happened? The Reichsmarschall despised us although the simplest calculation would have sufficed to show that a battle against such odds could only end in defeat. Did he really imagine that he could stimulate our will to fight by calling us cowards? Only a short time before he had rejected with contumely the possibility that four-engined bombers might penetrate the Luftwaffe's defences. In the meantime they had been reaching virtually every corner of the Reich. So now he was trying to make us responsible for his difficulties as well. He had meant us all, every single fighter pilot in the south. It had been a collective insult: 'One pilot from each of the Fighter Wings' – one pilot chosen at random!

Freiberg and Godert would be arriving shortly and I intended to tell them without delay. Abben and Meyers had flown back to their airfields, one to Sardinia, the other to eastern Sicily. I did not propose to pass the order on to them until I had spoken to the general. He could not and would not allow this absurd directive to be carried out.

Still holding the receiver which had long since gone dead, I sat staring straight in front of me. From the dining-room next door came the clink of glasses and china, and I could make out the voices of Bachmann and Straden speaking in undertones so as not to disturb me. Night had fallen abruptly. From my bed I could see a patch of star-strewn, velvety blue sky of a beauty and grandeur that only the south can offer.

I almost regretted now having gone for the group in North Africa when the general had given me the choice between a command in the Reich and one in the south. I had arrived on a short home leave from my fighter wing in the Crimea, having flown to Berlin in a Storch. The General of Fighters was expecting me. When he greeted me his mood was sombre. At first he had wanted to know how things were going with our fighter defence in the east but I soon realized that his immediate preoccupation lay elsewhere. Almost at once he came round to the subject of the Flying Fortresses, telling me about their first attacks on the Channel coast and their apparent invulnerability which had so surprised the German fighter pilots. He had warned the Reichsmarschall and had demanded a build-up of the fighter arm. In the same context he had pointed out that the armament of the Messerschmitt 109 and Focke-Wulf 190 was inadequate and had suggested certain improvements. When he had predicted that one day the Fortresses would be able to fly to Berlin itself the Reichsmarschall had brushed the suggestion rudely aside, declaring that he refused to listen to such defeatist tittle-tattle.

Without any transition, the general had gone on to talk about the death of Major M, almost as though his intention throughout the entire conversation had been to conclude with the startling words: 'I'm afraid you're going to have to cut your leave short. Replacements are needed for two cos. There's the choice of a group in North Africa or one in the Reich.'

Without hesitation I had chosen North Africa. I did not know the south and it attracted me, as did the prospect of combat with the chivalrous pilots of the west. At the time I had no inkling of how pitiless that combat was going to be in the face of such crushing odds.

'You'll be taking over the 77th Fighter Group in North Africa. The CO's been killed.' Not very encouraging, but in wartime this was the way promotion happened. We all of us moved up by stepping into dead men's shoes, we no less than those on the other side, those whom at every opportunity we tried to shoot down.

I flew to Munich and drew my tropical kit. Impossible, baggy trousers of khaki drill, some shirts and a brown tunic – all off the peg and all manufactured in accordance with the principle 'It'll fit somehow.'

And so in March I landed at Ciampino near Rome. For the first time in my life I set foot in the Eternal City. It was a marvellous spring day. On the way to the field marshal's headquarters I opened the windows of the staff car and breathed the prodigal scents of nature in full bloom. Frascati was, and still is, one of Rome's most luxurious residential suburbs. Outside the C-in-C's white villa I was met by the orderly officer who took me to the Chief of Staff. But first he introduced me to a real live receptionist, and a young one at that, looking like a vision of spring in her diaphonous wisp of a dress as she arranged carnations in a vase. And then I was standing in front of the 'Chief', a general who, clad in a white tunic, sat enthroned behind an enormous desk. Never in my life will I forget the Air Fleet situation conference which I was permitted to attend. There was I, a combatant officer, witnessing the prognostication and the synthetic portrayal of the future course of the battle in North Africa, a battle which the following day I would see enacted with my own eyes. The staff had assembled in a large sunny room. Officers in white stood round the situation table on which the maps had been spread out, maps whose characteristics were comparatively unfamiliar to me. Where land was shown, large, empty expanses of yellow predominated, but for the most part it was water, wholly blank except for the intersecting lines of the grid.

Dressed as I was in my badly fitting desert uniform, I felt ill at ease among these unbelievably gorgeous creatures. Not for ages had I seen so much glitter. Perhaps it was because two years of fighting in Russia had coarsened me and taught me to despise such things but this faintly pompous way they had of expressing themselves, indeed their attitude and behaviour in general, struck me as downright insulting to those at the front, and my distaste increased from minute to minute.

Was I allergic to the high command and to staff officers? That would have been unjust, for after all staff work had to be done just as we had to 'stick our backsides out'. But such admittedly vulgar expressions were no longer current among them, although nearly all must at some time have served at the front where language is not governed by the rules of aesthetics. I found their foppish affectation and general superciliousness insufferable. In their presence anyone honoured by an interview with the field marshal would be made to feel rather like a clumsy carthorse; with a condescending wave of the hand he would be offered a chair in one of the Air Fleet ante-rooms and there he would have to sit and wait. I had come from the eastern front and in the course of two Russian winters had learnt that we were 'human material intended for immediate consumption'. At Stalingrad I had watched an army die. I had witnessed the collapse of a front; I had flown, and flown again, and I had done my duty, as would any other soldier, wherever I happened to be sent. Then, almost without transition, I had found myself en route to North Africa to be at once actor in and spectator at the next catastrophe. But first of all I was to watch the prologue on the map table.

I had long since come to mistrust the value of the information provided by the flags and numerals on a map table. What was a battalion, exactly, or a fighter squadron? No one inquired into the real combat value of these entities. A squadron was something capable of shooting down ten of the enemy during a one-hour operation; therefore it had damned well got to do it. No one inquired into the actual condition of the infantry battalion whose command post was shown on the map as a small triangular flag. How could anyone tell that it was not a forlorn band, a captain and a hundred men, exhausted, desperate, half out of their minds, perhaps, and with fifty per cent of their number more or less severely wounded? Could anyone really tell? Yet all these generals and General Staff officers – at least the great majority of them – had themselves been in action; they must surely have been aware of all these things since their own experience must have etched them indelibly on their minds.

There was criticism of our Italian allies expressed in regretful tones; there was talk of reinforcements, of the tons of fuel and ammunition supplies required. I heard and watched the conclusion of a glorious campaign being presented with a matter-of-factness amounting almost to indifference. I found the attitude of these elegant colonels infuriatingly detached. Was I the only committed person there? And committed I certainly was, for the next day I was to land in Tunis to lead my fighter group in this final round against a more powerful enemy.

This, then, is what we had come to after having ourselves been the more powerful enemy in the early stages of the war. Now we had learned what the taste of defeat was like, but defeat itself had two aspects: one of them I had come to know at Stalingrad; the other had just been all but demonstrated to me on a sand-table in the spick and span headquarters of an air fleet.

When it was over we sat down at the large table to an excellent dinner presided over by the field marshal himself.

'As soon as you've familiarized yourself with the theatre,' he began, 'it is essential that you convince the people in your group that North Africa must be held – held at all costs. We shall be reinforcing the bridge-head and narrowing the front so that the position can be held without difficulty. But we must get the very best we can out of the air component. The most essential thing – and your first job – is therefore to carry the group's pilots along with you, to reinculcate the aggressive drive that inspired everyone during the advance to El Alamein.'

'Very well, sir.'

How did he think I should set about reinculcating an aggressive drive and restoring their offensive spirit? 'Very well' I had said but I was at a loss to know what one did when one took over a new command after arriving from a quite different theatre with experience that might well be no longer valid . . .

A day or two later I had come to grips with reality. Standing before the assembled pilots for the first time on the small airfield north of Sfax, I could read their thoughts by the expressions on their faces. It was with a friendly scepticism that they examined the newcomer who was henceforward to lead them. For leading a fighter group – this I knew for a fact which applied to every theatre – meant that you headed the formation, that you set an example, that you shot down aircraft. That was how a squadron commander, a wing leader and, above all, a group commodore was judged. They wanted to know what sort of a person this new arrival from the eastern front might be, whether he could cope with air fighting in their own theatre and how he performed in combat, for the eastern front was regarded as a 'cushy' front for fighter pilots. I felt ashamed of the strongly worded address I had prepared – one that would undoubtedly have met the field marshal's requirements – and said simply that I was proud to be able to lead the group and that our job was to fly and to destroy enemy aircraft. Thank you, gentlemen.

And already by the following day I had found out how they flew and how they fought here. I had also learnt not to forget that it was the enemy's task, too, to fly and to destroy enemy aircraft and that he had been making an excellent job of it for some time past. At all events this was the case with the Spitfire pilot who had riddled my radiator with some highly accurate shooting, so compelling me to make a belly-landing in the desert south of Kairouan.

They were sitting round the table when I came in. Their relaxed, carefree style, reminiscent of a peacetime officers' mess, never varied whatever the billet or the primitive airfield we might be occupying at the time. But this was merely on the surface and beneath one could see that they were deadly tired. It was much less physical exhaustion than the mental fatigue that comes of always being beaten. Godert had just arrived from Sciacca. As he greeted me, he looked at me sadly as though to say: 'I'm afraid I've no victories to report.'

Tubby served us with fried eggs and filled our glasses with wine. The conversation dragged on. We spoke of the operation and the abortive attack on the bombers. During lulls in the talk we looked at one another; in all our eyes was the realization of the inevitability of the event which no one could escape. There was no hope because miracles didn't happen and because there weren't any miracle weapons either, just men who kept on fighting until they dropped. The sequence of attacks on the island would proceed with deadly precision – a precision that once had been our speciality but which now seemed to have devolved upon the enemy. And we would have to keep hurling ourselves at our adversaries right up to the end which we knew was coming and could do nothing to avert.

Every pilot here knew it, even those who had only just arrived. But what they still did not know was that something had happened that evening which was to make it all more bitter still. They would have to be told – I could not keep it from them. And even as I debated how I could put it most gently, I had already begun to speak.

'I have to pass on to you an order from the Reichsmarschall. The general has just been on the telephone to tell me that the Reichsmarschall is displeased because, so he believes, we failed in our task today. One pilot from each of the wings taking part is to be tried by court martial for' – and suddenly the words stuck in my throat – 'cowardice in the face of the enemy.'

There was a deathly hush round the table. They looked at me in disbelief as if I had just told a joke in bad taste.

It was Freiberg who was the first to find his voice. Raising his glass, he said: 'Well, well, let's drink to that – I'll volunteer.'

I could have hugged him. With his cutting sarcasm, he had indicated the only possible course of action open to us, the commanders.

Shy young Bernhard, who was looking utterly miserable and had not yet touched a bite of his food, inquired in shocked tones: 'How's it to be decided, sir? What's in the Reichsmarschall's mind? Surely the Führer can't . . . ?' He stopped and looked round helplessly.

Oh worthy product of the Hitler Youth, I thought. But before I could say anything Freiberg replied: 'There's nothing in his mind. He just wants to frighten the pants off us. Perhaps it'll make us all the keener when the court martial has found a few of us guilty and we've been given the chop . . .'

I could not allow the conversation to go on in this vein; cynicism was not going to help the situation. So I said, evenly and unemotionally: 'The general asked me to tell you that he would intervene on our behalf and that we were not to worry. But he was really very disappointed himself. A hundred fighters in the air and only one enemy shot down – he just can't make it out yet.'

A bomb exploding near the house set the glasses on the table rattling. The electric light flickered once or twice and then went out for good. 'Nuisances here again,' Tubby called in the darkness. 'I'll take your camp-bed and sleeping-bag to the grotto, sir.'

We went thundering down the stairs and once in the open we could hear the sonorous drone of the Wellingtons' engines. The night was still hot. The glare from a burning house was reflected in the bay.

I straightened up after squeezing through the gap in the wall. The air in the grotto was heavy with cigarette smoke and the smell of sweat. Freiberg began to deliver a lecture on the subject of bravery. In his right hand was clasped a bottle of marsala, his favourite drink; he had dispensed with a glass this evening. Zöhler's face, in contrast to the extreme blackness of his hair, looked transparent and very pale in the light of the carbide lamp. Though he had had an attack of malaria not long before, he had nevertheless refused home leave so that he could stay with his squadron.

Godert, his eyes closed, was lying in a deck-chair. Straden and Bachmann, elbows propped on the table, conversed in whispers.

The fair girl, Teresa, was sitting in the semi-darkness near the narrow stone steps that led up to the villa. Beside her stood her *nonna*, as ramrod straight as ever and hardly distinguishable in her black dress and black veil from the surrounding shadows.

Bernhard and Zahn were in camp chairs, facing Freiberg. Tubby moved my deck-chair next to Freiberg's and poured me out a glass of wine. The conversation had just been interrupted by another explosion and all that could be heard was the hiss of the lamp.

Freiberg turned to me: 'Well, we've been talking it over,' he said. 'The wing leaders on the operation are going to step forward. It's us they'll have to court martial.'

'Yes,' Godert agreed, 'that's what we're going to do.'

'But doesn't that mean an admission of cowardice?' Zöhler objected.

Freiberg waved his hands in a gesture that was almost Italian. 'It's for the court to find out just what cowardly conduct is in a fighter pilot. They've got to tell us how to carry out an attack and whether everyone's a coward who comes home without having shot down an aircraft. Supposing you've closed from astern with a hundred machine guns shooting at you and you've fired off all your ammunition, yet the heavies keep trundling along like a bunch of airliners and nothing to do with you at all – then you've got to ram and if you don't you're a coward.'

'Yes,' Zöhler said, 'that's what he meant in his teleprint: we're supposed to ram the Fortresses.'

Suddenly they all fell silent and looked expectantly at me as though I should provide an answer. The Imp's large eyes, with their customary frightened expression, were gazing at me with peculiar intensity as if he wanted to ask: 'Is it true?'

But once again Freiberg got his word in first; he needed to let off steam, for he was much too angry to be able to remain silent. 'Of course. They'll print your name in the Wehrmacht communiqué and your old man will get a nice letter which we might as well have duplicated straight away so that all the CO has to do is sign his name at the bottom. And they'll be able to economize on useless rubbish like parachutes and life-jackets.'

'Come to think of it, you won't need cannons any more,' Zöhler said.

Bachmann had remained serious; all this cynicism was foreign

C

to his nature. 'Who can have put such nonsense into his head?' he wanted to know. 'You know him, sir, he was a fighter pilot himself once. How could he do that to us?'

'The Reichsmarschall hasn't yet realized that we've stopped flying biplanes with wire-braced wings,' I replied, 'and that we no longer sit in open cockpits muffled up in furs and wearing outsize goggles. He's certainly never worn an oxygen mask and he has no idea how we navigate or operate the radio. So how can one expect him to understand the nature of modern aerial warfare?'

'Maybe it's all one to him. As the C-in-C of the Luftwaffe perhaps he doesn't need to know anything about these things. At least so long as others are there to advise him . . .' Zöhler broke off pensively.

'Always provided he listens,' Freiberg said. 'I'll tell you what he's after. He's after kills. How, he doesn't care. And lately the Luftwaffe hasn't been doing so well. Earlier on there was Crete or Norway or, right at the beginning, Poland – then there were still successes. But now that the other side has discovered what it's all about and is beginning to show us how to perfect the kind of air fighting we adopted in the first place, there's only one course open to him: to chalk up kills!'

'But all those "raspberry pants" who swarm round him all the time,' objected Zöhler, 'don't *they* argue with him?'

'They stick pins in the situation map, and they say "Yes, sir", and they haven't the slightest clue about how we're fighting the war. They don't even have the guts to put him straight and tell him that things are different now from his memories of the way it was done in 1917. How can they be expected to? Only a few of them have ever heard a shot fired in anger, and after all, they want to be generals one day.'

'But he's been a fighter pilot,' said Zöhler, 'and if he doesn't understand the facts of our operation or of air fighting at 30,000 feet, then it's time someone explained them to him!'

'Who's going to explain them?' asked Bachmann. 'The Director of Luftwaffe Technical Services[1] was in the same

[1] Udet

66

squadron as the Reichsmarschall; he was also one of the great pilots of the First World War. Göring would surely have listened to him. But he shot himself. I'm certain he'd tried to do his best.'

'He certainly had,' I said. I felt compelled to intervene so as to extricate them from their self-destructive dialogue. 'But he was the only one to do so. I'll tell you why the Reichsmarschall thinks differently and how it's come about that he no longer understands our own particular world.

'When the war began I was commanding a night fighter squadron. Yes, we had them even then! We were stationed on a small grass airfield near Bonn and tried to catch the lone Blenheim bombers entering Reich territory on leaflet raids. It was a wearisome job chasing after those boys. The Blenheims, like the old Junkers, were fully equipped for blind flying which meant that we had to take our single-seater Messerschmitts up, whatever the weather. The blackout was being strictly observed by the civilian population, so taking off into the pitch darkness was a pretty weird experience. I still wonder how we screwed up the courage to chance it time and time again; we'd had precious little night-flying training and our navigational aids were extremely primitive. It was hardly surprising that with this set-up we never bagged anything. The British flew very high, preferably in cloud.

'Back in Berlin the thought was beginning to worry them that there might be serious intentions behind the British threat – that the leaflets falling on the cities of the Reich might be followed by bombs. They kept asking for combat reports. Above all they wanted to know why we weren't shooting the British down since our orders stated quite plainly that we were to do so.

'Towards the end of September a message came over the teleprinter ordering me to Berlin. I was to attend a conference concerned with improvements in night fighting. The Reichsmarschall himself was expected to be there. The following morning I reported at the Ministry of Aviation and was shown to a conference room where the small group of people taking part was assembling: the Chief of the General Staff of the Luftwaffe, the

Director of Luftwaffe Technical Services, the Commander-in-Chief of the Flak Artillery, the General of Fighters, officers of the General Staff and stenographers.

'While we waited for the Reichsmarschall I had a moment in which to examine the conference room. The style was modern and revealed the marshal's preference for oak, plain leather and furniture of imposing dimensions. The pale-coloured wooden panelling went right up to the ceiling from which hung an enormous lustre in the shape of a cart-wheel. Chairs, with seats and backs upholstered in light cowhide, had been placed round three sides of the oak table at the head of which towered a chair of a species all its own, a chair of truly Teutonic proportions. It was the Reichsmarschall's.

'A section of the panelling slid open and he came in. He was wearing a white uniform and while he settled himself down in his enormous armchair he lit one of those long Virginia cigars like they smoke in Austria. Then he started to speak. He talked of the British incursions and the failure of the flak and the night fighters. At that time there were no radio direction finders either for us or for the flak, which was dependent on sound locators. He thought it disgraceful that the Blenheims should be able to loiter about at will above the Reich.

'He talked himself into a thorough rage and all at once he was back in Flanders, and its air battles and the great fighter age of Freiherr von Richthofen. He raised his hands to demonstrate the tactics of the attack from below; moving his outstretched right hand in a swinging, circular movement past his face, he chased it with his left and finally shot it down. He enthused about flying in bright moonlight, about the stalking missions they flew along the roads of Flanders so as to spot the enemy's silhouette against the paler night sky overhead; how they had then increased speed and commenced the attack from below . . .

'He spoke vividly and he impressed me by the forceful manner in which he described the aggressive spirit of the famous fighter pilots and the way they fought. But gradually a feeling of bitter disappointment came over me, for an entire world separated the Reichsmarschall's elaboration of the tactics of night fighting from modern aerial warfare. This man, I thought, has absolutely no conception of air fighting as it is now. He's living in the past and doesn't know his Luftwaffe. He'll have to be told how things really are. That's why I've been ordered to attend. Quite obviously I'll have to put him right, it's what they expect of me!

'His tough phrases now sounded a bit pathetic as he droned on fancifully about the past. I began to shift about in my chair. The temptation to chip in and tell him what it was really like in practice became overpowering.

'As he paused to relight his cigar, I raised my hand. But at the same moment I got into a panic because the generals' faces, all of which had now turned in my direction as though at a word of command, expressed quite plainly what they thought of my impudence. But it was too late to retreat into my shell. The Reichsmarschall waved his cigar at me – his signal for permission to speak. I stood up and began to talk. First I explained that the dimensions of fighting as such had changed and then I went on to point out the difficulties of tracking down an enemy whose good navigational aids enabled him to fly in bad weather and at high altitudes. It was only possible for us to find and engage an adversary when he was caught in the beams of the ground searchlights. But since we had no means of navigating in bad weather, we were unable to carry out our task effectively. What we needed were better navigational aids in our aircraft and new methods if we were even to begin locating the enemy in the darkness. I had spoken concisely and, I hoped, convincingly. In any case it was all perfectly obvious, and surely if anyone knew at that time how night fighting should be carried out it was I.

'When the Reichsmarschall finally removed the cigar from his mouth to interrupt my flow of well-chosen words, he looked more amused than angry. "Sit down," he said as though to a schoolboy, "sit down on your little bottom, young man. You've still a long way to go before you can join in the discussions here."

'Then he turned to one of the generals of his directing staff and paid no further attention to me.

'So there I sat on my "little bottom", swallowing my humiliation, shamefaced in front of those old generals. One of them, however, the Director of Technical Services, gave me a surreptitious wink. He'd covered his note pad with doodled caricatures. And ever since then I've known that our Commander-in-Chief doesn't understand our war.'

The duty officer had been standing behind my deck-chair during the last part of my story. Although he had come with a signal, he did not interrupt me. Now he bent over my chair and said:

'Tomorrow's orders have just come in, sir. Our airfields are to provide the defence against raids from North Africa and Pantellaria. Armed reconnaissance missions are to be flown at first light to Malta, Pantelleria and Tunis.'

'First light,' I echoed, 'that's in three hours.'

Within a short while all was silent in the grotto. They had fallen asleep in their deck-chairs. Every now and again someone stirred restlessly. It was hot and humid in this cellar which ought, by rights, to have been cool. I longed for a refreshing bath and clean underwear, and I loathed this theatre with all my heart.

I would take off for Comiso as soon as it was light.

'Despite ground dissatisfaction with air plans, the Allied air forces actually performed their pre-invasion roles effectively. Furnishing all the fighter and fighter-bomber support and much of the light and medium bomber support, the NATAF moved three Spitfire wings from North Africa to Malta in June to bring the air strength on that island to twenty fighter squadrons. An American P-40 fighter group moved to Pantelleria, also in June, to cover the assault landings at Gela and Licata. American aviation engineers in the remarkably short time of twenty days constructed a new airfield on the island of Gozo, near Malta, to base another American fighter group. By the end of June, Allied planes based on the three islands totalled 670 first-line aircraft.'

UNITED STATES ARMY IN WORLD WAR II
SICILY AND THE SURRENDER OF ITALY

'The [Italian] coastal battalions... were composed of men of the older age groups, often badly commanded, and in some instances covering defensive sectors up to twenty-five miles in length.'

UNITED STATES ARMY IN WORLD WAR II
SICILY AND THE SURRENDER OF ITALY

'With the build-up of Allied air assaults on Sicily in the two final weeks of June, it was the task of the fighter units stationed in Sardinia and northern Sicily to engage the strong attacking formations of Allied bombers and fighters. Losses in the air and on the ground, as also the ever greater number of airfields destroyed, made increasing inroads on combat effectiveness.'

FRANZ KUROWSKI
DAS TOR ZUR FESTUNG EUROPA

Trapani, 27 June 1943

Comiso lies in the southern part of the island, about fifteen miles from the coast whose white, unending sandy beach can be seen from a great distance. It is a magnificent sight. In the days when we were attacking the port and airfields of Malta this bay offered the chance of an emergency landing to the crippled homecomer who saw no prospect of reaching the airfield at Comiso. The trick was to put the aircraft down on the water in such a fashion that, instead of going under, it skidded over the surface and reached the beach with the last of its way. Better still – provided that you got as far – was a landing parallel to the shore on the soft sand. Certain Me 109 pilots had carried out the experiment with great success; others had drowned in the attempt. Now it was with different eyes that I contemplated the lovely, sickle-shaped bay stretching far away beyond the town of Gela, for the place was ideally suited to a seaborne landing based on the techniques evolved by the Americans in the Pacific.

A chain of low pillboxes followed the line of the beach on the landward side. They were the same ludicrous loop-holed structures as could be seen everywhere round the coast and were built either of tuff or of soft-shell limestone; mortar had not been used in their construction since its essential ingredient was valuable and someone had flogged it. They were meant to give an impression of stubborn resistance, a form of self-deception typical of Italy under the Duce. Sights like these began to depress us badly because we were coming to suspect that we, too, saw things no longer as they were but as we wanted, or were supposed to want them to be. One example was the encounter with an Italian two-man sentry patrol during my previous visit to Gela.

c*

During the midday break Bachmann and I had been walking through the dunes on our way down to the beach for a bathe. Suddenly our path was barred by two men wearing the uniform of the Italian Army. They asked for the password, inquired into our nationality and were evidently quite satisfied when we showed them our German uniforms which we had left lying on the sea thistles. These two pathetic old men came from the neighbourhood of Enna in the centre of the island; despite the heat, they were dressed in olive-coloured uniforms of coarse, heavy cloth (known to German soldiers as 'asbestos'). They were armed with short-barrelled rifles of the pattern issued to the Italian Army. Their calves were bound with faded puttees and they wore shoes with laces. They said they were on patrol and that their task was to challenge unknown persons and establish their identity. If they found anything suspicious they were to inform their company HQ in Gela by telephone.

It had been depressing. So *that* was Italian coastal defence after the Italians and Germans had been defeated in North Africa and thrown back on to the island of Sicily! *That* was the much-vaunted iron determination to chase the enemy back into the sea should he be bold enough to set foot on the hallowed soil of the Romans!

Comiso had been an Italian Air Force operational airfield within the framework of what was proudly called the *Arma Azurra*. By reason of its convenient situation it had been a favourite jumping-off point for our bombers and fighters during the battles for air supremacy over Malta. Now, as then, it was occupied by one wing of the 53rd (Ace of Spades) Fighter Group. Nearby, in a grove of pines and fig trees permanently mantled with yellow dust from the arid plain, the Fighter Leader had set up his operations room.

As I made a wide left-hand circuit of the runway I took a mental note of its condition. The Allied bombers had obviously been carrying out frequent attacks for the brown, parched grass was dotted with bomb craters, the hangars lay in ruins and the wing's aircraft had been widely dispersed in blast pens round the edge of the field. A white cross pointed in the direction of the narrow strip of usable runway which, as the general had promised, had been marked with small red and white flags.

After touching down, my machine bumped over the uneven surface and the hastily filled-in craters before rolling to a halt. The airfield looked quite dead. It was only after I had opened my cockpit hood that I noticed an airman beckoning to me from the edge of the airfield where earth ramparts had been thrown up to protect the aircraft. Corporal Helbig had landed after me and followed me in the direction of the pens.

I climbed out and undid the straps of my life-jacket while the ground crew lifted the tail and turned my machine round to face the landing strip. Chocks were then placed against the wheels and the actual work of servicing began. The men were stripped to the waist, their deeply tanned bodies glistening with sweat as they worked in the blazing sun. One of them released the catches of the engine cowling to check the oil and coolant. My inquiry about transport or the nearest telephone was cut short by the telltale 'pop-pop' of flak bursts high above our heads.

'They're on the way!' yelled the fitter as he jumped down from the wing and raced off. Another shouted: 'There's a shelter over there!' He pointed at a mound of earth in the middle of a cactus hedge and then he, too, scuttled away. There was nothing left for me to do but take cover likewise.

'Helbig, hurry up!' I shouted to my corporal, before hastening after the airmen through the dried-out, knee-high scrub. By the time I reached the entrance to the shelter I could already hear the drone of engines. A steep flight of steps led downwards. Like the walls and roof of the shelter itself, they were made of yellow tuff, a stone which feels soft to the touch and leaves one's hands yellow after they have been in contact with it. The shelter was a tunnel with two exits and a head room of seven feet. Once my eyes had become accustomed to the semi-darkness I could see that it was packed as tight as an overloaded bus. The troops were either standing with their backs against the wall or squatting on the dusty floor. As I pushed my way in, some of them closed up, moving away from the entrance to a more protected position by the walls. Not a man attempted to salute me and indeed one would have had to be unutterably stupid to expect it in such a situation. Their expressions were stoical, almost indifferent, for by now they were long accustomed to this game of chance. Once again I realized how dependent we were on these unassuming craftsmen without whose careful attentions our machines would never have got into the air. They looked at me calmly and a little pityingly, as much as to say: 'You've got to sweat it out with us this time. The knack of shooting down aircraft won't be much use to you here.'

Suddenly the flak began firing rapidly. The men on the guns were little different from those in the shelter, the only dissimilarity being that the former were unable to take cover and instead had to, and did, keep firing as the carpet of bombs unrolled towards them. Each of these men had his own part in this drama devoted to destruction, his own brand of heroism, his own special way of achieving mastery over himself. These things were easy to forget when one was a privileged solo combatant, flying a powerful machine in the three-dimensional freedom of the sky, and it was only in a literally down-to-earth situation such as this that one remembered them. Now the soughing roar made by the first bombs as they fell could be heard plainly above the din of flak and aircraft. Involuntarily we hunched our heads between our shoulders. Helbig had taken hold of my arm with both hands, and as the bombs exploded with a gross and horrible 'crump' that pressed against one's eardrums, he gripped me so hard that it hurt.

Then came a pause in which only the flak was audible. The men on the gun nearest us had evidently survived. Now the roar of engines rose and fell again, punctuated by the bursting of delayed-action bombs. The faces of the men around me were covered with white dust blown into the shelter by the explosions. I heard someone say: 'The next wave . . .'

'*Mamma mia, mamma mia!*' wailed a hysterical voice close beside me and, before I could do anything to prevent it, one of the dusty figures on the ground had clasped me round my waist and was pressing against me in search of protection. '*Mamma mia, mamma mia!*' it kept screaming without a pause. And now, once again came the loathsome whistle of bombs. I found myself intolerably encumbered by the Italian but, at the very moment when the force of the explosion put us all on our knees, when I felt I might lose control of myself, a lanky German soldier dragged the man away from me and dealt him a resounding box on the ear.

Then it was quiet. Dust came drifting in through the two entrances of our dungeon and only an occasional explosion could now be heard. Circumspectly we climbed up the steps into the open where the scene of destruction brought us up short. Near the entrance, the patch of withered grass which extended up to the ramparts of the aircraft pens had been churned into a hideous landscape of craters, while above the spot where we had parked the 109s two columns of oily black smoke rose high into the air. Fragmentation bombs had perforated their fuel tanks and ignited the petrol. Above the burning aircraft the air shimmered with heat. An enormous dust cloud hung over the rest of the airfield like a white blanket, veiling it from sight. But we could see all too clearly what was left of our two burning aeroplanes, now beyond anyone's power to save.

In the end I managed to find some transport to take me to the Fighter Leader's operations room. My tale of woe made little impression on the general. Without beating about the bush he began to discuss the defence of the island.

'There's no longer any doubt in my mind that the island's being softened up for a landing. Now that Pantelleria has surrendered without a shot being fired, they don't need aircraft carriers any more. Malta and Pantelleria are ideal springboards for their fighters – you might even say they're unsinkable aircraft carriers. The bombers are being flown from further away, from Tunis, Bizerta and Tripoli.'

'So we'll have to reckon with fighters above every point in the island?'

'Indeed you will! Even when the bombers attack the Straits of Messina, the Lightnings will still be able to escort them.'

I had encountered the long-range P–38 Lightning fighter during the last few days of the North African campaign. Our opinion of this twin-boomed, twin-engined aircraft was divided. Our old Messerschmitts were still, perhaps, a little faster. But pilots who had fought them said that the Lightnings were capable of appreciably tighter turns and that they would be on your tail before you knew what was happening. Stories about their armament were undoubtedly exaggerated. The six machine guns mounted in the nose supposedly produced a concentration of fire from which there was no escape. Certainly the effect was reminiscent of a watering can when one of these dangerous apparitions started firing tracer, and it was essential to prevent them manœuvring into a position from which they could bring their guns to bear. For some time now the Americans had been using them for low-level attacks on the roads in the southern part of the island so that they would not have to return to base with their ammunition intact should they fail to encounter us in the air. Apparently they were already dreaded by the ground forces.

'How can we survive against such odds if we're destroyed on our airfields?' I asked.

The general began to develop the idea that he had mentioned to me on the telephone a few days before. 'We've got to employ the three fighter wings we have in a series of concerted attacks. We can only make an impression on the enemy if we concentrate our strength. It's a very considerable risk since we haven't enough airfields on the island. If we're going to engage the enemy with all three wings at the same time we shall have to assemble them on one airfield, if possible.'

'That's damned dangerous,' I objected. 'At Trapani yesterday we had a surprise raid by twin-engined bombers and we only came through because their aiming was so lousy. But one lot of carpet bombing, Fortress fashion, could easily mean the end of fighter operations in Sicily.'

The general was convinced his own idea was right: 'If we don't take this risk,' he said imperturbably, 'we'll merely keep on frittering away what little fighting strength we have at our disposal. If you try to conserve everything you end up by conserving nothing and if we take off every time we get a warning from the direction finders, it amounts to much the same as a midge bite – they just don't notice. At all events that's what you've been doing up till now, with about as much success. No, we've got to think up something new. We must establish two focal points. You will take command in the west operating from Trapani and the fighter wings will be moved to you at Trapani or else at Sciacca, depending on the circumstances.'

'But what do we do if Trapani and Sciacca are no longer usable?'

'You'll have to look for alternative landing grounds. Get hold of a Storch and reconnoitre the western part of the island. There are bound to be some fields and meadows which can be converted into makeshift airfields. And in case we can't hold out in the west, you'll always be able to find plenty of space for take-off and landing round Gerbini. It won't be too easy to eliminate that sort of airfield complex.'

This was what I had liked about the general: his decisiveness and resolution in carrying out a plan once it had taken shape.

I asked him: 'Can we count on reinforcements? I mean, is there a chance of one or two fighter wings being moved from somewhere else to give us a hand?'

'Somewhere else,' the general said, shrugging his shoulders, 'somewhere else! There's not enough to go round as it is. You were in the east not so long ago. What are you going to move from there? And Reich Air Defence? We're already short of several groups! Apart from that, where are you going to put them? There's no room left for any more fighters on the island.'

I remained silent for a few moments and looked the general straight in the eye. He returned my gaze gravely and unflinchingly.

'So, provided we're not destroyed on the ground,' I said, 'and at the most favourable estimate, we'll be putting a hundred Mes into the air. How's the Allied strength?'

His first reaction was a croak of laughter. 'For heavens' sake, who in fighters today still bothers about relative strengths? When I tell you that the Allies have about five thousand aircraft against our three hundred and fifty you'll be able to calculate the enormous number of chances you have of shooting them down.'

We went out on to the veranda to watch a flight of fighters from the Ace of Spades group take off for a reconnaissance over Pantelleria. The aircraft, dust clouds billowing out behind them, became airborne almost simultaneously. It all looked just as it did in palmier days when this group used to fly several missions daily to Malta.

Later on the general explained the overall situation to me: 'Control of the island's defence is in Italian hands. The staff of their Sixth Army is stationed at Enna. They have considerable forces available for the defence – at any rate the tactical symbols you see sticking in the map indicate two Army corps and six Coastal Defence divisions. But the vast majority of them are natives of the island, elderly chaps from the older call-up groups. The coastal defences are jerry-built and more of an ornament than an obstacle. The German forces in Sicily were not organized into fighting units – constituted as a Panzergrenadier division – until after we had evacuated North Africa and a landing seemed imminent. The Hermann Göring Division was moved here a few days ago. So much for the army. I don't believe we'll be getting any more reinforcements. There's a large flak group guarding the Straits of Messina. So far these people have been functioning in their normal role. They can, of course, also be of some use against tanks. But they've got to stay where they are – the straits are a dangerous bottle-neck and must be protected from air attack by every available means. Everything depends on where the Allies land. Fierce arguments are going on about it. There's been the wildest surmise about eventual landings south of Naples, in Sardinia or even the south of France, but on one point everyone is agreed – it's here that they intend to set foot on the continent.'

I asked him how the field marshal saw our chances of successfully defending the island.

'The field marshal? You know how he always tends to see

things in a positive light. He believes that we are bound to chuck the enemy back into the sea provided that our counter-attack is carried out with determination. The Italians, however, don't share his optimism.'

'How many Allied divisions are available for the landing?'

'Sixty. Yes, you heard me correctly: *sixty*, six-zero! At any rate that's what the intelligence people say. The American Seventh Army is in Oran, Algiers and Bizerta, ready to go, and the famous British Eighth Army is regrouping in Tripoli and Egypt. Both British and Americans have assembled a powerful fleet in the Mediterranean in preparation for a landing. The British alone have eight battleships which they can use to soften up the coast. In addition there are the aircraft carriers *Indomitable* and *Formidable* whose fighters are supposed to protect the fleet – which, of course, is quite superfluous since the enemy holds Malta and Pantelleria. On top of that there's a number of cruisers, destroyers and submarines, quite how many we don't know. Most of the landing craft have been provided by the Americans.'

While the general paused to attend to his black cigar, I cast my mind back. Only a year ago in the Mediterranean – it had been in June 1942 – the British fleet had suffered severe losses in a major operation for the relief of Malta. The bombers from X Air Corps in Crete had hammered away ceaselessly at the vessels sailing from Alexandria while the convoy approaching from Gibraltar had been attacked by II Air Corps based in Sicily. What price our fighting strength now?

I said something of the kind to the general but he brushed it aside. 'What we're experiencing now is the pre-landing phase. Their intention is to eliminate the threat presented by the Axis air forces, their main target, of course, being the bomber and Stuka units. It's an air offensive of dimensions as yet unprecedented in the war.'

Again he broke off and looked pensively in front of him as though seeking a solution. I took this opportunity of broaching a subject which we had been tacitly avoiding since our conversation had begun.

'Sir, I want to tell you that my wing leaders intend to offer themselves for court martial. They say that you can't after all pick out "one coward per wing" by casting dice and therefore insist that they themselves should be tried.'

I was about to add some bitter comment but he interrupted me with a violent gesture. 'I made it absolutely plain to you that you were to take no action! The combat report made a good impression on Air Corps. Their commander is doing everything he can to get the Reichsmarschall's order countermanded.'

'All the same he can't wipe the slate clean, sir. The pilots feel bitterly hurt and insulted. They think that no one understands them any more. Just now you were giving me an idea of the superior numbers we're up against every day. I'm positive that we can only make up for this lack of quantity by superior quality combined with a corresponding determination to fight back. But our fighter aircraft are no longer better than those of the Allies. You know yourself how the pendulum used to swing this way and that during the battles over England, depending on whether our own or the enemy's aircraft had the edge at any particular moment. That doesn't happen any more; it's been a long time since we had the edge. When I came here in April from the eastern front to grapple with the British again after two years of fighting a badly trained and technically inferior opponent, I was forced into the bitter realization that, in the game of cat and mouse over the North African desert, the roles had been reversed. Now we're quite definitely the mouse.'

'I know what you're trying to say,' answered the general in tones which showed that he understood. 'But in fighter operations conducted with skill and discipline, luck and success will still be on our side.'

'But men aren't machines, sir! Most of the pilots have long since reached the limit of their performance. I mean there comes a stage when orders are no substitute for moral standards.'

'What do you mean by that?'

'I'm trying to say that bravery, or better self-control, can't simply be produced to order, not at any rate if those orders are in fact reproaches, and insulting and degrading ones at that.'

'For heavens' sake don't let me hear any more about it! I've told you he didn't mean it like that . . .'

Unconvinced, I shook my head. 'I'm afraid, sir, that he did . . .'

Silently we sat facing each other, both of us aware that we were thinking the same thoughts. I understood the general and appreciated that he could not permit himself to drop his guard. As for me, I felt impelled to come out at last with something that had long been weighing on me and, indeed, on every group commodore.

Had anything really changed since I had last sought out the general in 1941 at his headquarters in East Prussia in order to enlist his help in preventing my fighter wing from being sacrificed as infantry on the eastern front?

At the time we were occupying an airfield on the edge of the town of Klin and a sudden cold spell had brought the temperature down to minus 50° centigrade. And it was just then that fresh, well-equipped, acclimatized troops from Siberia broke through the German front with hundreds of new tanks. The army was not alone in having to capitulate to 'General Winter'. The engines of our fighters refused to start for the oil had frozen in the lines. We destroyed the aircraft and began the retreat on foot. By the time the front became stabilized near Rzhev the wing had moved into reserve quarters in earth bunkers close to Smolensk. It was there that a signal arrived ordering the entire wing, officers and men, pilots and ground crews, to move at once and go into action against the Russians who were threatening to break through between Rzhev and Vyaz'ma.

I had lost no time in requesting permission to go and see the General of Fighters in East Prussia. This was granted and I flew to Insterburg. There I implored the general to intervene quickly before the wing was lost. I questioned the justification of the order, for the airmen had received no infantry training and would be no more effective in land fighting than the crew of a U-boat. The decimation of the wing, I told him, would mean an irreplaceable loss to our fighting strength.

The general – he had just taken over the appointment of General of the Fighter Arm – had remained silent as he heard me out. I spoke earnestly and with conviction for the latest happenings at the front were still fresh in my mind. Then, in his typically unruffled way, he began talking about the dilemma of our aircraft production. For a long while past he had been trying to impress on the Reichsmarschall the need for more fighter aircraft and more fighter groups. It would be Utopian, he had argued, to hope to conduct an offensive campaign in the air once we had lost the initiative. Finally it had been agreed, albeit somewhat reluctantly, to speed up the production of fighters and to form more groups. Yet now, they chose this very moment to let the pilots die in holes in the ground! He assured me that he would do all that he could to prevent the employment of a fighter wing in a ground role.

I had felt extremely optimistic as I left his headquarters and made my way back to the wing. But while I had been away some frightful things had happened. The wing's personnel had been incorporated into a Luftwaffe infantry division with whom they had plugged the gap torn by Soviet troops in the front between Rzhev and Vyaz'ma. Both officers and men had put up a brave and successful defence of the sector allotted to them although they were neither trained nor equipped for infantry warfare in the freezing, subarctic conditions. During one night attack the Russians had succeeded in penetrating the sector held by the wing, storming in on the inexperienced defenders with bayonet and hand grenade. At dawn our people had managed to win back the lost ground and were able to recover their dead who lay frozen stiff in the murderous cold, having been clubbed by rifle butts until they were unrecognizable. Among those killed were four young officer pilots, including the adjutant – some of the most efficient members of my wing. The General of Fighters kept his promise to release us from our infantry role. We transferred to East Prussia and were soon re-equipped with brand new Me 109s. But the loss of manpower took longer to make good and it was months before the wing reverted to the combat effectiveness and technical standard of the past.

That interview with my superior, a man revered by every fighter pilot, came back to me now as I talked to him in a way that is only possible between men who trust one another.

'What the Reichsmarschall is asking of the fighter pilots is inhuman!' I began. 'He won't realize that uninterrupted operations can exhaust a man's physical and nervous resources. Or if he does realize, it doesn't worry him.'

But the general realized it. And because he could not admit it, his manner hardened. 'You know how things are in the Reich,' he said tersely. 'Sentimental considerations are now even less appropriate than they ever were.'

'You may call them sentimental, sir, but you'll soon have no fighter arm left if the whole of the Luftwaffe high command also chooses to ignore the fact that we are human beings.'

'Whom do you imagine you're saying all this to?' he answered bitterly. 'Do you really believe that I don't know what can and cannot be demanded of you? The air battles against Britain, which we lost in a humiliating fashion, entailed too high a cost in sacrifice. You know as well as I do how badly we miss the highly experienced chaps who were either killed or ended up in POW camps. You people, however, have been taking things too easily for too long. You've been spoiled as much by the war in the east as by the easy victories during Rommel's heady advance towards Alexandria. Now, to your dismay, you've discovered that there's no more glory to be had and that all that's left are the daily air battles with their inflexible demand for the ultimate effort.'

'You must forgive me, sir, if I suggest you're oversimplifying matters a bit. An "ultimate effort" isn't something you can expect daily. I'm sure you don't want any German kamikazes. After all, a fighter pilot's main value lies in his ability to live for a while, to be able to shoot down an opponent tomorrow as well as today. You say we've been taking things easily. I think that the high command has always made things correspondingly difficult for us. The days of the big successes took as great a toll of our unit strength as did the Battle of Britain. When the going was good we savoured it to the full and once we had been turned into supermen and national heroes we gathered in the laurels which were there for the picking. It suited the high command perfectly that like anyone else of our age we should have been thirsting for success. Now that our victories and successes have become few and far between, they curse us for having taken things too easily. When Marseille and Müncheberg were killed neither Lightnings nor Flying Fortresses had yet appeared in the North African theatre and the easy victories you speak of could still be scored. And nevertheless those two, the best we had, were killed. The problem has reached its present dimensions not because we've become reluctant or cowardly but because men are being made to fight non-stop, like robots, and are then chucked aside when the spring can't be wound up any more. That's why we've nothing further to give. You surely don't imagine, sir, that we can beat the lads from Texas, fresh and rested as they are, in our good old 109s simply because we're scions of a warlike people with a warlike history and as such can be nothing other than bold, fearless and aggressive? Certainly we're miles ahead of them as far as experience goes but now our experienced veterans are more like worn-out, dilapidated pieces of machinery which no one has the time to maintain or repair. Most of them have been "on operations" as it's so aptly called for three and a half years, during which they've been flying a mission a day and sometimes several a day. They've been going along because there was no alternative. No one with any self-respect is going to stand aside while his comrades do the dirty work. Would you say, sir, that the group commodore who continues to lead his unit after losing an eye in an air battle does so either out of vanity or because he feels himself unfitted for staff duties? Or what do you make of the commodore with the smashed-up arm which he straps to his throttle control? He could always say "I can't carry on any more", and no one would think any the worse of him.'

While I was talking, it suddenly dawned on me that I was only able to speak to the general in this way because we were of similar age, because he must feel just the same as I did. He had scored the first successes in the Battle of Britain and had evolved anti-fighter tactics in concert with his predecessor. For a long time he said nothing, pulling at his black cigar and evidently reflecting on my passionate speech.

Then he replied as calmly as if he had been discussing the weather:

'Everything you say is true, yet at the same time it isn't. You criticize the higher command and the Reichsmarschall and you know as well as I that there are omissions which can now never be made good. You describe the higher and middle echelons of the command as distant and inhuman and maintain that they don't understand "your", or rather, "our" war. But where is the experience of modern aerial warfare to come from if fighter commanders refuse to serve on staffs or on the General Staff? Which is the better way to serve one's country when one is only half fit for active service is highly arguable. A unit that is led with desperate fanaticism but with failing powers and bad nerves is a badly led unit, Steinhoff. Consider, for a moment, what I myself am faced with: I request an immediate build-up of the fighter arm and I have reason to believe that my request will be met, yet at the same time I'm perfectly well aware that the number of properly qualified senior leaders can be counted on the fingers of one hand. A lot of groups and wings today are being led by people who are actually no more than competent squadron commanders. There are those who chase and fight and those who simply blaze away, as you yourself know . . .'

'But then it can't work out, sir!' I broke in agitatedly. 'How can we create more groups and wings and release experienced commanders for staff duties if there aren't enough of them as it is?'

'I said just now that what has been left undone can no longer be made good, at least in an arm which, rather like a fire brigade, must be constantly on the alert since there's always a fire to be put out somewhere. Don't ask me how the impossible can be achieved. Our reserves are not yet exhausted; we can retrain the bomber pilots and make use of their considerable experience, and there are many other things we can try. But we mustn't go on balking the real issue. Up to now we've failed in our attacks against the Flying Fortresses, the enemy's most effective weapon by far. The Reichsmarschall is angry about it and rightly so. You must all of you concentrate on one thing and one thing only – shooting down bombers. Forget about the fighters. The only thing that counts is the destruction of the bombers and the ten crew that each of them carries.'

That, I thought, was the nub of the matter: whether or not the Reichsmarschall was justified in being angry about our alleged failure. When an enemy acquires a new all-powerful weapon whose deployment should have been foreseen and which, better still, ought to have been made available to one's own side, there is little sense in blaming the soldiers who at first are helpless in the face of it. But it would have been futile to oppose the general with this argument, for he was perfectly well aware of it himself. Something of the kind ought to have been said to the Reichsmarschall but probably no one had had the courage to do so.

So instead, I said: 'A fighter arm is a fighter arm, sir. Fighter pilots are trained to fight and they're expected to do so whenever opportunity offers. It is an outlook that can't be altered on demand. During the Battle of Britain I belonged, for my sins, to a wing whose express task was to escort the bombers to London and southern England. I can think of no more idiotic occupation for a fighter pilot than this shuttle service to London and back. "Stay with the bombers at all costs," we were strictly ordered. "Don't engage in combat with the Spitfires. Don't let them lure you into attacking them even when they are in an ideal position. Remain with the bombers." That was hammered into us *ad nauseam*. And if a man had done that sixty times, as I did, if he had bumbled rather than flown alongside the Heinkels or Dorniers at between twenty-five and twenty-seven thousand feet as they crawled along at walking pace, if he had seen, time and time again, the gleaming contrails high overhead as the Spits' reception committee, forewarned by their long-range direction finders on the ground, waited for his procession above Dover, if he had observed their pilots' mocking grins as they flew beside him until the time was ripe to go for the formation, the escort first and then the bombers – if a man had experienced all that, how could he possibly fail to have doubts about the sagacity of the high command?'

I paused for a moment in case the general wished to say anything, for he himself had played this unnerving game over England. However, he looked at me without speaking and I had the impression that he wanted me to continue.

'Then on the eastern front, where crises seemed to follow one another almost uninterruptedly, we received strict instructions to confine ourselves to low-level ground attacks, using cannons and machine guns, and to desist from the "foolish" practice of shooting down aircraft. My protests against this method of boosting the ground troops' morale were as fruitless as my attempts to make Air Corps understand that the destruction of a Soviet bomber or an Fl 2 was of more help to the army than a spectacular blazing away of cannon above the heads of the infantry who were presumably expected to express their glee by throwing their caps in the air. But when, on more than one occasion, an experienced, reliable pilot came down in flames after being hit by a bullet from some idiot's rifle, my criticisms did, I admit, often overstep the mark. And today, sir, today our instructions are: "Shoot down the bombers, don't worry about the fighters." Next we're going to be asked why, after we've been expressly ordered to shoot them down, we're not doing so.

'They hold the Reich Air Fleet up to us as a shining example. But they seem to forget that here we first have to grapple with the Malta and Pantelleria fighters, which always have ample fuel, before we can get through to the bombers. What's going to happen once the Americans are in a position to use fighter escorts when they attack the Reich? There'll be some wailing and gnashing of teeth then, won't there?'

'Aha,' he suddenly interjected, 'so you do believe that a fighter escort serves some purpose! And so it does, in that it permits the bombers to approach the target and deliver their bomb loads without interference. But when two sides are both doing the same thing, then it's not the same thing, for the decisive factor will be success. And that, regrettably, lies for the moment with the other side. Do you imagine that I'm blind and can't see that it's hopeless to operate an effective air defence above Sicily? Quite apart from his sheer numerical superiority, the attacker has all the advantages. But that doesn't absolve you from the duty to adopt fresh tactics. If one lacks the material resources to counter a new weapon, then one has to try to bring it under control by new forms of combat. You must concentrate your few remaining battleworthy aircraft and you must shoot down bombers. The Americans and British may be able to turn them out like sausages but one day they're not going to be able to man them any more, provided you keep on disposing of their crews.

'Traffic with the mainland is vital to our existence whether, in the event of a landing, we manage to hold the island or whether we have to evacuate it. The flow of supplies must not be interrupted. And if we have to evacuate Sicily the ferry traffic must be maintained up to the last minute. At this stage of the war the Straits of Messina are crucial to our fortunes.'

The Straits of Messina. I repeated the words to myself. As so often before in the history of the West the Straits of Messina were once again in the limelight. Over on the mainland, in the 'toe' of Italy, lay a village called Scilla, and facing it, on the island, was Cariddi. Scylla and Charybdis.

Our truck broke down on the rough track leading to the Storch's airstrip. Helbig and I covered the last hundred yards on foot and joined an airman squatting beneath a canvas awning, who combined the duties of aerodrome commandant, mechanic and flight controller.

Bachmann was flying over from Trapani in the Storch to fetch me. Helbig would have to wait behind and leave on its next trip, but he should be in Trapani by the evening. Without our Storchs we would have been immobilized and helpless. The feats performed by these low-powered contraptions of fabric, plywood and alloy were almost incredible. They accompanied us into the limitless expanse of Russia and kept on flying in the burning heat of an Ukrainian summer and the bitter cold of the northern winter. They were not fast, indeed they were not 'proper' aeroplanes at all compared with our high-performance fighters, but they could nevertheless cover enormous distances in the course of a day. When flying against a strong headwind they gave the impression of being stationary. But it was a mistake to suppose that they would meekly submit to whatever an inexperienced pilot with little flying sense might choose to ask of them. Crashes involving Storchs flown by pilots unfamiliar with them were by no means rare. At the outbreak of war it was thought an especial privilege to be allowed to fly a Storch or even to have one in the unit.

The sight of one of these machines invariably recalled an incident unique in my flying career. After the Reichsmarschall's conference, having handed over my old night fighter squadron to my successor, I had taken over a new squadron near the capital.

Almost immediately I was summoned to Schönefeld to discuss technical problems of night fighting with the Director of Luftwaffe Technical Services. We stood on the concrete in front of one of the hangars and waited for the general to arrive. In addition to the squadron commanders, the CO of the newly formed Night Fighter Group was present as were officers from the flak artillery and the engineering branch. The general consensus seemed to be that night fighting was a question of co-operation between flak and fighters on the one hand and, on the other, of technical problems concerning location and navigation. We split up into small groups and walked up and down debating the matter while the bitter wind of a November day cut through us like a knife. Suddenly the general's Storch appeared over the far side of the airfield, circled the apron in a tight turn and came to a halt immediately in front of us, barely a moment after the wheels had touched the ground. The general wore a black leather coat which contrasted with the brilliant white of his trouser stripes. He gave us a friendly greeting, shook hands with us and at once entered into an informal discussion. Without reproaching us he maintained that our unco-ordinated and comparatively unsystematic night attacks against the British had so far been unsuccessful and he wanted to find out why this was so. We endeavoured to explain to him what I had already tried to point out to the Reichsmarschall in my ill-fated dissertation, namely that it was virtually impossible with the inadequate means at our disposal to seek out and engage a lone bomber. We spoke of lucky interceptions, of haphazard night patrols in single-seater Messerschmitts without reliable naviga-tional aids. The people from the flak pointed out that there were not enough searchlights and that these few, scattered about as they were at key points throughout the Reich, formed a net with far too coarse a mesh. An engineer officer, whom I did not know, talked of a 'new thing' called radio direction finding, which could locate an invisible enemy aircraft at night and in fog.

But I remembered clearly the perplexity revealed by these dis-cussions on how to prevent night incursions by the enemy. Evidently the danger of bombing raids on our cities at night was not yet being taken seriously, while the possibility of British attacks on Berlin was ruled out altogether.

After it was over I felt certain that nothing was going to change either for me or for my squadron and that we would go on flying through the pitch black night in our single-seater Messerschmitts – flying but never fighting.

As the general was preparing to leave, we gathered round his Storch. Suddenly he asked me – perhaps remembering the Reichs-marschall's meeting – if I would like to accompany him back to Staaken. Without a moment's hesitation I climbed into the rear seat and fastened my belt. Silently he passed his cap back to me to hold. I took it carefully, cradling it in both hands as though it was something extremely precious.

'Now I'm going to show you what a Storch can do.' So saying he applied full throttle and after a very short run brought the aircraft off the ground. Head to wind we rose like a balloon. Then this past master of the art of aerobatics started in on an im-peccable programme of daring banked turns and steep stall turns.

The whole performance took place immediately above the narrow confines of the apron from which we had taken off and where the remainder of the party stood watching us with upturned faces.

Eventually he had set course for Staaken. After we had flown for a time over the suburbs of the great city he turned round and asked me: 'Do you smoke cigars?' When I said that I did, he pulled out two, wrapped in silver paper, from his breast pocket and gave me one. It was thick and long, of marvellous tobacco, dark, moist and aromatic, and the small cabin had felt almost homelike as, smoking away contentedly, we flew over Berlin.

Bachmann's arrival jerked me out of my reverie. We needed to refuel and take off without delay. Our route lay over the centre of the island. Now that enemy fighters were able to range over Sicily virtually at will, it was advisable to keep a watch out for them. For that reason we wanted to reach the north coast as soon as possible since it lay at the limit of their range and gave us the chance to fly in comparative safety.

One of the Storch's bad habits was that it almost invariably refused to start if the engine was still hot. And here, with the sun blazing down vertically on to engine and cabin, any cooling down was out of the question. We took our seats knowing perfectly well that the old girl would not dream of starting at the first attempt. The mechanic stood on the left wheel and inserted the crank into the aperture in the engine cowling. I signalled him to start cranking.

He began to wind and while he wound I discussed our course with Bachmann in a leisurely manner, for we knew there would be ample time before the engine fired. Sweat started to pour off the back of the unfortunate mechanic who accompanied each revolution of the handle with an audible groan to make sure that his exertions did not go unnoticed. I gave him two more minutes before ordering: 'Switch off – suck in!'

The mechanic jumped off the wheel and began to rotate the propeller in the opposite direction. But he was quite obviously exhausted.

'Bachmann!' I said, with an appropriate jerk of the head. He had already suspected what was in store for him and now he levered himself, grunting and groaning, out of the rear seat. 'Bloody old cow!' he muttered, aiming a spiteful kick at one of the wheels of our valuable aircraft.

'Blow out – switch on!' I switched on both magnetos and Bachmann began his arduous task. The airman, still breathing heavily, stood to one side grinning, his hands on his hips. 'Rrr – click' went the engine after a couple of turns of the crank, but that was all. The back of Bachmann's tropical shirt became darkened with sweat.

They must have toiled for half an hour. And then Bachmann turned round, looked at me reproachfully with his large, mournful eyes and said simply: 'Sir?'

He meant in fact: 'Right – your turn!' Shrugging my shoulders, I climbed out. No doubt he felt it worth trying on but it was really rather an impudent suggestion to make to a group commodore. Bachmann settled himself comfortably in the pilot's seat. 'Switch off – suck in!' he shouted gleefully in an unnecessarily loud voice. It did not need physical activity to make one sweat; the sun's rays had been shining through the plexiglass straight onto my stomach. 'Switch on!' – barely had I turned the propeller with the crank through one complete revolution, at the cost of negligible effort, than the engine sprang innocently to life and kept running with no sign of smoke or sounds of misfiring.

'Out of the way!' I shouted to Bachmann, indicating that he should move quickly into the rear seat and fasten his belt. He shook his head in resignation. 'There's no such thing as justice,' was his only comment.

Thrown about by hot-air turbulence the Storch cleared the ridge and pressed forward through a rocky gorge on whose floor black cattle stood motionless in the scanty shadows between the oak trees. Then the valley opened into a gently rising plateau. On our left was a huge, bare massif. The engine hummed monotonously. When I moved the ignition switch down the drop in revolutions was barely noticeable. The cabin reeked of oil and dope. If I was going to clear the next ridge I would have to start climbing at once. But the oil temperature was very high, the needle remaining steady, a bare millimetre beneath the red mark. I pulled her up cautiously, keeping an eye on the altimeter; she must not be allowed to lose much speed.

Beyond the ridge, a plateau stretched away towards an escarpment which towered threateningly above the landscape. There was not a village to be seen in the whole of the expanse, only gentle undulations covered with low scrub. At the farther end of the plain the cliffs cast violet shadows. As I flew round them, there in front of me in this peaceful mountain solitude was the Temple of Segesta, its tall columns and pediments unearthly in the glow of the afternoon sun. Beneath our wings, in the wilderness, a stairway curved gracefully towards the mountain. Not a soul was in sight. Below in the valley ran the railway to Trapani, a minute station the only sign of human life.

'Segesta!' I shouted. 'Segesta, Bachmann. Ancient temple!'

He leaned towards the window and, like me, was immediately captivated by the beauty and magnificence of the scene. '400 BC,' he answered, drawing on what he remembered from his schooldays. 'Selinus – Carthaginian War.'

War, of course, as nearly always in Sicily. Greeks, Carthaginians, Romans. Foreign conquerors. And now us. Soon, perhaps, the British and Americans. Sicily is doomed by her geographical position: the conquerors come either from the mainland of Europe or from Africa.

But the mighty temple was already sinking behind the last mountain range. I spread the map out on my knee and measured off the distance to Trapani with my hand. Still about twenty minutes to go, I estimated. I intended to make for the narrow airstrip on the side of Mount Erice which could only be approached from the west and entailed an uphill landing. Departures in the same direction were impossible; we always took off downhill, irrespective of the direction of the wind.

I was not immediately alarmed nor did I take any action when I saw the broad, sharply defined shadows of aircraft flitting over the ground below. They sped beneath us like menacing phantoms and raced away up the slope at tremendous speed. Only then did I look upwards to discover the origin of these shadowy spectres. What I saw, barely three hundred feet above us, was a second wave of spruce fighters flying westwards on the same course. It was several seconds before I gave a horrified yelp – 'Kittyhawks!' – at the same time reacting automatically by wrenching back the throttle and putting the Storch into a steep turn. It was essential to get the machine onto the ground as quickly as possible and then run like hell. While Bachmann was twisting his neck to get a better view astern and shouting something like 'Another squadron's coming!' the Storch had flattened out and was almost at the point of stall. We just cleared a sandy track, its banks over-grown with huge agaves, and then our wheels were skidding through the soft earth of a tiny maize field. I held the stick close to my stomach, expecting at any moment that the aircraft was going to somersault. A stone wall at the far end of the field came racing towards us. Grimly I trod on the brakes and, as the final revolutions of the propeller swirled up sand and cactus leaves, the tail-skid smacked the ground. We hurled ourselves out and ran as fast as our legs could carry us. Where we went did not matter so long as it was well away from the aircraft. Both of us decided simultaneously that one particular sand-hill afforded suitable cover and we threw ourselves down breathlessly.

The throb of the Kittyhawks' engines died away in the distance. 'That was a piece of luck!' I said, still panting after our hundred yards' sprint. 'Our Storch would have made a nice titbit for those fighters. All the same she's too bent to fly now.'

'It's only the airscrew, I think,' Bachmann said.

'How are we going to lay hands on a new airscrew here? Where are we anyway? Would you fetch the map, please.'

While he made his way to the aircraft I reflected on the imponderability of fate and fortune in determining when a man's hour had come. I thought of the veteran fighter pilots with the illustrious names, the brilliant formation leaders and the cool-headed tacticians, all of them tempered by hundreds of aerial duels. What did their experience add up to in the face of the thousand and one tricks that chance has up her sleeve?

Why was it that not one American pilot had seen the helpless Storch flying along under his very nose?

According to the map we were only a few miles from the Palermo–Trapani road. Bachmann swallowed a couple of times when I told him I would walk to Catalafimi, leaving him alone in charge of the Storch until I had rounded up the local Carabinieri and brought them back with me.

An easy path led down to the road where, after I had been walking for a few minutes, a large Italian army truck stopped to pick me up. Everywhere in North Africa and Sicily the Italian drivers were noted for the spirit of comradeship in which they would invariably stop unbidden whenever they saw a German on foot. The Carabinieri expressed their readiness to take over the guard of the Storch without delay and within an hour Bachmann had been relieved. Then we both climbed into the Fiat that was to take us to Trapani.

There was not a great deal of traffic on the road. We met a few trucks carrying soldiers and stores. Outside every village stood the inevitable road block consisting of a few rocks and some ineffective barbed wire, and dignified by the sign *Posto di blocco*. The blocks were manned by elderly Carabinieri who conscientiously checked every vehicle. Beyond Catalafimi the road led down into the valley through thickly populated country and rich vineyards. In the villages the men, as always, stood idly talking in front of the cafés. The peaceful evening atmosphere that pervaded these villages and their naive, pious inhabitants was deceptive. They must, I thought, have some inkling of what was in store. How would they react, and what rumours might be circulating in this, the most rumour-prone of islands? As though they had guessed that the Allied air offensive marked the final phase of the occupation by the, to them, so alien Germans, they showed themselves amiably servile but made no pretence whatever of giving any effective help. Nor were the pithy slogans – *Noi tireremo diritto*, for example, or *Il duce ha sempre ragione*, painted in letters three

D

feet high on walls and the ends of houses – likely to alter this in any way. There were many indications which, with time, one learned to detect and interpret correctly as showing that here in Sicily the Duce was by no means always right . . .

We too, of course, had had our own experiences of the historic prognostications of our supreme war lord. On the other hand we had been carefully schooled to turn a blind eye to such experiences and to dismiss them as irrelevant.

Before dropping down to the sea the road made a final ascent in a series of hairpin bends through one of the few remaining oak woods on the island. We were driving slowly round one of these bends when the merry notes of a spirited military march suddenly fell upon our ears. We looked at each other in surprise. On the very edge of the road an Italian military band in olive green uniforms had set up their music stands in a semicircle round their conductor who stood with his back to a tall tree. They were blaring away cheerfully and the summer evening resounded with the music of their high-pitched wind instruments. Without consulting us our driver stopped. We got out, squatted on the bank and were entertained to a rousing programme of Italian military marches, music famed for its excellence and performed for our benefit with added zest. Caps on the backs of their heads, sweat glistening on their brows, the bandsmen flourished their somewhat tarnished brass instruments with considerable panache. Around them, sitting, squatting or lying, were hundreds of Sicilians with children of all sizes who had taken advantage of the unexpected evening's entertainment to turn it into an impromptu popular festival. This was characteristic of the Sicilian people who have invariably been the sufferers during the wars between the great powers. They have always had their festivals as and when opportunity has offered and have cowered away into hiding whenever foreign armies have been locked in battle. From far away the merry notes followed us as we drove round the last hairpin bends. Bachmann's only evident reactions to the interlude were a shake of the head and the remark: 'If the Führer only knew . . .'

We drove along the familiar route up to the villa. The white road gleamed in the dusk, reflecting the luminous sky. The many pedestrians and donkey carts hurrying towards the town stood out as black silhouettes; only the people's faces caught the last of the light. In the village on the saddle of the mountain the menfolk were standing in front of the *trattoria* as they always did at this hour. I reduced speed so as to turn into the narrow alleyway. My '*Buona sera*' was barely acknowledged, the only response being a listless murmur. On the house beyond the turning someone had painted in crude, three-foot-high letters still just legible in the falling darkness, the message:

VINCEREMO!

Tubby announced that the taps were working and that it would be as well for me to hurry if I wanted a shower before the water was turned off again. As I was undressing the telephone rang. It was the duty officer who reported that a general alert had been ordered following the sighting of a large force of warships off Malta. The group's task would be to fly a reconnaissance at first light and engage bombers. It was like any other day: forget what you've just been doing and think about how you're going to carry out tomorrow's task. Such had been the pattern of our lives for the last four years, had indeed been the pattern before the war from the time we had first learned to fly.

The Wellingtons were back with us again and the first bombs began to fall as I was making my way to the grotto. Again I found everyone assembled there, for it had now become the custom to spend the night in this way.

They listened to my account of the bombing at Comiso and the forced landing with the Storch as though neither event was in any way unusual. All that counted here were kills and destruction and death. Nor did they make any comment when I recounted my talk with the general.

'The doctor's back from Messina,' Tubby announced. 'He said he wanted to drop in and tell you about it.'

Dr Sperrling had been seeing the wounded on to a ferry and had brought back some medical stores which he had scrounged from a depot. He was our father confessor who looked after our bodily ailments and our spiritual needs, and we had missed him badly during the two days he had been away. As a gynaecologist he was actually a little out of place in this all-male community. He had been called up at the outbreak of war and, because he knew something about gliding, had been posted to the group where he had remained ever since.

His appearance in the grotto was greeted with cheerful yells. Flattered by the warmth of his reception he broke into a broad grin, revealing his bad teeth.

'Hello, Doctor, we thought you must have deserted. What are the girls doing in Messina?' someone laughed.

Dr Sperrling was never at a loss for an answer. 'What I'll do to you is keep on pumping atebrin into you until you're not only as yellow as a Chinaman but girls will be the last thing you'll think about!'

Whatever the temperature he invariably wore a khaki tunic with patch pockets. Immediately someone complained of an ailment he would rummage through them silently before producing pills of all sizes and varieties, pills for malaria, for desert sores, for diarrhoea.

'Messina's looking terrible. The heavies keep attacking almost the whole time. The ferries can't use the port either at Messina or at Reggio. They're being diverted to emergency harbours, but two large train ferries have already been sunk. Military traffic is crossing on landing craft and Siebel ferries, and that's been working quite well. Our flak's terrific. You've no idea of the barrage that's put up during every raid. The splinters whistling down make a noise like a gale blowing through the tree tops.'

'Sure, Doc,' said Zöhler amiably. 'We know what it's like, only we don't hear it as well as that. Come along some time when we're taking a close look at the heavies at twenty-five thousand feet, and those dirty grey bursts are there in front of your nose and the splinters are flying in earnest – if you don't mind my saying so. But if I was ever shot down by our flak I really think I'd go off my rocker.'

'If you still had a rocker to go off,' came a voice from the darkness.

'There's always an enormous amount of traffic on the road between Messina and Palermo,' the doctor continued. 'But their fighter-bombers are on the job too, going mainly for the road bridges and tunnels. Recently they've been attacking vehicles travelling alone. They're quite obviously enjoying themselves.'

Although dog-tired I was unable to sleep. Hitherto I had refused to admit to myself that I had already long been a prey to anxiety, a form of inward erosion that was something quite different from fear. Fear was something one experienced occasionally in a special situation, shortly before the interception of the enemy, for example, or in the middle of a battle when one knew that a Spitfire was on one's tail. But it arose out of the situation, could be combated by taking action and, with the passing of the situation, it, too, passed. Anxiety, however, came from within. It invariably returned at a specific stage of mental exhaustion when one was powerless to ward it off. Many of the bravest took to drink out of anxiety to dispel anxiety. Freiberg, clearly, was such a man. I had been familiar with this form of anxiety for a long time, indeed ever since we had ceased to feel assured of victory. It had spread among us that night when we had been cut off on the airfield at Kalinin and could hear the 'hurrays' of the advancing Russians without our being able to do the least thing about it. It had been there at Cape Bon – the last tip of Africa remaining to us – while we were preparing to escape and did not yet know whether we would succeed.

And here, once again, anxiety was robbing the men around me of sleep or else interrupting their light, uneasy slumbers on the uncomfortable camp-beds. Again, it had nothing in common with the kind of alarm that affects every part of a man's body, the abrupt contraction which paralyses him for a few seconds and makes his mouth go dry. Such reactions are induced by outside occurrences and can vary greatly. For instance, in my own case the previous afternoon when I had been flying along without a thought in my head, I did not immediately feel the alarm I really ought to have felt at the sight of the American fighters.

Shocks like these were part and parcel of air fighting and could be allowed for, once one had acquired a precise knowledge of oneself and one's own reactions. But it was impossible to foresee every kind of situation and all the ways in which one might react to them. One never knew what form the blow was going to take. Fate often allowed its victims time to prove themselves. As he flew his crippled aircraft, a pilot was under appraisal: would he be able to translate his astonishment or surprise into considered action or would panic gain the upper hand? Fate either granted him this time to prove himself or it struck suddenly and with overwhelming force, making him brutally aware of human impotence as his flaming aircraft plunged earthwards in an uncontrollable dive.

'Our own air forces dispose of too few aircraft to enable us to engage the enemy simultaneously and in strength over Sardinia and Sicily. The utmost concentration is therefore necessary.'

WAR DIARY OF THE OBERKOMMANDO DER WEHRMACHT (OFFICE OF THE CHIEF OF STAFF), vol 3

'Then for three days NASAF and the Ninth combined their forces in a smashing assault on the fields of eastern Sicily, while the mediums of NATAF pounded the airfields lying in the western and central parts of the island. Gerbini and its satellites received a thorough battering, the outstanding blow being delivered by B-17s on 5 July with an estimated destruction of 100 enemy planes.'

ARMY AIR FORCES IN WORLD WAR II
EUROPE: TORCH TO POINTBLANK

Gerbini/Trapani, 5 July 1943

We took off at first light, our task being to strengthen the eastern defences of the island. The Fighter Leader had decided to concentrate his fighters and establish a number of key points.

The organization of our fighter groups was very far from being capable of meeting the demands made upon it. After the Battle of Britain my unit had operated like a fire brigade, being sent in wherever the war happened to flare up. We had learned to subsist and fight with the help of a minimum of ground personnel – mechanics, armourers and signallers – for the main body, the workshops and headquarters, seldom caught up with the combat component as it moved from place to place. Altogether a fine example of wasted resources!

But it had always been like that: we had travelled through Russia with the spearhead of the army, hopping from airstrip to airstrip. On the day of the move three Ju 52 transports were usually available to carry the essentials. After several flights our few mechanics, our tents and boxes of rations would all be deposited in the new location. We pilots would then fly our first patrol over the new sector and land with our ammunition expended and our aircraft more or less badly damaged in combat. Usually a meadow or field of clover awaited us, a place which thereafter acquired the dignified appellation of aerodrome. These airfields took their names from the neighbouring village or group of shacks, names which soon became familiar to every member of the Luftwaffe: Pitomnik, Ljuban, Morossovskaya or Gigant. Meanwhile the main body of the group might be somewhere in Poland or the Crimea, where it would act as a depot and a transit camp for leave parties.

D*

On this particular occasion the Fighter Leader was virtually asking us to perform a miracle: we were expected to split up our ground crews even though we had not yet received replacements for the men we had lost in North Africa. The transport aircraft had been unable to operate for some days and it was felt that they would not survive the operation. Air Fleet were not generous with the few Ju 52s they still possessed.

Up to the previous day our aircraft had been maintained by the 55th Fighter Group whose two wings occupied Comiso and Gerbini. However, the number of unserviceable aircraft had risen so rapidly that a better solution had to be found.

On the night of 5 July a party of maintenance personnel from my group left by truck for the eastern portion of the island. West of Catania the plain broadened out at the foot of Etna. The fields, from which the wheat had long since been harvested, stretched away in arid desolation as far as the eye could see, dotted with parched, dusty olive trees.

A narrow track led between a few wretched farms, shown on the map as Gerbini. Hence the plain, which offered some ideal stretches for take-off and landing, bore the pretentious name Gerbini Airfield.

As my Messerschmitt rolled to a halt, I saw the mechanics motioning me to park beneath the olive trees. But as I was turning off the landing strip, a huge, swirling yellow-brown dust cloud enveloped the aircraft. I could see nothing at all and it was some while before the men, the trees and the hut reappeared. So thick was the dust that the colour of the wings had turned dark yellow. I opened the hood and looked round. In all directions dust-devils were rising up in the hot, shimmering air. The aircraft from my No 1 Wing had landed and taxied to the places assigned to them.

It was unbearably hot. Not a breath of wind disturbed the humid air; my shirt, dripping with sweat under my harness, clung to my body. The sun had made the cockpit like an oven. I detached my parachute and climbed on to the wing.

The hut was a few yards away, out in the blazing sun. Along

its length the earth had been excavated into a zig-zag pattern of slit trenches. Someone inside was telephoning; he kept shouting: 'I can't make out what you're saying . . . Which grid reference?'

Only then did I notice the sorry figure in the shade of an olive tree. Captain Kegel was squatting there motionless, his head bandaged and his right arm in a sling. He was looking at me almost reproachfully.

I jumped down from the wing into the dust, undid the leg-straps securing the flare cartridges and pulled my life-jacket over my head. 'Good lord, Kegel,' I said, 'you seem in a bad way.'

He made as if to rise.

'For heavens' sake, man, don't get up! What happened?'

Whoever it was in the hut was still shouting into the telephone. Mechanics, stripped to the waist, were running towards the aircraft and a refueller stopped with a squeal of brakes in front of my Me. The heat was murderous; the blazing sun felt as though it was battering down on one's head. From my knee pocket I pulled out my Africa Korps cap with its long peak to shield the eyes and put it on. I had to contact the Fighter Leader without delay and find out the latest situation. And the aircraft had to be refuelled immediately. I hoped that we would soon be ordered into the air because there was no protection against the bombers here.

'Sir . . .' Kegel said. I had almost forgotten about him. 'I was buried, sir, in that trench . . . We've lost the Storch – burnt out. What's left is over there.'

I saw the smoke-blackened skeleton of a tail section sticking up behind the hut.

Captain Kegel had only been with us for a few days. He belonged to the Reserve and in civilian life had been active in the National Socialist Air Corps – full time, so he said. He was older than we and, although he had completed a training course on Messerschmitts, he no longer flew missions. I had put him in charge of the operations room so that he could supervise the activities there and keep the combat reports and war diaries up to date. He had had to adapt himself rapidly to the small community at group headquarters. On the evening of his arrival it had seemed unlikely that he was going to do so, since he had been altogether too garrulous about his past achievements and his experiences in the Freikorps[1] and the Black Reichswehr.[2] It was hardly surprising that our young pilots, in action every day and having little time for past heroics, should have treated him in a somewhat offhand and ironic fashion. He had at once acquired the nickname 'Clever Claud' and had had to submit to Freiberg's repeated and innocent inquiries about what sort of an outfit the Black Reichswehr had been, exactly, and why he wasn't wearing the uniform of the National Socialist Air Corps . . . Before long the penny had dropped and ever since he had conducted himself in a manner appropriate to a non-flying officer of captain's rank in the headquarters of a fighter group. And now he, too, had come to grief, but on the ground.

The hut consisted of one room. It had been put up a few days before by the young lads of the Labour Service and gave off an aromatic smell of new wood which, had it not been for the appalling heat, might almost have been described as refreshing.

The furniture comprised two iron bedsteads against the rear wall, each covered with a palliasse, and a narrow table opposite the door. From the olive tree in front of the window, wires led to the dark brown box that contained the telephone apparatus. A field telephone, a map and a teleprinter completed the group operations room. The desperate, unrelenting battle in which we were involved permitted only the most essential equipment.

Korn, the operations-room sergeant, got up from the only chair as I entered. 'I'm in communication with HQ Fighter Leader, sir. I've already reported your arrival. Comiso airfield was bombed half an hour ago. You're to go into cockpit readiness immediately refuelling's over.'

A clear enough report. 'Why don't you take the telephone

[1] Paramilitary organization formed after World War I
[2] Armed forces in excess of the establishment laid down by the Versailles Treaty

outside, Korn? The heat in here is more than anyone can stand.'

'Right, sir,' he said. It had simply not occurred to him to try to make things easier for himself.

A Kübelwagen drew up in front of the hut, adding to the dust already in the air as the driver applied his brakes. Freiberg climbed out, nonchalant as ever, and reported that his wing had landed.

'Let's get into the shade behind the hut,' I suggested. 'We'll be off shortly. Comiso's just been attacked.'

'If they keep on like this we'll soon be having to walk. Spares are getting difficult. Even a 109's wheels are in short supply.'

As we exchanged essential items of information in the down-to-earth jargon of airmen at war, we kept breaking off, raising our heads as if to get wind of the approach of the heavies before the characteristic sound of their engines became audible. This complex of airfields was an ideal target for the Fortresses with their carpet-bombing technique. Just now the whole plain round Gerbini was covered with aircraft. Not far from our landing strip were a fighter-bomber group equipped with Focke-Wulfs and one wing each from the 51st and 53rd fighter groups, all of them dispersed under the sparse cover of the olive trees.

'The Malta Spitfires are back again,' said Freiberg, 'only this time they're the latest version with pointed wing tips. They're fitted with a high-altitude supercharger and at anything over twenty-five thousand feet they just play cat and mouse with us.'

'How often have you flown to Malta, Freiberg?'

'Oh, a good eighty trips. One time I was pulled out of the water close to Valetta harbour just as the British rescue launches were coming up . . .'

Those were the days when we flew escort for the Ju 88s and were still able to hold the enemy at bay over his own island. Freiberg talked of these operations as though they had been leisurely outings.

As he spoke, from time to time emphasizing his words with languid gestures of the hands, he stretched out his legs to rest his feet on the ammunition box in front of him. I noticed that he had on the usual snowy white stockings and yellow sandals although I had told him over and over again that he ought to wear stout shoes when flying . . . But now I said nothing, having no answer to his disarming excuses to the effect that his feet sweated or that in North Africa, when he had had to bale out, he had come to no harm . . .

Our equipment in this respect failed to take proper account of the possibility that one day we might meet the ground at a speed of ten feet per second. When the war began we still sometimes wore elegant, cavalry-style riding boots when we climbed into the narrow seats of our fighters. Then warm fur-lined boots became the rage, their soft tops, secured loosely round the calf, proclaiming to all and sundry that the wearer was a pilot. But when someone was compelled to abandon his aircraft while flying at high speed, it often happened that this type of boot was sucked off his legs by the force of the air stream. Such had been the case with 'Jonny' Schmitz, one of whose feet had become severely frostbitten as a result. For a night and a day he had walked across the ice of the Sea of Azov wearing only one boot.

At that time my wing had moved from the Kuban to an airfield at Kerch in the Crimea. The March sun had melted the snow in the streets and fields but the nights were still bitterly cold and the Sea of Azov, whose shore lay quite close to the northern perimeter of the airfield, was an uninterrupted expanse of dirty white ice. The wing's aircraft had returned from their afternoon patrol and the mechanics were preparing them for the next day's operations when orders arrived from Air HQ, Crimea, requesting the immediate despatch of a section of four Messerschmitts to Mariopol. When I objected that it was very late and that it would be difficult to land at night on a distant and unfamiliar airfield, I was told that the Führer himself proposed to arrive at Mariopol at first light and that fighter protection for his aircraft was absolutely vital. After a moment's reflection I chose Jonny Schmitz to lead the section and gave instructions that they should take off as soon as possible.

Following his matriculation and the completion of his flying training, Jonny had been posted straight to my squadron with the rank of leading aircraftsman. We were at Calais at the time and the Battle of Britain had reached its climax. Being more than usually endowed with the uninhibited high spirits of one who is barely twenty, he had been received with open arms into the small community of pilots who liked this tall, slim newcomer with his finely chiselled features and his engaging laugh.

In the course of the battle Jonny had fought valiantly in numerous engagements and soon showed a marked aptitude for flying fighters and for handling his aircraft in the countless precarious situations that arose in aerial combat between evenly matched opponents. Before long I was able to let him lead small formations. During the Russian campaign, in which he soon began to score victories, he was shot down behind the enemy lines but managed to make his way back to the group after six adventurous days. A little later he was promoted to second lieutenant.

On receiving instructions to fly to Mariopol without delay he had remarked that orders were orders but that a night flight to an unknown, possibly unlit airfield was asking rather a lot. Then he had taken off.

During the night I was woken by the ringing of the telephone; it was Air HQ who told me that Sergeant Nemetz, Schmitz's wing man, had seen him bale out as they were crossing the Sea of Azov. Night had almost fallen and his parachute had soon been swallowed up in the gloom.

Nemetz had reported back the following day and confirmed what I already knew, namely that there was no trace of Schmitz. A sea-rescue squadron had gone out to look for him during the night but had had to break off that morning because of mist. As soon as the weather permitted we began a systematic search over the ice in our Me 109s and continued searching until darkness fell. In doing so we observed that, with the coming of spring, the ice had been set in motion and high ridges of pack-ice alternating with narrow channels of open water were appearing in every direction.

On the following morning – by which time I had almost given Jonny up for lost – Air HQ informed me that Second Lieutenant Schmitz had been found in a small village on the north shore of the Sea of Azov, tucked up in a vast farmhouse bed where he was recovering from the ordeal of his walk on the ice.

That same day he had climbed out of a transport aircraft with his right foot heavily bandaged, overjoyed to be 'home' again. He told us that his engine had cut with a loud bang. He realized immediately that it was too dark for a forced landing, and in any case he had doubts about whether the ice would bear. No sooner had he jettisoned his hood and turned the machine on its back than the air stream pulled him out of the cockpit. Dangling from his parachute he noticed to his alarm that he had lost not only his right fur-lined boot but his sock as well. Thus ill equipped he landed somewhat heavily on the ice where his first act had been to sit down and massage a sprained ankle. Then, with his left sock on his right foot, he set off on a walk that lasted for a night and a day. The night had not been very dark so he made good progress northwards with the Pole Star as his constant guide. Some time later he discovered to his alarm that he had nearly fallen into a crack in the ice and realized that such hazards would have to be circumvented. But this also meant climbing over the high barrier of pack-ice which had formed at the end of each of these openings, and the added exertion had taken further toll of his strength. In the meantime his right foot had become raw and an attempt at wearing the left boot on the right foot had failed. From time to time he heard the sound of low-flying search aircraft but his Very pistol had been lost during his descent and he had no means of giving a signal. So the night passed without his knowing whether he had made any appreciable progress in the direction of his goal, the northern shore. He had become discouraged and utterly exhausted by the never-ending detours round the channels and the negotiation of the ice ridges. More and more frequently he halted to massage his raw, frozen foot and recoup his strength. And then, shortly before dawn, the mist descended. It had been nearly midday before he dared to set off again. Each time he scaled the top of a ridge he had looked eagerly ahead in the hope of sighting the shore which eventually came into view in the late afternoon. He had been very well aware that he must reach land before nightfall. By then the sock on his right foot had worn to shreds and the foot itself felt as though it was on fire. In the distance he saw low-flying 109s but he knew that they had no more chance of finding him in that icy wilderness than if they had been searching for a needle in a haystack.

He had been at the limit of his endurance by the time he stumbled up the steep shore in the falling darkness, to see in front of him a long Russian village street with its typical wooden houses and small kitchen gardens. Having made for the nearest door, he found himself in a warm room lit by a single oil lamp. His appearance had nearly frightened the peasant woman out of her wits but she quickly pulled herself together and, with the help of a neighbour, boiled some water and put the *nemetski* to bed.

In his snug bed beside the stove he had gone to sleep under a heap of eiderdowns, his right leg protruding from the covers and dangling in a pail of warm water.

When we asked him if the woman had been pretty and, perhaps, even compliant, he had answered: 'Even Garbo herself couldn't have stopped me falling asleep.'

Freiberg suddenly broke in on my thoughts by asking a question which all of us had been privately mulling over for days.

'How's it all going to end here, sir? They'll be landing on the island soon. In a day or two we won't have a single aircraft left to fly. And they'll leave us behind in Trapani. No one's going to get us out of here. This time the trap's going to close with a snap!'

He looked at me inquiringly as though I knew the answer. I wondered if the General of Fighters himself knew. However, as Freiberg's commanding officer, I had to tell him something.

'After Stalingrad and Cape Bon I've had all I want of heroic resistance and headlong flight. If, in fact, we do manage to get away from here in time, we'll see that on this occasion every man-jack reaches the mainland even if it means blowing up all the stuff we can't carry.'

'But how are we going to get across the Straits of Messina?'

The wing leaders, squadron commanders and their pilots were standing in a semicircle in the empty dispersal pen facing the narrow end of the hut. When I asked them to sit down, they made for the shade and sat, squatted or reclined in the position they found most comfortable.

Although I realized that the orders for the operation contained virtually nothing new and that the pilots were sufficiently experienced in the procedures of take-off, climb and the pre-interception phase to avoid tactical or flying errors, I had noted with concern that laxity was increasing and that some of them were no longer as attentive to detail as they ought to be. I felt I needed to hammer into all of them the basic principles that governed an operation from take-off to landing and to tell them that I had been watching them closely and had noticed how much their flying discipline had deteriorated.

'We take off,' I said, 'as soon as the direction finders report the approach of the enemy. I shall lead the formation on a north-westerly course so that we can reach our attacking altitude without fighter interference.

'But first one or two points about the take-off. I want you to take off in as tight a formation as possible so that we don't spend all day sorting ourselves out. As soon as I start taxiing for take-off, signals will continue to be fired from here until Group HQ and No 1 Wing are airborne. Only then will No 2 take off in the opposite direction.

' I shall climb at minimum speed in a wide left-hand turn and will not set course until the wings are in position. And for once, gentlemen, I would like the group to form up without any violent banking or overshooting. I shall expect to see you all on course in impeccable formation within five minutes of take-off.'

I should have liked to add some remarks about flying discipline and considered whether I ought not to mention by name the

114

people who, to my knowledge, had let their flying become so slipshod that they tended to drop back; often they would lag behind the formation and by so doing spoil an attack. On reflection it seemed likely that too much admonition would make them pigheaded, so I refrained. Besides, I knew that some of them were simply not capable of doing any better.

'Each wing will provide one section as top cover. The top cover will fly not less than two thousand feet above the formation and will dive instantly to protect it in the event of attack by Spitfires or Lightnings.'

I ought really to have ordered them to refuse battle with the fighters and confine their attacks to the bombers. But what were we expected to do if the fighters forced us into combat? Our formation was so ridiculously small that any tactics designed to tie up the attacking fighters, so that the main body could get through to the bombers, were bound to fail.

I stopped as the telephone in the hut began to ring.

'Yes,' we heard Korn shout, 'yes, understood, flying north!'

He appeared at the window, Very pistol in hand. 'Scramble, sir! Heavies south of Comiso, flying north with fighter escort.'

Scramble. The word immediately set in motion a chain of reflex actions in which there was no conscious intervention by the brain. Freiberg was gone in a flash and I found myself racing for my aircraft. While I ran I drew my life-jacket over my head and stumbled as I pulled the straps between my legs. I was vaguely aware of an airman, stripped to the waist, standing among the aircraft and firing a steady succession of red flares into the air.

My machine had been standing out in the sun and I felt the metal skin burning my hands as I gripped the edge of the cockpit to heave myself up. Two airmen stood ready to operate the inertia starter. During a scramble not a word was wasted – everything proceeded automatically. If a group commander was to lead he had to be first into the air.

I had lost count of the number of times I had run this race against time. The performance of the pre-flight drill with its intermeshing sequence of operations entailed a more or less automatic series of actions. What was one thinking about during that time? There must have been something in one's mind – the hope, perhaps, that one wouldn't be bombed to pieces on the ground, or that they wouldn't get you on take-off . . .

I know that during those long-drawn-out seconds I would sometimes whisper: 'Parachute straps – helmet – starter – quick, quick – close the hood – quick, quick . . .' until the engine fired and resolved the tension. With the engine running you could do something, you could taxi, take off, fly, shoot! Any pilot would prefer to run the risk of taking off through falling bombs rather than dive for a slit trench.

I sat in my glass oven. I was out of breath after my sprint and the haste with which I had arranged myself on my parachute pack had made the sweat literally pour down my face, chest and back. On my right the propeller of Straden's aeroplane began to turn. Immediately the engine fired, a cloud of dust, straw and leaves went swirling out behind, enveloping Bachmann's machine.

As soon as my engine was running, I closed the cockpit window and taxied forward. The dry dust rose up into the clear summer air like a sudden sandstorm and obscured the view to the south. I signalled to the man with the Very pistol, applied full power, moved the stick forward and now saw the airfield spread out in front of me. Silhouettes of Messerschmitts emerged from the curtain of dust.

I had given orders that Freiberg and his wing should begin taxiing for take-off as soon as Group HQ was airborne. Green Very lights were fired as soon as I left the ground to indicate that the commodore's flight was in the air.

With the engine at maximum revolutions, the airspeed indicator registering over sixty mph, the Me rose off the ground. Out of the corner of my eye I saw Bachmann and Straden climbing to my altitude. Undercarriage up, airscrew in coarser pitch, flaps up. Then I throttled back so as to muster the group behind me in a gentle left-hand turn.

It was a relief to be in the air again. After the doubts as to whether we would manage to take off unscathed there now followed a short period of carefree flight. We had escaped being bombed on the ground and we had not yet intercepted the enemy in the air. One had only to concentrate on the mechanics of flying, on navigation and on the interchange of messages with the controller, but these few moments were quickly over and already people's eyes were beginning to search the sky and to watch out for surprise attacks.

'Odysseus One, Comiso bombed – pantechnicons flying north, very high. Watch out for Spitfire escort.'

'Message received.'

Salty sweat was running into my eyes from underneath my open-mesh flying helmet. Closing my eyes I wiped the lids dry with the back of my glove which smelt strongly of petrol. Even when my sleeves were rolled right up I always wore gloves when flying, preferably an ancient dark brown pair which had become impregnated with petrol as a result of repeated contact with the fuel caps.

At three thousand feet we rose out of the haze which encircled the lower slopes of Mount Etna like a lake of delicate blue. Looking behind I could see the silhouettes of the emerging Messerschmitts sharply outlined against the haze. Today the British would have no difficulty in spotting us from a considerable distance for we were as though projected onto a screen. That wouldn't do at all and I would have to turn south into the sun. But we were still no higher than 18,000 feet.

The controller started speaking again: 'Odysseus One, pantechnicons twenty miles south of Catania. Your height, please?'

'Twenty thousand.'

'Message received. Alter course for Messina. Watch out for Spitfire escort.'

I acknowledged the warning and turned my attention to the group. They were now in looser formation. I had been unable to count how many aircraft had taken off but I thought about twenty-five. One of Freiberg's squadrons was on my right and I could see the others when I turned my head and looked upwards and astern through the plexglass hood into the dazzling sun. The cockpit had suddenly grown cold. Ice crystals were forming in the corners of the side windows. I rolled down my shirt sleeves.

My left hand automatically checked the fit of my oxygen mask. Ceaselessly, systematically and in accordance with a specific plan that had evolved out of the experience of hundreds of air battles we scanned the air about us. My altimeter was registering 25,000 feet. It was at this height that the bombers would be flying with the fighter escort above them at about 28,000 feet. By now I was heading north after making a wide, gradual turn. As Etna's snow-covered crater disappeared beneath the wing, the mountains of Calabria on the far side of the Straits of Messina rose up out of the haze.

Any minute now. 'Contact with the enemy' was truly an apt description of the commencement of an air battle. At all events it was the term used in our combat reports. Once the adversary had been reported, either by yourself or by someone else, then a new phase began involving a different mental attitude. This did not necessarily mean that you had opened fire with your cannon or become embroiled in a dogfight. Rather it meant the irrevocable end of the approach flight; you were released from what might have been preoccupying you during that short spell and, at the same time, you had reached the point of no return. For there could be no disengagement now, no breaking away. All had to be involved when the battle began, for the individual who turned aside from the fight because on that particular day his offensive spirit failed him would be lost.

During the approach you were mainly occupied with routine tasks: checking instruments, switching over magnetos to check the plugs, watching the oil temperature, checking the boost pressure and, every so often, feeling automatically for parachute straps and oxygen mask. You were flying in formation with others to the left and right above you. Nevertheless you were alone, very much alone in your thundering glass-topped box, a prey to the thoughts and temptations that war brings. You still had some personal choice; you could still decide whether or not you were going to carry out the orders for the attack, whether or not you would remain with the formation until there was no pulling back from the battle. Was the engine a bit rough? Was it misfiring? Were the revs dropping? Engine trouble would be a plausible excuse for falling behind and having to turn back. It was a temptation to which all pilots were exposed.

As the minutes passed the screeching voices in the headphones kept up their merciless commentary, feeding the already heated imagination with fresh images: 'bombers', 'lots of them', 'look out – Spitfires . . .'

All at once you were aware of the immensity of the sea and the forbidding nature of the mountains and you began to wonder about your chances of survival. These were four-engined bombers and to bring them down you had to get in very close. Even when you were only attacking a section of three aircraft, about thirty machine guns would be firing at you. Moreover the Spitfires, which were still manœuvrable at very high altitudes, would be above you so that you were at a disadvantage from the outset. And when this particular mission was over, you would be sent out on another and yet another, all in one day. Provided, of course, that you were still alive . . .

Usually the report that someone was turning back came shortly after take-off and before there was any real danger. It was invariably accompanied by an expression of regret; for instance: 'Oh sod it, my engine keeps cutting. I'll have to turn back.' In some cases the regret was perfectly genuine, in others less so, and it needed long experience of command to distinguish between them.

Those who turned back could be divided into three categories. First of all there were the genuine cases which were by no means rare since technology is a law unto itself and cares little for the reputation of a fighter pilot. The reliable veterans of numerous campaigns, the old hands, knew their aeroplanes and made little of it when they had to turn back. Instead of profuse explanations, they simply gave the leader a factual report of the trouble. They knew that what they said would be accepted without question.

The second category consisted of experienced pilots who, having suddenly reached the end of their tether, either could not or would not acknowledge the fact. Having survived hundreds of patrols and battles, each time learning more about how to master themselves, how to circumvent the perfectly natural instinct of self-preservation, they had all at once found themselves unable to cope any more, unable to resist the temptation of making a timely excuse. Thereafter they would turn back more and more frequently. In such cases it was better to take them off operations before they were killed.

The third group was composed of young pilots posted to the front from fighter replacement wings. Among them there were always a few who would yield to the temptation of a minor deception so as to avoid a battle. They were horrified and utterly overwhelmed by the pitilessness of the air war in the Mediterranean. Many had been misled by communiqués which, though full of heroic deeds, said nothing about the superiority the enemy had gradually achieved. None of the fighter training schools was in a position to prepare the young pilots for what really awaited them.

When someone in this category turned back, the older, experienced pilots would test his machine after their return from the operation. As often as not they found no sign of the alleged trouble, thus instantly demolishing the boy's fragile edifice of petty lies. Some never repeated the attempt; others reappeared, much later, in category two, while the majority were either killed or posted home 'for other employment'.

Thoughts like these were going through my head as my eyes continued their mechanical search of the surrounding air. Suddenly, in an instant, the enemy appeared and events began to follow one another at lightning speed.

Hurtling head-on towards us at the same height, the elegant fighters went racing through our formation. For a split second I seemed to see – though it may only have been my imagination – the colourful insignia on the Spitfires' fuselages, the pointed wing tips, the bellies milky blue like those of fish.

And suddenly the old bitter taste was back on my tongue again and my mouth went dry.

Then, out of the corner of my eye, I saw the bombers below us. They appeared to be stationary for they were flying in the same direction as ourselves. Seemingly unperturbed they proceeded on their course calmly and majestically. They were flying in their customary, stepped-up battle formation which allowed every machine a free field of fire above and astern. But this was hardly the moment to dive on them. Each of us would very soon have had a Spitfire breathing down our necks, for the protective role of the enemy fighters demanded that they should swing round at once and attack us.

At 28,000 feet the Spitfire could turn in an astonishingly narrow radius. We, on the other hand, in the thin air of these altitudes had to carry out every manœuvre with caution and at full power so as not to lose control.

Utter chaos reigned on the R/T. The medley of reports and exclamations had suddenly turned to an unintelligible and ear-piercing screech. I was glad that I could see my flight – Straden, Bachmann and Bernhard – who were keeping station behind me. Freiberg's wing was evidently at grips with the escorting fighters. It was they who were making the din in the headphones: 'Watch out, pull up', or 'Jochen, he's on your tail – look out!'

There was no rational explanation for my decision to attack when I saw the two Spitfires flying below me. Possibly the experience of earlier and similar situations had told me, without my having to think, that I was in an ideal position – I had the advantage of height and was approaching out of the sun. I have no idea whether I informed the formation of my intentions; at all events I found myself suddenly in a steep dive with the speed building up enormously. Already the outlines of both my opponents had appeared in my sights. The number two, however, as if hearing a warning shout, suddenly turned his aircraft on its side and broke away to the left in a tight spiral. By now I had lost sight of his number one.

Without hesitating – it was against all common sense – I

decided to fight it out. There was no time to look round. Bach-mann ought to be behind me if he had been following my manœuvres in accordance with the prescribed drill. As I banked steeply the acceleration pressed me onto my parachute with ele-mental force and my neck ached as I tried to keep my opponent in view. The tight turn had caused the wing slats to jump out while the shaking of the stick indicated that the aircraft was on the point of spinning.

Yard by yard I worked my way towards the Spitfire. It would quiver across my sights and disappear again. I set the firing lever on top of the stick at 'fire'. One more full circle and then, perhaps, I would have him properly in my sights. Like one possessed I rode this carousel, the final phase of a duel in the air. I did not need to worry about anything behind or above – Straden, Bachmann and Zahn would surely be covering me, and a whole fighter wing as well . . .

There was a thud against the fuselage and I wrenched my head round. Looking past the armour-plate I saw a Spitfire in a steep turn a few yards behind. Smoke from his tracer groped towards me like fingers. My engine stuttered violently. Bullets shattered against the armour-plate behind my head with appalling cracks. Immediately the cockpit was filled with the smell of cordite. His shooting was damned good! Almost as though on an exercise I broke out of the circle, half-rolled and went into a vertical dive. Rigid in my seat I felt almost of a piece with my aircraft as I put it through the classic evasive manœuvre. It spiralled steeply earth-wards as though into a vortex. With almost complete detachment my eyes took note of the wildly oscillating instruments, of the failing engine which these gyrations conveyed. The controls were ominously heavy while the fabric-covered ailerons began to balloon, inducing a virtually uncontrollable spin. Escaping coolant had covered the windscreen with a milky, opaque film. I was now in a state of cold, considered purposefulness, as though observing the behaviour of one who has landed himself in a hopeless predica-ment. Only for a second or two had such thoughts as 'this is it' or 'it's all over' impaired the powerful instinct of self-preservation.

Then I began to talk to myself, suiting action to word as I always did in an air battle. I may even have spoken aloud, saying: 'now', 'faster', and 'flatten out'.

At 6000 feet it became apparent that no one was shooting at me any more. The windscreen was a little clearer. What I could see lurching towards me must be the slopes of Etna. I switched off because the oil and coolant temperatures had risen dangerously. The propeller windmilled idly in the air stream. My rate of descent was very high indeed. Small details could now be discerned: narrow strips of cultivated land surrounded by vine hedges – not the best of country for a belly-landing.

However, I made a successful approach between tall trees towards a long, narrow field that sloped up towards Etna. Only when the tips of my airscrew struck the ground did I notice that the land was strewn everywhere with lumps of rock. But it was too late to do anything about it now. I had tightened my shoulder straps shortly before touching down. There was a heavy impact – the hood flew up and away in a high arc while lumps of earth came thudding down on wings, windscreen and fuselage. I was thrown forward violently but my harness held. The aircraft finally came to a halt with a sudden jerk which tipped it on to its propeller boss, nearly causing a somersault. There was one last almighty crash as the fuselage fell back onto the stony ground.

When I came to my senses everything was quiet. The only sound was a gentle hum – the radio was still switched on.

In a daze I undid my harness, switched off the radio and climbed out of the cockpit onto the wing. Once on solid ground I walked a few paces to a rock. Not until I reached it did I feel a sharp pain in my back. I slowly lowered myself to the ground, easing myself down with my hands on the rock. Leaning against it with my back to the sun I worked myself out of my life-jacket, undid the straps round my calves that held the Very pistol and the flare cartridges and pulled my cap out of my knee pocket.

Exactly an hour earlier we had taken off from Gerbini. It was now midday and the sun was directly over the barren field. Not a sound was to be heard. Shading my eyes, I looked up at the sky and saw there, gradually dispersing, the pattern of the air battle described in the innocuous-looking white tracery of condensation trails.

The field sloped up the side of Etna. It was covered with rocks. One of these had been in the way of my 109 and had nearly caused it to somersault. When, after tipping forward, the aircraft had fallen back on its belly, the heavy impact had obviously done little good to the base of my spine. The pain was bearable provided I kept quite still but any movement sent it shooting all the way up my back. However, I had to move whatever the consequences, for though I was so exhausted that I could hardly keep my eyes open, it was out of the question to go on sitting here in the scorching sun.

Why had I accepted the Englishman's challenge to a dogfight? He had offered to take me on in single combat although he had certainly had plenty of time to escape my fire by turning and diving away. Probably he had felt safe enough because his friends had been above to cover him.

That must have been it – otherwise the second Spitfire pilot could never have attained the margin of speed that enabled him to manœuvre into the position behind me from which he had shot me down. But my first adversary had accepted the risk of holding on in close combat until such time as help should arrive, and that was characteristic of the tough, sporting British; they were made of a fibre quite different from that of the Russians with whom I had been having dealings not so long before.

My sums hadn't worked out properly. If only my people had covered me for a few minutes longer and prevented that Spitfire from getting on my tail, I would have been able to fire and break away in which case the Englishman would now be sitting in some field beside his aeroplane, or he would have come down by parachute – or else he would be dead.

As the rules of the strategic bomber offensive came increasingly to dictate the nature of air battles, so the duel in the air, the classic dogfight, was becoming correspondingly rare. There was no time for a trial of strength, no time to measure your flying skill against an adversary's when the bombers flew in streams and the fighters provided the protective umbrella. Our job was to dive through this screen and attack the bombers while the job of the escorting fighters was to prevent us from doing so by pulling up and opening fire as soon as we had begun our dive. But the dogfight as such was becoming ever less frequent.

Alarm would often incapacitate our young pilots and sap their resolution when they were attacked by fighters so that they would go into a tight spiral without due tactical consideration of how to come out of this manœuvre in the position of advantage. Fights like these did not last long; before one could go to his help the victim would be spinning earthwards in flames, having flown no more than one full circle with his antagonist.

Every now and again, however, two equally matched masters of the craft suddenly found themselves locked in combat. When this happened the old hands, while still participating in the main battle, would watch enthralled, awaiting the outcome with bated breath.

They would come to look for me soon. Evidently my forced landing had not been observed; otherwise they would surely have circled the field. I would have to try to make contact with the group operations room on the R/T. Or perhaps one of the group's pilots was still in the air and would hear my distress call.

Groaning, I pulled myself up, one hand pressed to my spine, and bent laboriously over the cockpit. I operated the usual switch and the radio came on. Holding the throat microphone in position with one hand, I worked the transmitter button on the stick with the other.

'Odysseus One to Odysseus . . .'

No answer.

'Odysseus One to Odysseus. Have belly-landed south of Etna. Please come . . .'

The radio was obviously unserviceable. Indeed it would have been a miracle if it had survived the heavy impact. I switched off and slowly covered the hundred yards to the edge of the field where some stunted trees cast a little shade. As I entered a patch of long, dry grass, swarms of small locusts rose into the air on all sides, settling on my shoes and trouser legs. I started back in disgust and shook my feet to rid myself of the pests. There was shade elsewhere – higher up by the hedge, for instance.

If only it wasn't so infernally hot! But they'd find me in due course. I wondered if Gerbini had been bombed. By now they were probably getting ready for the next mission.

Meanwhile I had found a shady spot at the foot of an olive tree. I unbuttoned my shirt down to my stomach, pulled my cap over my eyes and fell into a doze.

I was half asleep when I heard the clink of metal on metal followed by men's voices. Opening my eyes I saw two Sicilians in grimy white shirts and black trousers beside the aeroplane. They were leaning over the cockpit and tugging at the parachute.

'Hey!' I shouted. They gave a start whereupon I picked up the Very pistol and shouted again.

They looked in my direction but it seemed that, although they had heard me call, they had not yet spotted me under the olive tree. Only when they slowly straightened up did I observe the two long-barrelled shotguns propped against the fuselage. Carrying their guns they came towards me, then halted without saying a word. There was nothing particularly formidable about them. The older of the two had a kindly look in his eyes. He was a scrawny man, toothless, with bony arms upon which the veins stood out prominently. The younger one – he could not have been more than thirteen or fourteen – kept gazing with round, astonished eyes at the strange flier.

'*Buon giorno.*'

'*Buon giorno.*'

'*Tedesco?*'

'*Si, Tedesco.*'

Both sat down beside me in the shade. For a moment I felt curious to know what they would have done had I been an '*Inglese*' or '*Americano*'. But at that moment the boy was pointing out two more figures who were advancing towards the wrecked aircraft. And then I heard the unmistakable sound of a Storch's engine.

Yes, there it was: a Storch circling above the slopes that rose to

Etna's summit, the high slopes where the vegetation began to get sparse. I fired a red flare and shortly afterwards the slow-flying aircraft was banking over the field searching for a suitable place to land.

It came to a halt near the 109 and Bachmann and my chief mechanic, Sergeant Schwarz, climbed out. Immediately both aircraft were surrounded by curious spectators of all ages. Indeed, every single inhabitant of the neighbouring villages must have turned out to watch the event. No doubt we provided a welcome diversion for these people who clustered about us, chattering loudly and gesticulating. I had a feeling that they would be seeing rather more of the war before very long.

'I'm sorry, sir,' Bachmann said, 'about our losing sight of you . . . You attacked so suddenly . . .'

'Yes, Bachmann, it wasn't exactly a masterpiece either of combat drill or of co-operation. You must all hang on whatever happens.'

'The Imp was shot down. Everything happened so suddenly – before we knew it there was a general mix-up . . .'

He faltered. What more could he say? Again it had been one of the younger ones who had gone. Turning away I, too, remained silent.

Schwarz had already begun to dismantle the aeroplane. We decided to remove the radio and the clock and take them with us. Schwarz was to remain with the wreck while we would reconnoitre an approach route from the air so that a recovery vehicle could be sent out.

My back hurt as I climbed in. I was thirsty and the sweat was pouring off me. As usual the Storch's cabin was like an oven. It was two pm when we took off. The Storch bumped over the dry field and after a short run left the ground in a cloud of dust. Our passage through the air brought some relief from the heat. The oil temperature gauge was showing the maximum permissible reading but I had no wish to climb into cooler air, for up there we would have been at the mercy of the Spitfires and Kittyhawks.

We were probably about thirty miles from Gerbini. The plain with its fields of yellow stubble extended to the horizon. Conditions were hazy and the air was shimmering in the heat. I was trying to pick out some landmarks when Bachmann suddenly shook my shoulder and yelled into my ear: 'They're attacking Gerbini! They're bombing . . .'

Then I, too, saw the brown fountains of earth and all at once the whole of the vast plain seemed to erupt into eerie motion. On the fighter-bomber group's airfield, where continuous sticks of bombs were ploughing up the ground, all hell was evidently being let loose. As I approached our own landing ground the view ahead became obscured by a curtain of dust. It was impossible to tell whether or not our own fighters were in the air, but to land there now would have been madness. I had sufficient fuel to reach Trapani and in any case the group would be arriving there that evening. On the other hand Schwarz was waiting beside the wreck of my aircraft at the foot of Etna, and would have to remain with it until help came.

Making up my mind I turned round to Bachmann. 'I'm going to Trapani,' I shouted. 'We'll telephone the Fighter Leader's people about recovering my aircraft and leave them to look after it.'

As I spoke I turned the Storch northwards so as to cross the mountains and reach the coast. Once there, and flying low along the coast road towards Trapani, we would be safe from enemy fighters.

Glancing astern shortly afterwards, I saw that a brown cloud of dust had spread like a blanket over the plain. From it emerged blue black mushrooms of smoke of the kind produced by burning aircraft.

I flew over the parched fields beside the mountain before turning the Storch towards the bare slopes and the crest. The midday heat had created extremely turbulent conditions so that I had to work hard to control the aircraft. To our right rose the snow-capped cone of the volcano. Then the ground fell away steeply in a delightful wooded slope which ended abruptly where the deep blue expanse of the sea began. I reached the coast near

Cefalù – identifiable by its distinctive cliffs – and flew westwards at low level towards Palermo. The air was smooth now; the engine hummed monotonously and the hot midday sun shone into our faces through the plexiglass of the cabin. I shifted about on the hard seat to try to overcome my fatigue. But my limbs felt as heavy as lead, while the effect of the heat and of over-exertion created the illusion of a firework display before my eyes. I had been on my feet since four that morning.

The Englishman who shot me down had riddled both radiators under the wings. The protective armour behind my head, however, had stopped a complete burst. Some of my pilots had, I knew, removed this plating because they wanted an uninterrupted view astern and I decided that I would order them to have it replaced.

Had the group been caught on the ground, I wondered? That was the worst and most inglorious thing imaginable for a pilot, yet it was only two years ago that our own bomber crews had been daily and successfully pursuing the same object: the elimination of the enemy air force on the ground . . . I thought of poor Freiberg who would go half out of his mind when he had to squat in a slit trench impotently listening to the whistle and crash of the bombs.

How many aircraft would reach Sciacca and Trapani that evening? The improvisations achieved by our gallant mechanics had been little short of miraculous. Unserviceable aircraft were ruthlessly cannibalized, for the spare-part situation was truly catastrophic.

We would have to evacuate the established airfields before we were entirely destroyed. I decided that on the following day I would take the Storch to the upland portion of the island and reconnoitre possible landing grounds. There were sure to be suitable fields between Trapani and Enna where we could conceal ourselves from the bombers. I would have to inform the General of Fighters of my scheme and I hoped that his telephone line was still intact. But in reality I was only deceiving myself, in the same way that I had deceived myself in Tunisia three months before

E

when the remnants of the group had been ground down during the hopeless battle in the Cape Bon bridge-head.

How appallingly apathetic we had all become! During our last night in North Africa we had had to destroy our vehicles, air-craft, radio sets and spares. The operation had degenerated into an orgy of vandalism, and it was perhaps then that our attitude to the value of these things had changed.

If I didn't do something I was going to fall asleep. In wartime no good could come of thinking. Abruptly I put the Storch into a steep bank and swept low over the shore. At that moment we found ourselves being tossed about in the slip-stream of a fighter overtaking us at the same height. Wrenching the Storch round in alarm I identified it as a 109 bound for Trapani.

I landed some way from the group operations room in the early afternoon on a field which sloped upwards towards Mount Erice. Once the airscrew had stopped turning, the tension of the flight fell away and my one desire was to close my eyes and remain sitting where I was.

Bachmann opened the door at the side of the cabin and instantly it was hot again; once more there was the chirping of crickets, the smell of oil and dope under the burning sun. My back hurt as I straightened up and heaved my left leg over the door ledge in order to climb out.

Groaning I set both feet on the ground and steadied myself, supported by Bachmann. Clouds of grasshoppers rose up as we walked through the thistles and wild radishes towards the tent where a Kübelwagen was waiting. The ride to the operations room was agony for the vehicle was virtually unsprung and went bumping from furrow to furrow on its way to the track.

The duty officer in the operations room reported that my HQ flight and No 1 Wing had left Gerbini and were just about to land. The news of the day's events was confused and uncertain. Moreover the line to the Fighter Leader was temporarily out of order. The group had shot down six Fortresses and one Mosquito. Second Lieutenants Bernhard and Flick were missing. The damage caused by the bombing raid on Gerbini could not yet be assessed but the fighter-bomber group had borne the brunt of the attack.

Freiberg telephoned shortly afterwards. 'We're just back from Gerbini, sir, we were worried about you . . .'

'I only sprained my back. How are things with your wing?'

'Flick was shot down. It happened during the fight with the Spitfires. He went down in flames off Catania. All the airfields round Gerbini have taken a pasting. The fighter-bomber boys must have lost the hell of a lot of aeroplanes. Four Focke-Wulfs were already on fire as we took off.'

'How many aircraft can you put in the air, Freiberg?'

'Impossible to say at this moment,' he answered unemotionally, 'but if things go on as they are, there soon won't be any left to send up.'

'The Freyas report enemy aircraft approaching from Pantelleria. I want you to have two flights on defensive patrol west of Marsala as soon as you can.'

'Right, sir.' He acknowledged his new orders in the same un-emotional tone and confirmed with three short rings of the telephone that the conversation was over.

In the meantime the duty officer had been trying to restore our telephone link with the Fighter Leader to whom I now sent a wireless signal. The line might well remain out of order and I wanted to inform him of the latest state of the group. Godert reported from Sciacca that the airfield had been attacked by a number of bombers and that the wing had shot down five of the Kittyhawk escort at a cost of one aircraft.

Eventually I managed to get through to the general on the telephone and informed him about the group, the air battle and my forced landing.

After he had heard me out, the line was silent for a moment. Then he gave his instructions which were brief and to the point: 'Keep both your wings in the west tomorrow and go for any heavies that attack your airfields. And start using advanced landing grounds so that your group isn't destroyed on the ground . . .'

Then we were cut off.

I would rather have remained in the villa and slept for a few hours. Still half asleep I plainly registered the Wellingtons' arrival, the rhythmic noise of their engines, the whistle of the first bombs. But my limbs were as heavy as lead and I felt as if it was I who was falling at high speed towards the ground. When a bomb burst close by and the windows rattled, I remained rigid on my back. I was soaked with sweat.

As I sat up to pull on my shirt, I felt a savage stab of pain in my back. Tubby was standing in the doorway holding up the carbide lamp.

'Wouldn't you rather sleep in the grotto, sir? They're here again . . .'

Laboriously I crawled through the hole in the wall in Tubby's wake and entered the grotto. Before my eyes had become accustomed to the light, I heard Straden saying:

'The Imp hit the sea like a torch.'

Freiberg's voice replied: 'They must have got him from ahead. Nobody saw the Spitfires coming. As soon as I'd cottoned on they were Spitfires, he was already going down in flames.'

Tubby moved up a deck-chair for me and I lowered myself cautiously into it. The lamp on the table was shining full in Freiberg's face, his features harshly illuminated by the crude light. Never before had I seen him in a state of such utter exhaustion. His eyelids were puffy and the heavy bags under his eyes made his face look old. It was obvious that he had been drinking too much again.

'Sorry I couldn't come to your help, sir,' he said rather thickly. 'By the time you made that sudden attack we all of us had our hands full.'

'Perhaps it was a mistake to do it,' I said, 'but I thought you'd be covering me. A dogfight is a temptation I just can't resist. Only one more time round and I'd have had him for sure.'

'They dived on us – about eight Spits. Before we could look round each of us had one on our tail.' Straden's tone was almost apologetic and his remark ended the discussion.

They were quite right, I thought. But I had long been aware

that they had ceased taking unnecessary risks. Would they otherwise have left me on my own? Now they only went for the easy kills – the solitary flier, the inexperienced pilot who had broken away from his formation, the crippled straggler. During the air battles over England, whatever the mistakes that had been made, things could hardly have come to such a pass. But now we were tired, worn out and dispirited.

All the same I wondered if I could describe any one of them as a 'coward in the face of the enemy'. And then I realized that for some time I had been observing Bachmann who was sitting quietly opposite me. But he was avoiding my eyes as though he had a guilty conscience. Perhaps he, too, was thinking about the Imp's death.

'Will you see to Bernard's things,' I asked him. 'We can put them on a transport aircraft if one lands here.'

He nodded silently. Such procedure was a matter of course and no longer needed orders for its execution. It was something he'd done often enough already . . .

I asked myself why it was that our younger pilots survived so few missions. We old hands had also started in much the same way as they had but perhaps we had gradually accustomed ourselves to the present situation and for that reason were now immune to the shocks it induced. When the young replacement pilots first arrived they were still very sure of themselves; they were full of panache and they talked a lot. But the first few missions scared the life out of them and of their own accord they became much quieter. Usually they flew at the tail end of the formation or on the outer flanks where they were particularly at risk. It was only after a very large number of missions that a fighter pilot was given command of a section or even a pair. And so they flew in their appointed positions, for long remaining as it were in blinkers because they were simply not capable of taking in the situation as a whole when contact was made and the enemy engaged, and also because they had not developed an instinctive feeling for combat in three dimensions. It was during this period that most of them met their deaths since the way they handled their aircraft when under attack instantly revealed them as beginners to any escort pilot with a reasonable amount of combat experience. Whenever they had to bale out or make a forced landing, it was essential to send them up again at once on another operation, for if they were given too much time to reflect, they would fail to get over the shock.

'How many missions had Bernhard flown?'

'About ten, I think,' Bachmann answered.

'During the last week before the Allied landing the bombardment assumed massive proportions. Every airfield, landing ground and advanced airstrip was so heavily hit that only by the deployment of all available resources – including army units – was it possible to restore a few airfields to their operational role on a makeshift basis. The German and Italian anti-aircraft batteries shot down a large number of machines but they were unable to halt the massed air attacks. Moreover during the last days before the invasion the Allied air forces carried out heavy attacks against coastal defence installations in the south and the southeast of the island. These large-scale attacks indicated the eventual place of landing.'

FRANZ KUROWSKI
DAS TOR ZUR FESTUNG EUROPA

'By the end of D minus 1 (9 July), then, the Allied air forces had cleared the way for the invasion of Sicily. The enemy's air arm had been driven from the island or largely pinned down on battered fields, and his lines of supply and reinforcement had been so hammered that the normal flow of material and personnel was seriously retarded. With superiority in the air established, NAAF and the Ninth Air Force stood ready to assume the additional duties the actual invasion would impose upon them.'

ARMY AIR FORCES IN WORLD WAR II
EUROPE: TORCH TO POINTBLANK

'At 0430, 10 July, the first enemy planes appeared over the Allied

shipping massed in front of the assault beaches . . . The air raids inter-
fered but little with the landings.'

UNITED STATES ARMY IN WORLD WAR II
SICILY AND THE SURRENDER OF ITALY

'By nightfall on D-day, 10 July, the Seventh Army was firmly
established in Sicily.'

UNITED STATES ARMY IN WORLD WAR II
SICILY AND THE SURRENDER OF ITALY

Trapani, 10 July 1943

The airstrip ought to be just beyond the next range of hills. I put the 109 into a left-hand turn and swept low over the sun-scorched surface of the meadow towards the farmhouse which stood beside the dried-out river bed. Close by was a yellow cloth marker spread out on the ground and pointing up the valley. This indicated the point where it was essential to touch down.

I wondered why today this parched, yellow strip with dark oak trees sparsely covering the slopes on either side should seem so small. Yesterday the area had looked much larger when I had landed there in the Storch and taxied over the rock-hard ground. Pacing it out, I had had to make my way through a knee-high scrub of grass and thistles which had crackled as it broke and crumbled away under my feet. The length of the runway had seemed to me adequate provided that one approached the marker at minimum speed and touched down beside it.

With the wing behind me, I wanted to make a good landing so as to give them confidence. Then I would have to taxi quickly to one side to make way for Bachmann and Helbig who were not far behind me and were likewise banking prior to straightening out for the final approach. There was no wind nor, at this early hour of the morning, was there any turbulence. Just before I set the aircraft down, men in khaki came into view outside the farmhouse door and as the wheels touched the ground I saw airmen with Very pistols close to the landing marker. Their orders were to fire a red signal immediately if anything should seem to be amiss with a landing. Straden had chosen experienced men for this duty.

Breasting the slope the aircraft came quickly to a halt. And then

E*

I realized that the runway was too short for a pilot to take off again if, having misjudged his landing, he took more than a split second to decide to go round and make a second attempt. My mechanics were signalling to me from under the shade of the trees. I switched off the engine, undid my harness and sat down on the edge of the cockpit. From there I had a good view of the activities on the airfield and could give landing instructions over the R/T to Freiberg's wing.

The things we did with our Messerschmitts on this tiny patch of earth we called an advanced landing ground bordered on the realm of aerobatics. With the engine in high revolutions, just sufficient speed had to be maintained to control the aircraft. Immediately before the marker the throttle would be wrenched back and the heavy machine would alight in a cloud of dust on the rock-hard but far from even ground. It was a bold manœuvre to which our years of wandering had, however, accustomed us. For me the only difference lay in the fact that as a squadron commander I had still been able to curse the choice of this or that wretched strip of land from which we had been expected to operate. Now, however, the choice had been mine and that was quite a different affair! But it all seemed to be proceeding satisfactorily: everyone knew the landing sequence; the intervals between aircraft were adapted to the conditions and the younger pilots had been repeatedly briefed about the hazards of landing in these circumstances.

One of the latter took off again immediately after touching down because he had misjudged his speed. Quite correct. The red flares sank slowly to the ground and went out. There were the usual dust clouds, the crescendo and diminuendo of engines, the taxiing aircraft, the refuellers moving up, the bustling mechanics: a kaleidoscope of war invading this peaceful valley with explosive force. To us it was all quite commonplace, even though the hair-raising inadequacy of the landing strip – whose existence here would be unlikely to occur to anybody – was somewhat exceptional.

From time to time I spoke into the microphone: 'No 2

Squadron taxi off to the left!' for example, or 'Open out more', or 'Go round again!' About twenty Messerschmitts had landed safely. Only two were circling the field: in one case the pilot was having trouble lowering his wheels; in the other, one of the new men had failed to land at his first attempt. I took off my helmet and was reaching into the cockpit to switch off the radio when I heard agitated shouts from the mechanics: 'Too far to the left . . . he's coming in too steep!' As I straightened up I saw a 109 touch down well to one side of the marker. Travelling much too fast it ran some way with the tail up and then, under violent application of the brakes, went rumbling up the slope in a lurching movement.

At a time like this everyone pauses to watch. The mechanics ceased work; the pilots in their cockpits swivelled their heads to follow the progress of the machine as it tore past them, while the airmen by the door of the farmhouse stood with folded arms. The veterans, the experienced ones, knew that something was going to happen, yet their faces were impassive as they awaited the inevitable end. He's going to smash into the trees, I thought to myself. Perhaps he'll fetch up in the oak coppice or maybe he'll risk wrenching the aircraft round so as to tear off his undercarriage.

But before he reached the trees, the tail suddenly reared up and the aeroplane, after balancing momentarily on its propeller boss, went over in a somersault. All that could be seen now above the tall scrub were the wheels and the slender legs of the undercarriage pointing skywards.

He had obviously hit a rock, but how was that possible? Yesterday I had made a thorough examination of the ground, taxiing the Storch in all directions . . .

Several vehicles were already racing to the scene of the accident as I jumped to the ground and called for transport. Well before I arrived I was aware of a strong smell of petrol. A party of airmen was clustering round the rear of the aircraft, preparing to lift the tail in a combined effort. I listened to their shouted exchanges.

'Watch out, there's a fuel leak!'

'Have the extinguishers ready!'

'Altogether – lift!'

Bachmann suddenly appeared at my side.

'It's probably one of the new officers,' he said.

'Christ – d'you hear that? The generator's still running. That means the ignition is still switched on.'

One spark somewhere in the maze of wiring could cause an explosion. Already the ground round the aeroplane was saturated with petrol. One of the mechanics, armed with a heavy tool, knelt down beneath the wing and knocked out the side window of the cockpit with furious blows. Groaning, the other airmen supported the tail. First a pair of arms appeared outside the cockpit and then a head in a flying helmet; finally the entire body, soaked with petrol, covered with abrasions and with its shirt in tatters, was rudely hauled out by the arms and dragged on to the ground. By now several of the onlookers were sighing with relief. During the operation a number of fire extinguishers had been aimed at the wreck. We were well aware of the dangers of the undertaking and had kept at a respectful distance from the pool of petrol.

'Pull him clear!' someone shouted. The pilot got to his knees, striking his head against the edge of the wing, and was urged forward on the arm of his rescuer.

'Now the extinguishers!'

It almost seemed as though the jets of foam had ignited the petrol vapour, for with a dull 'whoof' a red wall of fire as high as a house suddenly appeared immediately in front of us. Stumbling and falling we raced for safety. We were out of the danger area when we saw a running figure, blazing like a torch. It was the pilot. After a few yards he halted and suddenly collapsed. The firemen rushed to give assistance and emptied their extinguishers over the writhing man. By the time I arrived the flames had been put out.

'It's one of the new officers as I thought,' Bachmann said. 'He's been very badly burnt.'

Abruptly the whole infernal makeshift nature of these advanced landing-ground operations came home to me. In any case the group now only possessed a single ambulance and that was else-where. We had destroyed all our transport in Tunis and when we had been re-equipped one ambulance was all that Air Fleet could make available.

Everyone was shouting for a medical orderly but so far none had arrived. Only the most essential transport had set out from Trapani and the small patch of pasture land that constituted our airfield was difficult to find. We had left Captain Sperrling, the MO, behind to look after the wounded, for the uninterrupted raids had filled our small sick-bay.

The burned man had been placed on a stretcher and brought into the shade. He was a terrible sight. Several of the airmen were discussing ways of alleviating his pain.

'It's Behrend from my squadron,' Reinhold told me. 'He's only been with us for a week and hasn't yet done an operation.'

As I bent over the prostrate man I was hit by the stench of burnt flesh. The flames had made ghastly work of his head and the upper part of his body. His hair had melted into a nauseous mass and his face was puffy with blisters. Shreds of clothing had burnt their way into his arms and chest.

Between his groans the boy was screaming:

'I can't bear it – give me something to stop it hurting!'

Over and over again he repeated his appeal while we stood round helplessly, for in the absence of either a doctor or a medical orderly there was no one who knew how to give a morphine injection.

'Send for Straden,' I ordered. 'He's done an injection before – that time with Hofmeier. Take the first-aid kit from one of the aircraft; there'll be a syringe and ampoules inside.'

Straden arrived panting for breath. His duties were now in the improvised group operations room. He knew at once what was expected of him and set to work in professional fashion.

'Gently, lad,' he said as he broke off the top of the ampoule with a steady hand and filled the syringe. 'Gently, it'll only last for a moment or two. It'll be over in no time . . .'

Then the injured man quietened down. He moaned softly to

himself, murmuring words we could not make out, while an airman kept off the flies which had appeared in repulsive swarms. His eyelids had swollen together; his face was a featureless, liquefied mass.

At last the Storch we had summoned from Trapani by radio appeared above the field. It would take Behrend back to our sick-bay. There was also a field hospital in Trapani. Perhaps they would succeed in flying him to the mainland if a Junkers happened to arrive during the night to bring in urgent spares and evacuate the wounded.

I got into the Kübelwagen and drove down the slope to the farmhouse where we had set up our operations room. For a long time I was unable to shake off the impression of what had just happened. In between telephone conversations and aircraft-state reports the boy's face kept reappearing before me and I thought I could detect the stench of burnt flesh.

The operations truck was standing outside the farmhouse gate. Tent canvas had been rigged up between the truck and the wall to make an awning. Beneath the canvas stood our deck-chairs. The gate, heavily barred, was locked and securely bolted. By reaching to the top bar and pulling yourself up you could look over into a quadrangular inner courtyard surrounded by tiled lean-to shelters for the cattle. Rusty agricultural implements lay scattered about. This was rural Sicily, a peaceful sight. It was now harvest time and you would have expected to find some activity in the yard, but most likely the people had fled in panic as soon as they had got wind of what we planned to do here. For wherever we appeared in the land, death and destruction followed in our wake.

Freiberg and his squadron commanders together with Straden, Bachmann and Helbig had gathered in the shade of the awning. It was hot and windless.

'What information is there about the Allied landing?' Freiberg asked.

'Not much,' I answered. 'Very little more than we can find

out for ourselves. I managed to have a further word with the general this evening before the line was cut. He talked about air landings and parachute operations in the Augusta–Cape Passero–Gela area. You know the cool, detached way he has of viewing and sizing up a situation – the sort that would give anyone else a nervous breakdown. But this evening his voice sounded edgy and overloud when he said, "We're putting up an unbelievable barrage . . ." And then the line went dead.'

'Nice situation,' Freiberg commented.

'Bachmann, let me know, please, when all the aircraft are refuelled. How many have landed?'

'Twenty-four, sir.'

Twenty-four. And how many of those would be serviceable? No 1 Wing had remained in Sciacca. Godert was to take off from there at first light to attack landing craft near Gela and would only move to our advanced airfield if it became impossible to remain at Sciacca.

The previous evening we had all forgathered in the grotto, as had been our custom since the beginning of the Allied air offensive. Now that Tubby had set up an improvised kitchen in the place, we had taken to eating our monotonous evening meal here.

During the past few days reconnaissance had revealed the presence of a powerful force of warships of all sizes in Valetta harbour and surrounding the island. That, combined with the violence of the bombardment and the enemy's non-stop reconnaissance flights, pointed to an imminent landing.

Towards midnight the guns out to sea had begun firing with unusual intensity. The bursts shook the floor and roof of the grotto. Roused from the sleep of the dead, we lay open eyed on our camp-beds, all of us aware that the final phase had begun.

The telephone began ringing: first the monitoring section on Mount Erice reported that traffic on the Allied R/T wave lengths had assumed unbelievable dimensions. But apparently the people who were shouting out orders, information and warnings to each other and talking to their controllers on the ground were not the commanders of the bomber and fighter squadrons with which we were already familiar but entirely new arrivals whose squadrons and wings had hitherto not been encountered in the Mediterranean.

Next the operations room came on the line followed by the radio section and finally No 1 Wing from Sciacca, and all this information combined to form a picture of a battle upon which the Allies had embarked with the intention of taking the fortress of Europe by storm.

The occupants of the grotto lay motionless, waiting till the grey light of dawn should drive them from their beds to prepare for the day's missions. Their eyes were riveted on my lips whenever I was at the telephone speaking to the operations room or receiving reports from the radio section to hear how the situation was developing. Afterwards they would converse in undertones, or pull maps out of their knee-pockets and point to Gela, for instance, or Syracuse, or else run their fingers over the coastal strip near Licata.

As we got up, the first light of dawn was filtering through the archway in the wall. Before we went across to the trucks to drive down to the airfield, Captain Kegel issued the briefing for the day:

'Morning reconnaissance of Gela beach-head. Reconnaissance of sea areas extending to Malta, Pantelleria and Tunis. Interception of approaching bomber formations. Operations will commence after diversion to advanced landing ground.'

'CO to the telephone!'

Groaning I got up and climbed the steps into the operations vehicle. Once inside, it was impossible to stand upright without banging your head on the roof.

On the map which covered the table by the window, numbers of red arrows pointed from the south and east towards the southern portion of the island. These represented the pincers movement which was enabling the enemy – who enjoyed air and naval superiority – to cut off the southern tip of the island at his leisure.

144

'Sir, we've picked up a large formation of heavy bombers approaching from the southwest.' The call was from the operations room on Mount Erice. 'If you take off straight away you'll meet them as they cross the coast.'

'Thank you – we'll take off. I'll call you up again when we're airborne.'

The pilots standing beside the truck had heard my reply and were ready to go. The drivers started their engines.

'Heavies approaching from the direction of Pantelleria,' I announced. There was no need to preface the information with the word 'scramble'. That was generally understood. They hurried towards the vehicles fastening their life-jackets, stuffing flare cartridges into the lower leg pockets of their overalls and exchanging remarks about the take-off.

A well-drilled unit always took off in a predetermined sequence which had been rehearsed on numerous occasions, for the procedure during take-off governed the assembly in the air and the departure in formation. When our squadrons were dispersed round a circular airfield – and most of the airfields with the exception of the advanced landing grounds were laid out in this way – take-off was controlled by visual signals in the form of Very lights fired from the squadron dispersals. It was not always possible to adhere to the normal sequence and during a scramble aircraft would often race about wildly with their tails already off the ground. Then, as if by a miracle, the chaos would somehow sort itself out. A casual onlooker, witnessing this hurly-burly for the first time, might well have been inclined to close his eyes in alarm, but careful observation would soon have revealed that the whole was a curious combination of drill, intuition and experience. In Russia a squadron of Pe 2s would often appear over the airfield unannounced because one of our aircraft-observer detachments up forward with the infantry was moving into a new position. The result would be one of these precipitate take-offs in which, of course, everyone took part, firstly because they wanted to shoot down the enemy, secondly because, even in Russia, one tended to be safer in the air than on the ground. Obviously air fighting on the eastern front was little more than a harmless game compared with this hell, but on the other hand it could produce some unpleasant shocks.

As I made a wide, left-hand turn I looked back and counted the aircraft behind me. Sixteen – in other words the remnants of No 1 Wing and HQ Flight. Perhaps after this operation there might be ten, maybe less.

'Pantechnicons approaching beach-head. Crossing coast at Selinunte.' The transmission from our signals office on Mount Erice came over loud and clear and I found it in some way reassuring.

'Message received,' I acknowledged.

The morning sun was shining directly on my face. I shifted sideways a little on my parachute so that the windscreen division shaded my eyes. Spread out beneath me like an exquisite water-colour in blue and green lay the southern part of the island, its coast delicately outlined by an undulating ribbon of white foam where the azure waters of the Mediterranean were breaking on the beaches. The air was crystal clear and so close did the villages, the blue green olive groves and vineyards look, so slowly did they slide past below me, that they seemed barely an arm's length away and I to be motionless in the air above them. Over to the left where the fertile coastal strip gave way to bare, dry, barren country, the painting took on tints of dark yellow and gold. The altimeter was registering 26,000 feet.

A delicate white condensation trail, plainly visible against the blue of the sky, began to form behind Bachmann's machine. Clearly I would have to lose height at once; otherwise we would give away our position to the Spitfires and Lightnings. Far ahead towards the southeast, where the sun was reflected back from the sea as though from a mirror, lay the enemy's beach-head. My eyes travelled along the coast road until they picked out the white smudge that was Gela. In that direction, too, there were ships, innumerable grey shadows dotted about the surface of the sea. They were manœuvring at high speed and their long bow waves wove upon the surface of the water a web-like pattern extending as far as the eye could see. What an enormous fleet! If only we had some bombers and intact airfields! But the ships were no concern of ours, for there was nothing we could do about them.

'Odysseus from top cover. Pantechnicons should now be crossing your course.'

And immediately afterwards Bachmann came on the R/T:

'Odysseus, lots of pantechnicons, nine o'clock!'

Then I, too, saw the orderly formation making for Messina. They were echeloned to left over a considerable distance and layered up through three thousand feet. It would take a few minutes before we overhauled them and mechanically I began making the usual calculations relating to the approach, the preliminaries to the attack, the battle and the withdrawal. But where could we withdraw to? It was more than likely that Comiso would not be usable since it was already threatened by ground forces, while Gerbini, with its many satellite airfields, had been laid waste only the day before. So it would have to be either the advanced landing ground or even Trapani. As I made a wide turn to port I saw that Freiberg's wing had already set off in pursuit. Behind me were only Bachmann and Helbig.

At that moment I caught sight of a lone Boeing about three hundred feet below me, a late starter, perhaps, or one which had experienced technical difficulties during the flight. Now it was flying along bravely to the rear of the main body. I knew that I ought to pursue the formation and not leave Freiberg on his own. If the solitary aircraft continued on its way, we would in any case be able to deal with it later. On the other hand, the general's words were still sounding in my ears: 'You've got to shoot down bombers. It's the ten crew they carry that counts!'

By now I had half-rolled and was diving from an ideal attacking position. My feverish concern for a kill had banished all other thoughts, apart from the brief reflection that the pitiful remnants of my group would now be mounting their assault on the armada of Flying Fortresses . . .

The Boeing was steady in my sights. I had moved the firing lever from the 'safe' position well beforehand and now I opened fire although it was still much too early for my shots to take effect. As I closed rapidly there was a 'pop' – my cannon had jammed; only my machine guns kept firing. The smell of cordite filled the cockpit.

On pulling up I saw the Fortress continuing on its course, apparently unscathed. Then, like long fingers, smoke from Bachmann's tracers began groping towards its wings and engines, and already a thin white trail of escaping fuel could be seen streaming out behind the starboard outer engine. But the big aeroplane remained on course as though nothing had happened. Helbig opened fire at 3000 yards, well outside the range of his weapons.

Then it was my turn again. Almost as though I had a guilty conscience and wanted to put a speedy end to the unequal contest while at the same time giving him a chance, I dived down, text-book fashion, and closed to within a few yards. But why wasn't anyone firing from the rear turrets? As the bomber's tail-fin loomed up tall as a tree before the armoured glass of my windscreen and the turbulence created by its engines threw my aircraft about, my hand closed on the stick and I pressed the firing lever. 'Pop' went the cannon and jammed again. My machine guns sprayed a shower of sparks over the aluminium skin of the giant aircraft before I had to pull up and over. My speed took me well ahead of my adversary and as I turned my machine on its side I looked down and saw that he had gone into a majestic turn. Then Bachmann was on to him again. He might almost have been flying in formation by the way he hung on without wavering a few yards astern of the banking aircraft while he fired at the damaged engine with everything he had. A white spray of escaping petrol registered his hits. The propeller of the engine he had made his target revolved more and more slowly and finally stopped. By now the American had turned half-circle and was seeking to escape in the direction of Pantelleria. We fired a few more bursts into his fuselage but with no success. We were still at 13,000 feet when we crossed the coast. The bomber was a flying wreck with petrol streaming out behind two of the engines.

It was unbelievable that there should be no flames after all the tracer we had fired. I wondered how many of the ten men in this airborne coffin were still alive: the pilot, for certain, protected by the armour-plating at his back.

But I had forgotten that our time was running out. 'Break, break!' I ordered and set course towards the northwest and our advanced landing ground. As the airfield appeared below me and I began the approach I could hear scraps of speech and the hubbub of battle. Freiberg's wing was still fighting.

A quarter of an hour later, twelve out of the sixteen Me 109s had returned from the operation. 'Captain Freiberg's missing,' I heard someone say. The news, passing from mouth to mouth, had reached the operations vehicle well before the pilots arrived to give their reports.

'We flew right into the middle of the Spits,' said von Köster, a lanky young lieutenant. 'After that I lost sight of Captain Freiberg. It was more like a piece of slapstick than an air battle and everyone was shooting from every imaginable position. The Spits were as startled as we were.'

'Did anyone see a parachute?'

'No, sir – at any rate not during the fight with the Spits.'

'But the Spits funked it,' Köster went on. 'They beat it, going like the hammers of hell, and left the bombers on their own. And the bombers' formation was so lousy that they were just asking to be attacked. We pitched into them and a bit later six of them were going down in flames and there were parachutes all over the place.'

'Will you dictate your combat reports to the operations clerk, please, and after that make sure your aircraft are ready to take off again as soon as possible.'

The midday heat was becoming unbearable. We had taken to our deck-chairs and now lay silent and lost in thought. The airfield telephone kept ringing as the squadrons came on the line to report technical defects and the completion of refuelling. We would fly one or two more patrols and then return to Trapani.

We had long ago given up discussing our operations – the formation in which we had flown, say, or the attack, or the battle itself. We had been so stultified by the hopeless routine of the daily round that we now performed like automatons and, although we registered what we saw and experienced, we did so without comment. In any case, what was there to discuss or put right? We were the few who, for whatever reason, still survived; to some extent we were the lees of the once-renowned fighter component in the south, a component that had been graced by the famous names of Marseille and Müncheberg. Yet again, calculations were going wrong, as they had at Stalingrad and Tunis. In the eyes of the Reichsmarschall we were simply good-for-nothing punishment battalions whose exploits were no longer evaluated in terms of praise or blame but were deserving only of contempt.

The news about Freiberg oppressed me. I had taken the easy way out by attacking the solitary aircraft instead of pursuing the main formation and thereby strengthening our position.

If he were here he would undoubtedly have made some ironic comments on my action. They would have been well chosen yet within what to us were the acceptable limits of informal give-and-take between superiors and subordinates. Perhaps he would have said: 'That was a nice titbit you picked for yourself', or 'It's incredible what those heavies will stand up to. Three fighters blast off all their ammunition and what happens?'

Bachmann was lying in the deck-chair on my right. He was a young man of happy disposition and hitherto he had faced events calmly and serenely, but now his face had grown so thin that it looked almost pinched. His fingers were drumming out a nervous rhythm on the edge of his chair. When I placed my hand on top of his to restrain him he turned to me and came out with the last remark I would have expected in the circumstances.

'If I ever get out of here, sir,' he said, '*if* I get out, I'm going straight to Berlin. I've got to have a woman. I've been looking forward to that ever since Alamein . . .'

'You ought to have done something about it when you were in Bari, sport,' suggested Straden.

'Oh, don't talk to me about Italian women . . . That's the sort of great adventure they promised us when we were boys and used to read Karl May. We were going to be conquerors in distant lands in the service of the Führer and the spoils would be there for the picking, like they were for the Greeks in the Trojan War . . .'

The operations clerk came up to report that twelve machines were now ready to fly. A little later the group's technical officer climbed out of the Kübelwagen and lowered himself groaning to the ground to lean against the wall opposite me. He wiped his brow with the back of his hand which he dried on his trouser leg.

'The spares situation is catastrophic all along the line, sir,' he said. 'There's even a shortage of ammunition and not much coolant or hydraulic fluid either. If nothing turns up within a couple of days, we'll have to close the shop.'

'In a couple of days, my friend, the shop will be closed anyway,' said Straden in hollow tones.

After that the conversation petered out again. The telephone rang continuously. We could overhear occasional words as the operations room carried on its usual business: 'serviceable' – 'coolant' – 'plug change', for example, interspersed with scraps of conversation with the operations room on Mount Erice. The way the signallers kept restoring the line was little short of miraculous.

Several of the pilots began conversing in low tones. 'Didn't anyone see what happened to Freiberg?' someone might inquire, or 'Behrend's machine hit a rock. He was going much too fast and touched down to one side of the landing-strip.'

Tea, melons and white bread arrived from the field kitchen. We ate listlessly and without appetite. The sun, a fiery ball, was directly overhead.

What, I wondered, could I do with the remnants of my group? Ought we to fight 'to the last machine'? Rather than fritter away my last effectives against enemy formations of squadron strength, it would be better to find a worthwhile alternative suited to our limitations. We were due to return to Trapani at dusk provided that they had managed to keep a runway clear. On the following day our tasks would be the same: reconnaissance over the beach-head, ground strikes (it had come to that again!), protection of the Straits of Messina against bombing attacks. Traffic across the straits was vitally important if the intention was to hold Sicily, and it would become even more so if the island was going to be evacuated. In the event of the general moving north with his staff, our operation orders would be transmitted by radio. They would be short and simple, and would include information about the situation but, in contrast to the Wehrmacht communiqués, there would be nothing about heroic resistance or the crippling losses suffered by the enemy. I feared that the island was going to be 'held at all costs' because the Supreme Commander of the Armed Forces had so ordained it and that once again the evacuation order would arrive when there was nothing left to evacuate and nothing left to salvage.

'Telephone – Lieutenant Bachmann!'

A little later the adjutant returned and said: 'No 1 Wing want permission to join us here. They've just had a terrific doing-over by some Marauders and say they would like to find a peaceful spot in the country where they can enjoy the air.'

'There are too many machines on this pocket handkerchief already,' I reflected aloud. 'Where are we going to put them?'

Straden was sceptical. 'That's about the last straw. If the Kitty-hawks spot us here when they're out ground strafing or on armed reconnaissance, that'll be that.'

On the other hand, to refuse the request would be contrary to my view that we needed to concentrate our effective strength. Far too much valuable flying time was lost when we had to proceed to an assembly point from different airfields.

'There can't be many of them left,' Bachmann said.

I gave my permission. In this leaderless situation every CO had to decide for himself and accept sole responsibility for his actions.

It must have been about an hour later when No 1 came into view, made a circuit of the airfield and landed, fortunately without incident. Godert and Zöhler were there, together with thirteen other pilots – all that remained of the wing. Godert ducked under the canvas awning to report his arrival, after which he pulled his life-jacket over his head and unbuttoned his soaking shirt as far as his belt. In doing so he revealed a stomach adorned by a pale blue tattoo depicting a well-shaped lady in an attitude of voluptuous repose. We had met this lovely before; apparently she had come into the world either in Hong Kong or Shanghai when her owner was serving in the merchant navy. Godert's forehead was covered with beads of perspiration.

'Sorry I'm sweating so much,' he said, 'but I was anxious about the landing . . .'

Zöhler squeezed in after him and made a feeble attempt to salute. By now this gentle, sensitive man was a mere shadow of his former self. In the diffused light beneath the awning his face looked almost chrome yellow. He was waging a remorseless struggle against malaria with the aid of massive doses of atebrin but he nevertheless flew on every possible operation.

'I got one of those slow American Storch-like jobs this morning,' he said. 'It was utter chaos when we ran into the anti-aircraft fire. We were supposed to shoot up landing craft and find out how far inland the Yanks had got. Everyone up there is firing at everyone else! There are colossal gliders on the beach and in the shallows. We were shot at all the way to the Agrigento road.'

'It was an artillery observation aircraft directing the fire from the warships. He was swanning happily up and down the coast road. Armin lined him up quickly and he went down like a ball of fire.' The imperturbable Godert betrayed a hint of elation as he spoke.

'We were right down on the deck when we crossed the hills on the way to the coast and we could see their tubby-looking fighter-bombers on the job. So we could tell where our own chaps were. But it's all a hellish mix-up and you can't make out any actual front. The light anti-aircraft shoot at anything they see and if you get anywhere near the larger ships it seems as though mountains have started chucking up fire at you. The fighter-bombers are from Malta and Pantelleria, Grumman Martlets most of them. They're fat, unmanœuvrable crates and they carry an incredible bomb-load. On the first patrol, we went for the landing craft. When they're low in the water and packed with troops they make fine targets.'

'How many aircraft can you put in the air?'

'I'd be more than happy to settle for ten, sir,' Godert said. 'They really ploughed up Sciacca for us today. We were already in our cockpits ready to take off on the second patrol when our old Marauder friends from North Africa turned up without warning. Their aiming is still as rotten as ever. Our eighty-eights opened up and did damned well and soon there were ten parachutes above the runway. Two of the bombers crashed beside the airfield. In exchange they left me with a hole in my wing big enough to shove your head through.'

'Very well, then. We'll have to get ready to take off again as soon as possible. Erice operations keep reporting the arrival of one wave after another, and Trapani has already been bombed twice.'

Kittyhawks! We had not heard the sound of their engines but suddenly there they were, right over our airfield in line abreast at no more than three hundred feet. They were obviously returning to Pantelleria. Their bellies were painted a harsh shade of blue and as the leader put his aircraft into a vertical bank we could see the dappled desert camouflage on top. Down below everyone remained motionless, hoping that we had not been spotted. If we had opened up with our machine guns and rifles we would have given our position away. In any case our airfield defence was largely improvised and consisted of a few MG 15s on tripods posted along the landing strip and the rifles which our mechanics kept ready to hand.

'They're coming!'

Strung out like beads on a necklace the Americans were now in line astern and coming up the valley. Stumbling over chairs and cables we made for the protection of the wall in a series of mighty leaps. The enemy's weapons hammered out as though at a word of command and then our own machine guns joined in. We leaned against the wall panting for breath while bullets raised spurts of earth from the hard ground round the farmhouse. As the pointed-nosed fighters – there must have been about ten of them – roared over the airfield, the unfamiliar sound of their American engines filled the long valley. By now our men had opened up with their rifles as they had been trained to do, from trenches, from holes in the ground and from places of concealment under trees. It was not, I thought, a particularly effective mode of defence but at least it was good for morale. Only if everyone fired, so that the maximum possible quantity of lead was directed upwards, could there be any prospect of success. The Russians had also been trained in the drill and they used to irritate us, if nothing else, when we carried out ground attacks against them.

'Watch out! They're coming back!' yelled one of the look-outs.

They had departed in a climbing turn and now they were racing in from the east, opening fire at long range. As we dashed round the farmhouse to take cover on the west side, we began to see the humorous side of these antics. There could be no doubt that they were going for the farmhouse and operations vehicle, imagining, perhaps, the presence of some radio installation vital to the direction of the battle. But surely they couldn't fail to see our thinly camouflaged aircraft under the trees?

Swearing and gasping for breath, we threw ourselves into hollows in the ground as a hail of bullets tore into the earth round the farmhouse and through the dry grass of the landing strip.

'Stupid idiots!' someone cursed. 'If only we could take off.'

'Watch out, they've split up. They're coming in from both sides!'

Seemingly intent on shooting the innocent farmhouse to pieces, the Americans were now attacking from different directions, chasing us round the barn. We kept jumping for our lives, cursing and laughing. Fortunately none of our adversaries had a bomb slung underneath his fuselage so we could afford to treat the proceedings with a certain amount of levity. All at once, after a wild, furious crescendo, they disappeared in a westerly direction and very soon afterwards the sound of their engines died away.

We gathered round the operations vehicle, brushing the dust from our sweat-soaked shirts and trousers and contemplating the sorry, bullet-riddled truck and its shattered windows. It was leaning over to one side on burst tires and we would probably have to abandon it if the engine had also been damaged.

Bachmann was the first to find his voice. 'Bloody amateurs,' he said scornfully, and we all of us laughed in agreement.

'Karl's been hit!' someone shouted from the other side of the landing strip. 'We want some bandages – and we'll need a Storch!'

'Karl of all people,' I said. 'Come on, we'd better hurry.'

They had laid him on a groundsheet with a seat cushion under his head. There was a frightened look in his eyes and he tried to say something, but all that came out was a gurgle.

'You mustn't talk,' said Flight Sergeant Hamann. 'Lie quite still; the Storch will be along soon.' He turned to me: 'A bullet went diagonally through his chest. We've routed out all the bandages we can find but he's still bleeding.'

Karl Ramhart had been with the group when it went to war in 1939. His home was in Munich. He had grown up in the *Viktualienmarkt* before starting work with a coal merchant. More precisely he had been one of those specialists with blackened faces and a sack worn like a cowl over their heads who deliver bags of coal to people's cellars, and he possessed a physique to match his calling. He had been posted to the group as a 'non-tradesman' and in this capacity had worked in the cookhouse and, later, in the clothing store. Then he had been taught to drive and had developed a preference for the large refuelling vehicles. Before long he had become one of the most indispensable members of the group.

But what gave Karl his special status among us was his highly individual form of social intercourse. He said *du*[1] to everyone, his superiors included. It was not that he paid no heed to questions of rank, but he had this effortless knack of combining the intimate

[1] Equivalent to the French *tu*

form of address with the customary courtesies when speaking to a superior. And all of it in the ripest of Munich accents. Evidently there had been some conventions which his teachers had failed to instil in him at school.

Not only was he generally popular but he also set an example by his selfless devotion to work and his readiness to help others. Among those for whom he had a particularly soft spot was myself.

'Karl,' I said, bending over him, 'lie quite still and don't talk. We're going to fly you to Trapani. It's not as bad as all that; just enough to get you nicely home.'

His face looked shrunken and he was breathing with difficulty. His massive hands, which had manipulated the heavy fuel caps with such ease, stirred restlessly. It was clear that he wanted to speak to me.

Placing my ear close to his mouth I heard him say hoarsely: 'I want to tell you something, sir – when I'm OK again I'd like to get back to the lads. D'you promise, sir?'

'Yes, Karl, don't worry. You'll be back with us again in a few weeks.'

We reached Trapani just before nightfall, 'we' being the handful of pilots still with serviceable aircraft. Unable to make up my mind where to touch down, I made several circuits of the churned-up airfield and did not begin the final approach until green flares had risen from the dispersal indicating that the runway markers could be depended upon and that I was cleared to land.

It was truly astounding how much punishment this airfield could take, I thought, as the propeller came to a stop after several loud backfires. For the past fourteen days the enemy had been attacking it several times a day with bombs of all calibres, yet we could still take off and land. Here, I thought, was a lesson in air tactics but I doubted if it would be any use to me – the lesson, namely, that there is little point in smashing an enemy's airfields unless you hit and destroy a large proportion of his aircraft as well. Admittedly our opponents had succeeded in fulfilling this requirement, but we were still flying and still inflicting losses on them, which in turn compelled them to carry out further attacks against our airfields. However, the British and Americans possessed such ample resources that they had no need to husband them; they would be unlikely to rest until they had either destroyed us or driven us out.

The sun had just set and in the lurid light which made the rocks, fields and houses on the slopes of Mount Erice look as though they had been painted with luminous pigment, the area round the dispersal pens had the appearance of a spectral landscape. One side of the hut had been torn away and the roof, having parted from its supports, reared skywards. Wrecked aircraft had been piled together, forming a whitish heap near the ravaged trees, and the earth ramparts were littered with cans and step-ladders. Evidently it was no longer possible for a refueller – assuming we still had an undamaged refueller – to enter the pens. The airmen had rolled petrol cans into position and were beginning the arduous task of refuelling by hand pump.

'One of those bleeding days today, sir,' said a corporal without pausing from his work. It seemed almost as though he had no need to watch what he was doing, so practised were his movements.

These were the few minutes in which a ground crew had their pilot to themselves. On such occasions the reality of the common task banished all differences of rank and degrees of responsibility and they would talk to him in the same brisk, economical phrases that they used among themselves. In this way they came to know something about the fighting and could participate in the fortunes of the group to which they belonged.

'Just what happened to Captain Freiberg?' they might inquire, or 'What's going on at the beach-head – how far have the Yanks got?' Nor did they hesitate to express their views on the conduct of the war in the most forthright terms: 'It's one right bloody shambles, just as it was in North Africa two months back. What do they think we're going to do with the few crates we've got left? Talk about rose-tinted spectacles!'

I was not happy about my engine and had sent for Flight Sergeant Hackel who had a magic way with the 109's Daimler Benz power unit. He was like a diagnostician and rarely failed to find the cause of the trouble after the symptoms had been described to him. If at dusk one heard the sound of an engine somewhere on the perimeter being run up to maximum revolutions, then suddenly dying away again, and if this happened three or four times in succession, one could be certain that Hackel was examining one of his patients and that should one approach him, he would poke his head out from its entrails, his hands and forearms covered in oil and grease.

'The engine still isn't right,' I told him, 'even after the change of plugs. As soon as I go over five thousand it begins to get rough. But there's no drop in the fuel pressure. The mechanics set the injection pump a bit leaner yesterday and it didn't do any good.'

In the meantime the airmen had changed the subject of their conversation and were now discussing Foggia, our base on the mainland, where there would not be just rubble and corpses but drinking places and real live girls. But these, alas, were no more than soldiers' day-dreams, for here and now the reality was quite different.

'Let's try her now,' Hackel said. He climbed on to the wing and thence into the cabin. 'Switch on!' he called. Whining, the inertia starter gathered speed and, as the engine fired, a dense cloud of sooty, blue black smoke belched from the exhaust-stubs.

By now the members of the ground crew – usually referred to by us pilots simply as 'the mechanics' – had gathered round again, for they were as much involved with the fortunes of their aeroplane as they were with the fortunes of the man who flew it. By referring to this inanimate masterpiece of aluminium, steel, plastics and many hundreds of yards of wiring as 'she', as though it were a woman, they endowed it with a living personality. They would also ascribe the pilot's successes to 'her' and it was they, too, who kept up to date the tally of victories on the rudder unit – at least they had been doing so until quite recently.

159

From constant observation, they knew a great deal about an aircraft and its peculiarities and they made no allowances when one was destroyed or damaged through carelessness or inexperience. The disapproval of his ground crew often proved a more effective factor in a pilot's training than disciplinary action by his squadron commander. I remember how on one occasion a ground crew walked away shaking their heads when a young 109 pilot, who was impervious to advice, had failed to correct the swing induced by the torque reaction from the airscrew on take-off, and had broken his undercarriage as a result.

Even now, when aircraft had long been expendable items, their sense of responsibility and their pride in their work had remained. Ever since we had returned to Sicily they had been toiling and sweating almost uninterruptedly, surrounded by dust and by oil and petrol fumes and deprived of sufficient sleep. On the frequent occasions during the day when they were chased into the slit trenches, it was always with the thought that they might emerge to find the object of their hours of labour reduced to nothing by one small bomb.

Since the time in North Africa when we had evolved the scheme of stowing our mechanics in the fuselage so as to take them to Europe, a special relationship had sprung up between the airmen who had thus escaped death or captivity and 'their' pilots. I do not know who evolved the plan to use fighter aircraft for a kind of airlift to Sicily but it was first hatched when we began to reckon up just whom and how many we would have to leave to their fate should we receive permission to evacuate the North African theatre.

On the eve of the initial attempt, specialists from the different branches formed an interested group of spectators round the aircraft which was about to be used for a trial loading with a prospective passenger as guinea-pig. First the armour-plate behind the pilot's head was removed and then the floor of the minute baggage space aft of the cockpit cut away. This enabled the guinea-pig to kneel in the 109's narrow fuselage, looking over the pilot's shoulder. Boarding was an acrobatic feat, for he had to be pushed feet first through the narrow hatch which gave access to the radio for maintenance purposes. We soon realized that nailed boots or shoes could not be permitted since the passenger's feet lay close to the master compass and the metal would cause it to give a false reading.

With his legs drawn up beneath him, our man had begun to suffer pins and needles but for a flight time of less than an hour the arrangement would do well enough. Then one ingenious soul discovered that room could be found, if need be, for 'a very small one' in the darkness of the far end of the fuselage where the wires leading to the rear control surfaces came together and the tail wheel recess projected upwards. Here again the experiment proved successful but it was, of course, necessary to keep to a pre-determined sequence both in boarding and in the disposition of the limbs. These activities caused a great deal of hearty laughter although there were few grounds for merriment either in the circumstances that had made them necessary or in our future prospects. We then began our search for 'very small' mechanics and set about preparing detailed passenger lists.

With the aircraft loaded in this way, the centre of gravity was in a quite different position so that take-off and landing became dangerous operations demanding great flying skill. Reinhold earned everyone's admiration when, despite his heavily loaded aircraft with two mechanics on board, he accepted battle with the enemy and shot down a Kittyhawk. Many of the fitters and radio mechanics, however, who had begged so fervently to be flown to Sicily, were later blown to pieces during the bombing raids on the island.

Since these flights the members of the ground crews had always talked of 'their' pilot. Even if he was no longer alive.

That evening nearly everyone who had landed at Trapani from the advanced landing ground was in the grotto. Godert and the pilots of No 1 Wing were also with us because Sciacca airfield was no longer useable.

At nightfall the warships out to sea began their bombardment.

F

'Pretty big stuff they're chucking over,' said Godert, 'from cruisers or battlewagons almost for sure.'

There was an unnerving regularity about the dull thudding of the bursts, a noise quite different from that made by bombs. We had not been in touch with the Fighter Leader since midday. The signallers kept tapping away on the various frequencies, now making contact with II Air Corps, now losing it again before resuming their search of the ether. The British fleet were obviously bombarding the coastal defences, which could mean either the prelude to a landing at Marsala or else a feint to divert our forces. Although every one of us was dead tired, nobody thought of sleep. The thunder of the warships' guns rolling in from the sea and the noise of the bursts put paid to any rest or relaxation.

At first light we would fly another reconnaissance even though we did not know to whom we were to report the results. And with our few remaining aircraft we would continue to attack the bombers. We needed no orders for that. Not far from the advanced landing ground which the Kittyhawks had discovered that morning, Straden had found a meadow he thought would accommodate the remnants of the group. We intended to make for it after taking off at dawn and to operate from there, provided that the Allies had not landed at Marsala in the meantime and provided also that we still had enough aircraft to fly an effective mission. It was essential for me to make contact with the Fighter Leader and find out if it was true that the Americans had pushed on well to the north and had reached the centre of the island, thus threatening to split our forces in two. With this eventuality in mind I had given orders for a plan to be prepared whereby the group's ground personnel, in so far as transport was available, were to withdraw to Messina by the northern coast road, while the pilots were to continue flying until no aircraft were left to fly. If I was unable to find out anything about the situation, I would have to rely on the information revealed by our own reconnaissance.

That evening even the customary grim humour had dried up. Anxiety, admitted or concealed in varying degrees, brooded over us like a nightmare. All of those present, having followed the same uncomplicated train of thought and having weighed the chances, now knew that the situation had become extremely serious. They looked on Freiberg's departure as an evil omen. None of us had ever really allowed ourselves to believe that anything could happen to him when flying or fighting. If he had been lucky enough to bale out and come down on dry land, we would undoubtedly have heard long before now, for anyone in those circumstances made every possible effort to inform his unit.

Today, as always, he had been wearing his spotless white stockings and those yellow sandals which had so often been the object of my criticism.

Teresa shed a few tears when told of Freiberg's uncertain fate. She was a girl with a curiously vacant and stolid nature, a simple child of the Sicilian countryside and people, and the experience of this ghastly war was perhaps too much for her few wits. Now she was sitting silently beside her *nonna*, staring blankly in front of her.

No one in the grotto felt any desire to drink more Marsala or vermouth than was necessary to quench his thirst. In any case most of the contents of the bottles set out for us by Tubby had always been drunk by Freiberg.

Towards midnight, the enemy evidently decided to give their crews some sleep as well, for the bombardment slackened until only a few guns kept firing. Eventually these, too, fell silent, by which time even our 'nuisances' had gone off duty and flown home to Tunis or Bizerta.

As the noises died away the tension eased, and exhaustion combined with the healthy constitution of most of those present allowed them to fall into a brief, dreamless slumber. Only a few were unable to sleep but they remained in the grotto for there seemed to be little point in returning to their billets for the rest of the night, and in any case the Wellingtons might have been bombed up again and now be on their way back.

Captain Kegel arrived and sat down beside my camp bed to tell me about his inspection of Gerbini airfield. He spoke in whispers so as not to disturb the sleepers, polishing his glasses the while. In the sing-song tones of his native Saxony he described his flight to Gerbini and the shocking picture of devastation that had met him there.

'I think we should be able to land at Gerbini,' he said, 'because the commandant and his people keep on clearing one or two runways. They've even got some Labour Service units there and they, too, have had casualties. Just boys they are – it's a damned disgrace! If you're going to fly defensive patrols over the Straits of Messina you should only jettison your drop tanks in an emergency, of course, or break off the battle in good time because I doubt if you'll be able to land again. One lot of heavies has hardly left Gerbini before another takes over. You'd almost think they'd got too many of them. The air is likely to be a safer place than the ground tomorrow.'

'The ground organization in the island had been badly disrupted by massive and continuous air attacks and for this reason it was no longer possible for the fighter and close-support units to provide decisive support for the army or to protect it from bombing attacks. A contributory factor was the irresolute conduct of the Italians . . . Among the laudable exceptions were the torpedo units which performed magnificently and a few fighter squadrons led by outstanding commanders.'

FRANZ KUROWSKI
DAS TOR ZUR FESTUNG EUROPA

'The Italian Air Force was in a hopeless situation because of obsolete and inferior aircraft . . . Italo-German co-ordination of air matters was poor, the German fighter units taking over the protection of Sicily from their own fields as though the Italians were not even present.'

UNITED STATES ARMY IN WORLD WAR II
SICILY AND THE SURRENDER OF ITALY

'Within the limits of their capabilities the fighter units also took part in the defensive battles. Indeed they were particularly heavily engaged in the protection of traffic across the Straits of Messina where, in combination with the flak artillery which had moved into position in the area, they cleared the airspace of enemy aircraft. The flying units of Air Fleet 2 stationed in Sardinia were transferred to Sicily.'

FRANZ KUROWSKI
DAS TOR ZUR FESTUNG EUROPA

11 July 1943

On the morning of 11 July at about five o'clock Straden and I taxied towards the runway preparatory to leaving for Sardinia. While taking off he burst a tire and after informing me by radio he returned to land. I decided to carry on alone and soon the coast of Sicily was sinking into the sea astern. I climbed slowly to 20,000 feet so as to pick up the Sardinian shore as soon as possible. The night had been short; the bombardments had allowed us little sleep and as the CO of a fighter unit I was compelled to attend to the essential paper-work during the hours of darkness. But the further I flew towards the northwest, the more my tension eased, and before long a sense of almost tranquil security came over me. For what was a flight over more than three hundred miles of water when there was little likelihood of trouble from Spitfires or Lightnings? It was simply a relaxing excursion.

I adjusted my position on the hard parachute so that I could stretch out my legs more comfortably and then I checked my oxygen mask. The propeller, its pitch set at 10.40, was adjusted as perfectly as possible to the revolutions of the engine which kept humming away without the slightest hint of vibration. At 20,000 feet it was obviously very cold outside, probably about $-30°C$. Slowly I closed the radiator flaps. Although the rise in the coolant temperature was barely noticeable, the air speed increased by about four mph.

Directly below, the sea looked green as grass, changing to an inky blue towards the horizon. To a seaman the complete absence of foam crests would have indicated a wind force of 1 to 2. It was agreeable flying with the sun at one's back. The armour-plate protecting the head and neck cast a broad shadow on the instrument panel. The propeller, a glittering transparent disc, reflected the brilliant sunlight, for dust and sand had scoured away the original coating of black paint to expose the bare metal.

Suddenly my headphones came to life, making me start. 'Heavies in grid reference one-two one-seven heading one-two-zero. Fighters escorting.'

It was the group operations room on Mount Erice giving instructions to the fighters in Sicily. I could also hear the indistinct voices of some of the pilots and then all went quiet again. The cold began to penetrate my spine somewhere about the level of my kidneys. My shirt, which had been wet through when I took off, now felt like an ice pack in the small of my back. I rolled down my shirt-sleeves and spread the map out on my knee. Another hundred miles to the coast of Sardinia, I estimated, and then a further forty to No 3 Wing's advanced landing ground. Abben did not know that I was coming, so it was to be one of those snap visits that are part of a CO's duties.

In days gone by such visits by senior officers had created much agitation, if on occasion a good deal of hilarity, but we had long since abandoned military antics of that kind. After our abortive massed operation on 25 June, Abben had had to return to Sardinia with his wing because the ports of Cagliari and Olbia were favourite targets of the four-engined bombers and also because the possibility of a landing in Sardinia could not be excluded.

Now, at the moment of crisis in the battle, he was to fly to Gerbini on the following day in order to help guard the Straits of Messina. Admittedly this was robbing Peter to pay Paul and we might yet have to answer for our action in leaving Sardinia unprotected, improbable though it was that the Allies would be able to launch two major landings almost simultaneously. But we were expecting the impossible of our ground organization. Only a few of my group's mechanics had been transferred to Gerbini overland since it would have been inadvisable, in the absence of transport aircraft, to despatch more than a minimum of technical personnel on a journey that took several days. They could not be spared for as long as that. At Gerbini the 53rd Fighter Group would have to look after our aircraft in addition to their own. At Trapani there would have to be sufficient ground crews and workshops personnel to refuel, rearm and maintain our machines on our return. And finally we would still have to keep some men on the advanced landing ground so that we could at least land there, refuel and take off again. We simply had not got the right type of ground organization for this kind of warfare, but it was no use thinking about that now.

My drop tank was empty. I depressed the ignition switch to check the magnetos and saw that the engine revolutions remained constant. Each time I breathed, two pale yellow discs on top of the oxygen equipment opened and closed like a pair of lips, indicating that oxygen was reaching my mask. I felt unspeakably tired. To prevent myself falling prey to hallucinations I shook my head and moved my shoulders as energetically as the tight harness would permit. And I began to talk aloud. 'Gentlemen,' I said, 'I've come here to tell you about the situation. I've been speaking to the general and he's completely on our side. As soon as he gets back to Berlin, he's going to speak to the Reichsmarschall . . .'

What nonsense! As though it mattered to us any more what the Reichsmarschall or anyone else might or might not think about us. Why couldn't they leave us to do our blasted duty on this coffin of an island until the last pilot was killed and the last aircraft was a pile of wreckage? If that was what the high command wanted, all well and good. But they might at least stop pestering us!

I was not, of course, going to say anything of the sort to the pilots although it was probably the kind of speech they expected of me. These were simply the words of a man speaking privately to himself when alone in an aircraft 20,000 feet above the Mediterranean.

I was struck by the emptiness of the sea. Not a single ship was in sight anywhere. These waters had long been an Allied preserve, the Italians venturing out of their harbours only at night.

Far ahead the coast of Sardinia, a thin, delicate blue line, rose up out of the dark blue water. Now I could begin to lose height.

As I approached the landing marker, barely half an hour later, I could see the air shimmering above the gentle hills and their sparse covering of trees. The character of the Sardinian landscape was quite different from that of Sicily; it was softer, more even, and in its monotony somewhat resembled the steppes. The tall grass was parched and yellow; the humid air danced under the pitiless, burning sun. They had pitched their vast, sand-coloured tents in the shadow of the squat cork oaks. For one such as myself, accustomed to nothing but churned up airfields and shattered buildings and aircraft, it made a peaceful scene.

To the accompaniment of several backfires, the propeller came to a stop and a waiting mechanic climbed on to the wing to help me undo my harness and climb out. Captain Abben was standing nearby and as I jumped to the ground he reported: 'No 3 Wing on active service . . . Seventeen aircraft available for operations!' Then in less formal tones he added: 'The sirocco started blowing today; it's over a hundred in the shade . . .'

The hot breath of the desert wind blew over the plain. The sky was yellow and the trees cast diffused shadows. It was something I had not noticed as I approached.

'I'd better have a word with the pilots,' I said.

'Very well, sir. Perhaps you'd care to come to the ops room over there under the trees. It's a bit cooler inside. Meanwhile I'll have the pilots called.'

In the tent I was handed a glass of lemon tea; it was lukewarm, strong and unsugared – we had been drinking it like this for weeks past. Shortly afterwards the pilots, the wing's MO and the technical officer were sitting in a semicircle round my chair. The hot wind swelled the yellow awning rigged up between the oaks. The sunlight suffused the canvas with a tawny glow and the colour was reflected on their faces.

I gave them an unvarnished account of the situation in Sicily. The Allies, I said, were attacking our airfields by day and by night and hence it was necessary to remain constantly on the alert if we were not to be destroyed on the ground. I explained to them in detail the plan the general and I had devised for this eventuality, which was to make flexible use of airfields and advanced landing grounds and to concentrate our strength in so far as a massed assembly of aircraft on one airfield seemed permissible. There was little hope, I continued, of making much impression on the heavies with our relatively few machines and, since the arrival of the Fortress, sheer weight of numbers meant that any air battle was now a major engagement. We could, however, compel the enemy to keep diverting part of his strength in order to pin us down, and that might assist in the defence of the island.

They listened quietly and asked no questions. There were exactly thirty pilots – officers and NCOs – sitting in front of me and looking at me with an open expression on their faces.

I knew most of them by name. Three months before I had stood in front of them in North Africa and discussed the prospects of the battle. I had not, I thought, said anything then that would have been better left unsaid, for I had not made any attempt to raise false hopes. No commander worthy of the name did that any more after all these years of war. We left such pronouncements to the high command whose sole wisdom consisted in ruinous exploitation and excessive demands. As on the previous occasion, I held out no hope that things would get any better. The old hands among them recognized as well as I did the unmistakable portents of defeat.

On this occasion, however, a number of the younger faces were new to me. Ought I to say something to these newcomers? Cheer them up, perhaps? By now most of them must have realized why they had been sent here from their fighter training schools. But the really essential lesson, namely how to stay alive without being unduly cautious, could only be learnt from the veterans in the course of daily operations.

There was little point in talking about how hard things were on the other fronts, for that had always been the case anyway. To spout sentimental and high-sounding phrases at these men would be no better than telling them lies. They knew what they had to do on the following day, and the day after, and the day after that, and all they wanted to hear was whether they still had a chance or whether inhuman demands were to be made of them. Moreover they were sceptical, and from their expressions it was evident that they were weighing and evaluating my words. They were asking to be told what the situation really was, to be told whether the battle held any prospects of success, and even if there were no such prospects and everything looked black they still wanted to know the truth. Well, why not tell them? I knew I would not be misunderstood.

The older pilots, those who had been flying since the early days of the war, had in any case understood my brief account of the situation and our fighter operations against superior forces. They knew what 'diverting to advanced landing grounds' meant, and 'flexible in our operations' and 'concentration of our remaining strength'. They knew that these words meant the endeavour to survive in the face of weakness, improvisation and experiment. They knew too that you had to fly in tight formation if you were to force your way through to the bombers and that these tactics were both necessary and propitious. But they also knew that such measures could no longer balance the scales. And because they knew all this, only a few minutes were needed to say what had to be said. When I had finished I dismissed the pilots so as to speak to Abben about the next day's flight and about operations in Sicily.

The three fighter wings that formed my group were all quite different even though their victory scores were much the same. No 3 had always been detached from Group HQ and had fended for itself, and it was this which gave the unit its special stamp. They were evidently aware of their privileged position, for the officers and NCOs were more self-confident, more reserved than their opposite numbers in the other two wings. One had the feeling they wanted to say: 'Just leave us alone, we'll manage things all right . . .'

Now once again they were out in the wilds, miles from the nearest town and without any German supporting units. Their home was this patch of Sardinian plain and from it they flew against an apparently invincible stream of four-engined bombers

and they did so without grumbling. On the following day, however, they would be faced with something new: the constant
endeavour to achieve the unachievable, the wild hopping from
airfield to airfield for as long as this still remained possible.

Sardinia's long eastern coastline slid past the edge of my right
wing as I climbed slowly prior to setting course. In twenty
minutes the southernmost tip of the island ought to appear to
starboard, but the sirocco had veiled everything in a cloud of
yellow dust that extended right up to the sun, now in the south.

No. 3 Wing's operations room came through on the R/T to
warn me about the Lightnings which had recently been penetrating as far as the island. The headphones crackled; a transmitter
kept coming on and going off the air; a female voice began to
count: 'Uno, duo, tre . . .'

I ought not to have left at noon when the day was at its hottest
And I had not made up any sleep during my visit to 3 Wing. As
I had taxied towards the runway and turned my 109 head to wind,
the sweat had been pouring off my face, chest and back. Now at
my present altitude, I began to feel the cold again.

Flying was a vile business when there was no horizon or visual
point of reference to show the aircraft's attitude, and it would
still take me an hour to reach Trapani. Ample time for reflection
on the events of the morning during which discouragement and
depression had been constantly lurking at the back of my mind.
Now that I was flying alone over the sea, these same feelings
assailed me with such suddenness and force that I was horrified.
Had I really come to that stage? Mental stability, we had always
been taught, was the prime requirement in a CO. Anyone unstable
or subject to depression was unfit to lead.

My eyes travelled over the instrument panel and paused at the
oil-pressure gauge. The reading struck me as unusual yet somehow I could not make out what this indicated. Why had the
engine become so noisy all of a sudden? I must have dropped off
for a few seconds. My head felt heavy and the pressure of the
headphones was hurting my ears.

I corrected the course, checked the magnetos and adjusted my oxygen mask. I wondered what would happen if I fell asleep. Would I be woken by the aircraft's unusual attitude? Perhaps pure oxygen might help to dispel this deadly tiredness.

In the knee pocket of my trousers there was a strip of cotton about six inches long protected by a cellophane wrapper and containing five or six milky white tablets the size of lumps of chocolate. It was labelled 'Pervitin'. Dr Sperrling had told us the tablets were intended to combat fatigue. Opening the packet I pulled out two, then a third and, briefly displacing my oxygen mask, I began to chew them. They tasted revoltingly bitter and were floury in consistency but I had nothing with which to rinse my mouth out. From now on, I hoped, I would stay awake.

The engine was running smoothly and quietly. If it began to give trouble I could still reach land near Cagliari. After that there would be a long haul over the sea and it would make no difference where I baled out or, for that matter, where I put the aircraft down on the water. Once in the dinghy I could, perhaps, last for forty-eight hours, becoming more and more badly burnt. And then I would die of thirst and sunstroke. But this was nonsense! Why should the engine pack up today of all days?

As soon as I sighted the coast of Sicily I intended to turn eastwards so as to keep out of the way of the fighters near Trapani. The ground controller would tell me if the air was clear.

Those specks straight ahead of me at the same height looked like Spitfires or Lightnings. Yes, Spitfires! Four – six – and then I lost sight of them. By now I was wide awake and my ears were throbbing in time to my heartbeats. Why was the sky so bright all of a sudden? The brilliant light hurt my eyes. If they were Spitfires I would have to climb above them – that was the time-honoured rule – but what were Spitfires doing over the sea area between Sardinia and Sicily? The brilliance was almost unbearable but I could see better when I shaded my eyes with my free hand. The engine was very noisy now and sounded as though it was exceeding the permissible revs. But surely each instrument was giving the normal reading? Oil temperature, oil pressure, coolant temperature, revolutions – or were the revs much too high?

There were aircraft below me in the haze. Fortresses perhaps? They were on the same course as I was and I had to strain my eyes to see them. I dropped one wing slightly so as to look down, but the aircraft tilted steeply sideways. And then I lost sight of them. But how had I got as high as 26,000 feet? I found breathing difficult and the cockpit felt very cold, particularly round my knees. I flew on through the high-altitude haze created by the sirocco. The sun, a pitiless yellow disc, shone through the cockpit roof and the side windows, its harsh light flooding everything that was usually in shade: the instruments, the armament panel between my knees, the oxygen equipment with its telltale indicator. The windows were getting streaky and ice crystals had started to form in the corners near the armour-plate. My eyes were glued to the altimeter and its luminous needle, beneath which I could read the letters VDO. The engine was running sweetly now with a complete absence of vibration. So remote was the sound that it seemed almost that silence reigned up here. Everything was becoming ethereal and abstract. It was as though I had left my body and was myself flying above my aeroplane, able to observe the fastest German aircraft and one-time holder of the absolute speed record as it tore across the Mediterranean, drawn onward by the immense power transmitted to its airscrew: an elegant, streamlined thoroughbred, fashioned by the hand of man for purposes of destruction.

There was an art in relating the engine's thousand horsepower to the airscrew and the controls so as to ensure a perfect balance between speed and climb. The controls passed on my orders, whether harsh and abrupt or again so gentle as to be hardly noticeable; they could cause the aircraft to dive, climb, roll or corkscrew. And they could cause it to crash if the wings were no longer capable of withstanding the 'g' stresses imposed on them. Just then I remembered what I had long since forgotten: how gloriously blissful it was to fly . . .

I had trained on the Heinkel 52, a biplane, and it was perhaps for this reason that I was still reluctant to put on an oxygen mask and take my 109 up to altitudes where the controls became flabby and unresponsive. Shortly before the outbreak of war Messerschmitts began to replace the biplanes, for the latter were little more than relics of the First World War and better suited to portray the romance of flight than to participate in fresh advances in the sphere of speed and altitude. In those days we used to take a light-hearted view of the condition known as oxygen starvation, dismissing it as a momentary but not serious personal weakness or else as a comparatively harmless imperfection of the human frame. We were still too much wrapped up in aviation's romantic period, not least because the station libraries were chock full of literature about knights of the air whose sole concern was chivalry, sportsmanship and good honest single combat. In our hearts we resented an aeroplane with an enclosed cockpit because it made us feel shut in, and also because the attributes of the intrepid aviator – helmet, goggles, scarf streaming in the wind, leather jerkin with thick fur collar – had had to give way to a more functional and hence less dashing outfit.

On our first exercise we flew from a satellite airfield to shoot our fixed machine guns at a target towed by a Junkers aircraft. There were three of us, all young second lieutenants, and we belonged to a maritime fighter squadron. We regarded flying fighters as a sporting occupation, rather like motor racing, which combined aerobatics, air fighting and formation flying. During a break in the exercise our squadron commander suddenly remembered that we second lieutenants had not yet passed our altitude test and he therefore ordered us to fly round for half an hour at between 16,000 and 19,000 feet. Dressed like flying cavalrymen in breeches, elegant riding boots and brown leather jerkins with fur lining and fur collar, we settled ourselves behind our windscreens and prepared to climb to what was then a very considerable altitude – without oxygen, be it noted! Each of us, of course, was anxious to go higher than the others and to prove that he had done so by means of the barograph carried in the aircraft. I still remember how, up there in the thin air, flying felt like riding the Atlantic rollers in a sailing boat, how appallingly cold my hands and knees were, how I gasped for air and suffered from improbable hallucinations. Back on the ground we compared our barographs and boasted of our imaginary adventures, regarding the whole thing, in fact, as great fun.

Later our squadron commander led us into the air for a close formation flight to 18,000 feet. The exercise had to be broken off, however, firstly because he was nearly rammed by his wing man, and secondly because one of the biplanes went into an uncontrolled dive. When the pilot eventually came to above the airfield at 6000 feet, he had no idea how he could have got there.

We were witnessing the irrevocable departure of the romantic period and we tried vainly to delay its going because we were still unaware that it was just this process that was opening the door to much bigger things in the field of aviation. Oxygen masks had to be worn more and more often because our engines only reached their peak efficiency after we had entered the layers of thinner air. At that time the masks were still unwieldy objects which badly restricted both vision and movement. This gave rise to a sudden craze for carving a wooden mouthpiece, like that of a saxophone, which was fastened to the end of the oxygen tube in place of the mask. The life-giving elixir could then be elegantly inhaled as though from a Turkish hubble-bubble. But this affectation was, of course, also an unconscious defensive reaction against technology's prosaic realism. Again, it was considered rather good form to know nothing about the technicalities of the engine and simply to switch off the R/T whenever it proved disturbing. (I must admit that I was often tempted to do this myself, for it was virtually impossible to regulate the volume, and the incessant battering of one's eardrums was truly nerve racking.)

In front of me Mount Erice reared its head out of the haze like some friendly apparition. I had thus kept strictly on course despite my state of euphoric unconcern and my feeling of weightlessness. Once again the group operations room came on the air, the words resounding overloud in my headphones: 'Watch out! Twin-engined pantechnicons crossing Palermo heading for Trapani with fighter escort.' The report, however, seemed to have nothing to do with me and left me quite unconcerned.

The airfield, when I landed, looked absolutely dead. Nothing moved; not a soul was to be seen. Near the battered olive trees between the bomb craters, the forlorn ruins of the hangars pointed skywards. It seemed as though I had arrived on the moon or some dreadful planet.

The dust from the last attack had barely settled. As I taxied towards HQ Flight's dispersal my right tire burst, probably because I had run over a bomb splinter. I switched off the engine and climbed out, noting as I did so that it had not occurred to anyone to help the CO out of his machine. The hut, or what was left of it, was a hundred yards away and I walked towards it under the burning sun.

The operations clerk looked at me as though I was a ghost, saluted and reported that the all-clear had been received from Mount Erice the moment before my arrival and that the attack had been mainly directed against the eighty-eight-millimetre flak.

Some time later, meeting Captain Sperrling, I asked him what, exactly, the terrible stuff was that went into Pervitin and suggested that the pilots should be warned about it. When he discovered that I had taken three tablets in quick succession, he nearly threw a fit and forbade me 'to lay hands on an aeroplane, even the outside of one' for the rest of the day.

On the same day three new arrivals joined the group. They had been flown to Vibo Valentia, the airfield in the 'toe' of Italy, and from there had crossed by ferry to Messina, arriving in time for the first of the day's raids. They had then hitch-hiked to Trapani.

The two second lieutenants were about twenty, and the three NCOs even younger. They held themselves very erect when reporting and generally made a soldierly impression. Our requirements dictated that the officers should be posted to No 1 Wing and the NCOs to No 2. Every month the replacement wing had sent us sufficient pilots to make good our losses. But it was now no longer possible to keep up the supply and in any case we could not really use them. To allow them to fly on operations here would be dangerous not only for themselves but also for the others. As Bachmann had said: 'We can't let them go like lambs to the slaughter!'

It was no longer possible to introduce the newcomers to the enemy by degrees, for the Spitfires, Kittyhawks and Lightnings were almost constantly over our airfields. Nor were we able to initiate them into the methods of attacking Fortresses because the closeness of our formation demanded both skill and experience, neither of which they possessed.

'They're awfully young,' Straden observed after they had reported.

'You mean they keep getting younger,' said Bachmann. 'I'd give something to know what they're thinking when they arrive here. It's a pity we can't ask them. And obviously they're not going to say anything off their own bat – they're too unsure of themselves for that.'

Once again, as we had so often done before, we began to discuss their faces, their bearing and their general appearance. And once again, as on so many past occasions, we summed them up, making predictions about their futures that were mostly inaccurate and unjust. I ought to have known by then that such attempts to classify a man were fruitless because the gifted, success-ful fighter pilot did not belong to a recognizable type. It was a great temptation to single out those to whom one took an imme-diate liking because of their natural endowments. But a manly appearance and a bold presence seldom coincided with success in flying fighters.

There had been one occasion in Tunisia when two new NCOs – mere boys – had reported to me. Superficially they were both completely different and it soon turned out that they also performed quite differently in the air. Whereas one of them – a lad of athletic build and erect carriage – had gazed at me with a candid look in his blue eyes, the other had kept glancing about with a watchful expression, as though making an inventory of the contents of my living-caravan. In contrast to his companion he was slight, lean and sinewy and his head was crowned with an immense quiff of hair as favoured by Wilhelm Busch's barbers. Altogether he reminded me of Busch's caricatures each time I looked at him.

'It's really incredible what they're sending us,' I had remarked to Bachmann as we watched the pair walk away. 'Just look at that skinny little chap! And he's expected to attack and shoot down aeroplanes while all hell is being let loose in the sky.'

'Yes,' said Bachmann, 'I'd plump for the tall fair lad, too. A good games player, I should imagine, and altogether more likeable.'

Later in the day I was sitting with Bachmann, Straden and Zahn in front of the tent by the edge of the airfield, waiting for orders to take off. The two newcomers were trying out their aircraft, practising landings and taking the necessary precaution of familiarizing themselves with their place in the pattern of operations. Bachmann and I were attending to paperwork, 'bumf in deck-chairs' as he called it. He passed me the papers, orders and files, giving a few explanatory comments about each, while I read, dictated, signed, and issued instructions. Whenever the increasing sound of an engine indicated that an aircraft was approaching the landing marker, I looked up and followed it with my eyes, for no CO of a flying unit can prevent himself watching one of his pilots coming in to land. The landing is the crucial moment in which aerodynamic flight abruptly ceases and gives way to that temporary, uncontrollable situation which is neither 'flying' nor 'taxiing'.

There are good landings – and there are bad ones, some consisting of a series of bounces and others being simply a violent impact between aircraft and ground. A humorous aviator once said that 'flying means landing', while an Englishman – a colleague except for his different address – who was being entertained in our mess after a forced landing on the Channel coast, had remarked about his manœuvre: 'Any landing you walk away from is a good one.' Watching aircraft land had always fascinated me, and my interest was, of course, particularly keen when a newcomer was familiarizing himself with his machine.

I had been observing an approach and was on the point of jumping up in consternation when Bachmann called out: 'He's forgotten his undercart! Look, sir, he's forgotten his wheels!'

At that instant the propeller struck the ground and the aircraft slid forward on its belly before coming to a standstill in a fountain of spurting dust.

'Come on!' I shouted. We jumped into the Kübelwagen and raced over the hard sand to the scene of the accident. There we came upon a sight that took my breath away. The pilot was kneeling close to the sorry object with its bent airscrew, trying to get the wreck in the view-finder of his camera. It was our barber!

'Idiot!' I roared at him. 'You must really be past all hope – wrecking one of our priceless 109s like that. Aircraft are like gold out here and you go and bash one to pieces just because you're incapable of using your five senses. And what, on top of everything else, induced you to photograph this monument to incompetence?'

He looked at me utterly aghast, stammering something about 'memory' and 'be more careful next time'.

As we drove back I said to Bachmann:

'Freiberg had better check and find out if we can send the barber home. I could tell from the first that that boy wouldn't be any good.'

Not long afterwards, perhaps a week later, we met up with our Marauder friends from Tebessa, but this time they had no Spitfire escort. Their attacks on our airfields had been getting too impudent of late and they didn't seem to give a damn about our fighters. This time we managed to restore our battered image in the eyes of our opponents by splitting up their formation and chasing them individually at low level across the desert. Over Kairouan we suddenly encountered a strong defensive patrol of fighters. The Spitfires, having the advantage of speed, dived on us to prevent us pursuing the bombers. Then the merry-go-round began, a huge spiral pattern, revolving anti-clockwise, of battling 'Mes' and 'Spits'. The Spitfires dived and the 109s broke away to gain height and return on a reciprocal course with weapons blazing. For some time neither side succeeded in scoring a victory. Then I saw an Me that was being hard pressed by two Spitfires. The pilot went into a steep dive, pulled out gracefully, climbed and, in a manœuvre that betrayed consummate flying skill, positioned himself behind one of his pursuers, fired a short burst and brought him down in flames.

After we had landed I asked who the marksman was and heard to my astonishment that it was our aircraft wrecker, the barber. Freiberg, to whose wing he belonged at the time, confirmed that he was a gifted flier and predicted a great future for him as a fighter pilot. Apparently he was one of those blithe spirits who are always light hearted and cheerful and he had quickly become popular with everyone. In fact he soon afterwards scored a second victory before meeting his end in appalling circumstances. On the day before we evacuated Tunisia, he was about to take off from the narrow runway when he was rammed by a fighter forced-landing from the opposite direction. He died miserably of burns while still in his cockpit.

During the afternoon I tried to rest so that I could at least fly another mission in the evening. But I did not stay long on my camp-bed in the villa. My heart was beating violently and an inexplicable feeling of nervousness made me restless. I had to move about, do something. I therefore filled in the time until evening preparing for the move which now seemed inevitable. If no move was ordered I intended to make the necessary dispositions myself, depending on the situation. In company with Captains Kegel and Tarnow, my administrative and technical officers, I went through the vehicle loading lists and discovered that, if the transport was used to its maximum capacity, there would be just enough room to carry our personnel to Messina. Hence, once again, tons of material – all the stores and equipment which we had drawn from the depots immediately after our withdrawal from North Africa and which had only just been placed on our inventories – would have to be destroyed to prevent it falling into the hands of the enemy.

As we sat down to supper the heavy naval guns began firing again. The house shook and the windows rattled to the bursts. Shortly afterwards the night bombers arrived and we repaired, as we did every evening, to the grotto. Day fighter pilots, we used to say, were there to fight by day, not to make a night of it. Very soon all was quiet and we felt reasonably secure provided that some fool of a bomb aimer didn't catch the villa with a lucky hit. We all of us tried to use the short hours of darkness for sleeping.

The drug was evidently still circulating in my veins for I kept tossing restlessly on my camp-bed. Over and over again I went through the sequence of the move, so crucial if the group with its pilots and aircraft was still to represent a viable fighting formation on reaching the mainland. This time we wouldn't even be able to salvage the tool cases. The orgy of destruction could begin within the next few days and, if we succeeded in assembling the group in Foggia, it would take months to procure replacements for the thousand and one items necessary to a fighter group's operations: aircraft, tools, lifting tackle, tents, engines, spares, cook-house equipment, radios, telephones, typewriters . . .

The telephone rang. Captain Kegel reported that Major Temme, the CO of the fighter-bomber group, was on his way to the grotto. Apparently he had had to bale out of his Focke-Wulf near Corleone after a squadron of Lightnings had set on him and shot up his engine. A little later Tubby showed Temme into the grotto. Leaning on a stout stick, he hobbled forward and introduced himself.

With a deprecating gesture he waved aside my apology for our rough and ready sleeping quarters. I proposed that we should move to the villa if the bombardment slackened so as to get a few hours sleep. The major was a sturdy, thickset, muscular-looking man with close-cropped curly hair. He looked like a countryman, one of his most agreeable features being his dark, humorous eyes.

He needed little prompting to begin his story: 'Round about midday we were attacking the shipping off Gela. It's always a good moment after your bomb has gone and you can pull up and climb out of range of the murderous fire from the ships. Then we ran into the Lightnings . . .'

'But how did you come to arrive at Trapani when it's Gerbini you belong to?'

'As I told you, the Lightnings were waiting for us. With the few serviceable aircraft we could scrape together we had dived from 16,000 feet carrying thousand-pound bombs. Up forward the sea is covered with fine targets.' His voice was a trifle too loud and his gruff tones caused the occupants of the deck-chairs and camp-beds to sit up and observe him with interest.

'They tucked themselves in behind us straight away and began to chase us inland at low level through the valleys. It ended up in a whole lot of single battles. Fortunately the Focke-Wulf isn't exactly a sluggard. I saw some aircraft going down but I was having to watch out for my own skin. I wanted to turn north so as to shake them off. In the end I found myself all on my own, twisting through valleys and hopping over mountains, but still the Lightnings kept after me. Eventually they got within range and damaged my aircraft, but before they could finish me off completely I pulled her up and jumped. I'm surprised in a way that they didn't keep on loosing off at me while I was dangling from my parachute. I came down near a small town called Corleone. It's due south of Palermo and about forty miles from here as the crow flies. Corleone means lionheart, which I thought rather appropriate . . . After that I walked and took lifts on Italian trucks. There are Italian army lorries all over the place with odd-looking civilians on board – in other words the glorious Italian Sixth Army on its way home to mum.'

'What does Gerbini look like? We're expecting to take off from there tomorrow.'

'The airfields have been ploughed up like arable in autumn.

184

They've been laying their bomb carpets everywhere as though intending to destroy the place yard by yard. We were forced to pull out and were having to move our aircraft almost hourly, concealing ourselves in the stubble in between times. Then the whole area started blazing and the flames drove us out. Only a few of the group's aircraft are still serviceable and anyway we can't do much damage with one miserable bomb slung under our bellies. Now if you watch a Boeing opening its bomb doors and see what comes out – that's what I call efficiency . . .'

'D'you think we'll still be able to land at Gerbini tomorrow morning? How can we be expected to protect the ferry traffic if there are no airfields left in the east?'

He shook his round head doubtfully. 'You should be able to get down provided you arrive before the first wave. The commandant has people from the Labour Service who repair the runways during the night so far as they're able and so long as the night bombers give them time to do it. What *we* planned to do came to nothing because of the bombing. We intended to knock out the ships with 2000-pound bombs. We would certainly have sent a few to the bottom if we hadn't been picked off one by one. By the time the enemy landed on the island my group was already done for, smashed on the ground. Now they're showing us how we ought to have fought the battles over Britain in 1941 if we'd had the right aircraft for the job. I've just been reading a manual, usually the last sort of thing I do. LdV 16 is the one and it describes exactly how to set about it. Written by General Wever himself . . .'

'The orders issued by the latter [the Reichsmarschall] to the units were so harsh as to be tantamount to a demand that the German fighter pilots immolate themselves. Individual pilots whose aircraft had not been damaged or who had not themselves been shot down were threatened with court martial proceedings if they were unable to produce evidence of success in aerial combat.

Because of the high command's refusal to understand the factual reasons for the fighters' lack of success against four-engined bombers, and also because of the outrageous measures outlined above, morale among the fighter pilots sank very low indeed. It was obvious to any sensible person that the Commander-in-Chief of the Luftwaffe had lost his nerve when faced with the facts as they were, and was burying his head in the sand.'

PAUL DEICHMANN
DIE LUFTSCHLACHT IM WESTLICHEN MITTELMEER

'. . . in a series of twenty-one air battles from the latter half of May through the early days of July, the Germans sustained heavy losses. Göring, who recognized what was happening but not the cause, brought heavy pressure to bear on the German Second Air Force, calling for incessant commitment of long-range bombers and fighters. But the German aircraft were not able to match the speed and armament of Allied planes. Göring added insult to injury by sending a special message to the fighter pilots of the Second Air Force:

"Together with the fighter pilots in France, Norway and Russia, I can only regard you with contempt. I want an immediate improvement in fighting spirit. If this improvement is not forthcoming, flying personnel from the commander down must expect to be remanded to the ranks and transferred to the eastern front to serve on the ground." '

UNITED STATES ARMY IN WORLD WAR II
SICILY AND THE SURRENDER OF ITALY

The remorseless jangling of the telephone dragged me from my sleep. The noise was unpleasantly loud and in a daze I felt for the receiver in the darkness.

'Teleprint from Air Corps, sir. We made contact at midnight but we've lost it again now. Shall I read it out?'

'Wait a moment. I'll have to turn the light on.'

I looked for the switch in the dark, but when at last I found it, I turned it in vain. There was no current. Eventually I managed to find some matches with which to light the candle stump on the plate beside my camp-bed. My movements were slow, for I was unspeakably tired. As I lay down again in my sweat-soaked pyjamas and picked up the receiver my limbs felt heavy as lead.

'Will you read it out, please.'

In expressionless tones the teleprinter operator, a leading air-craftsman, began to read: ' "To the Second Air Force. Together with the fighter pilots in France, Norway and Russia, I can only regard you with contempt. I want an immediate improvement in fighting spirit. If this improvement is not forthcoming, flying personnel from the commander down must expect to be remanded to the ranks and transferred to the eastern front to serve on the ground. Göring, Reichsmarschall" . . . Are you still there, sir?'

'Yes, thank you. Will you bring it over to the ops room.'

As I replaced the receiver, the airman gave the three short rings prescribed by regulations. Then the room was deathly still. The candle's flickering flame cast grotesque, dancing shadows on the walls. All at once I could hear my own breathing. I held my breath and remained quite motionless. Everywhere in this small house people were wrapped in soothing sleep, wholly unaware of this fresh insult. As yet the aircraftsman on the teleprinter and I were the only people here to know of the strictures passed by the most senior officer in the Luftwaffe. I tried to imagine what the man on the other end of the line looked like, for I must have seen him often enough. Perhaps he had been a schoolmaster in civilian life; he might even be old enough to be my father. All at once I was conscious of a strange bond between this invisible airman and myself.

But the mood passed quickly, thrust aside by the realization of the sheer brutality of the unbelievable message I had just heard. What ought I to do about the signal? Ought I to read it out in front of a muster parade? But if I were to appear before them and talk about 'fighting spirit' they would look at me in mute reproach. Their expressions would tell me that my duty as a CO was to spare them such phrases.

So this was what had come of our general's efforts to save us from court martial. Fighting spirit indeed! In an hour's time another day would begin and with it yet another feat of improvisation such as had been demanded of us every single day since our return to Sicily. With what we could scrape together of the remnants of the group, we would fly along the north coast and over Etna's crater towards the Straits of Messina where we would fling ourselves at the Flying Fortresses in a series of uncoordinated attacks. Our numbers were so few that we would do little damage, and even that little depended upon our breaking through to the bombers.

Afterwards we would land in Gerbini if the airfield was still usable, or else at Catania. We would refuel our aircraft by handpump, rearm and top up with oil. We would leap into slit trenches and shelters and wait for the bomb carpets to unroll over us. And then we would crawl out again, haul the wrecked aircraft to one side, repair any minor damage and, provided we still had enough machines to make up a modest formation, take off on the next patrol. This was what all these men had had to go on doing day after day. And now I was expected to talk to them about fighting spirit!

I doubted whether we would be able to hold out in Trapani for the remainder of the day. The bombers appeared without warning since they came in too low to be picked up by our direction finders. Flying in close formation, they had been showering down bombs on the airfield until it resembled a lunar landscape. The advanced landing ground near Corleone would therefore have to be our last refuge. Up to now, however, it had been nothing more than a long field covered with yellow wheat stubble and marked out with whitewashed stone slabs.

We would be like hunted animals seeking cover. And without either telephone or supplies we would be cutting ourselves off from the outside world. Nor was there another airfield left in western Sicily.

I must have fallen asleep, for again the telephone jerked me out of a brief spell of blissful unconsciousness. 'Four o'clock, sir.'

The first light of day was filtering through the Venetian blinds as I got up to open the shutters. I still felt utterly exhausted; indeed, I seemed to be in a permanent state of fatigue. I had but one desire and that was to sleep.

In the next room Tubby was opening the shutters, putting the chairs in place and rattling the breakfast crockery. It had become a little cooler. In the wan light before dawn, the sickle-shaped bay, the terraces, gardens and white houses were lightly shrouded in mist through which black pines thrust upwards and smoke from chimneys rose perpendicularly into the sky.

Bachmann and Straden, who were sitting at the table when I entered the day room, answered my 'good morning' in low, morose voices. None of us felt any desire to converse. What we really wanted to do, as we drank Tubby's strong hot coffee, was to cradle our heads in our arms on the table and sleep.

Kegel came in, sat down and pushed the teleprint over to me without speaking. The white strips of printed text had been pasted neatly on to the pale pink paper of the official form. The first words to spring to the eye, appearing as they did well below the main portion of the long signal, were 'Göring, Reichs-marschall'.

'. . . regard you with contempt . . .' I had no wish to read to the end. It was not my habit to shirk what was unpleasant but this repelled me. It seemed to be directed at myself alone; I was the man responsible for this group and I, personally, was the object of his contempt.

I handed the signal across the table. Straden took it and he and Bachmann began to read. Then, slowly and carefully, he put the paper down on the table, rose, took his cap from its hook and left the room without a word. Bachmann looked after him uncertainly, then at me and Kegel, eased his chair back and followed Straden. On his way out he said quietly: 'I'm driving to the ops room, sir.'

The telephone rang. 'It's the general, sir.'

The general's voice came from a long way away and was overlaid with crackles and hisses. So as to hear him better I held my breath and motioned to Kegel and Tubby to keep quiet.

'We're near Taormina,' the general said. 'We're surrounded – d'you understand me? Comiso is no longer usable.'

'Yes, sir.'

'I wanted to call you last night before that signal went out but I couldn't get through to you . . .'

'Yes, sir.'

'Listen, you're not to take it seriously. I did what I could. I've been urging him to abandon the whole business, but then he sent this signal to Air Corps.'

He did not continue and I remained silent. Finally he asked: 'Can you still hear me?'

'Yes, sir.'

'Collect all the aircraft in western Sicily and go to Gerbini. The airfield is usable. By now your 3 Wing will be on its way from Sardinia and they will also land at Gerbini. Your job is to protect the Straits of Messina. Can you tell me how many aircraft will be arriving?'

'Between fifteen and twenty belonging to 2 Wing and Group HQ. No 1 hasn't reported yet.'

'Have you any questions?'

I had indeed, lots of them, but in terms of German military tradition most were not of the kind a major can ask a general.

'Yes, sir. What's the situation? How far have the Allies got?'

'The pressure on our ground troops has increased enormously and we shall be concentrating our defence in the eastern portion of the island. It's possible that you'll have to move soon. The enemy is pressing on towards the centre of the island.'

'But where is the group to move to, sir?'

'I don't know yet,' was his somewhat irritable reply. 'For the time being no German soldier may leave Sicily. But you should get all your vehicles ready for a move. There'll be no transport aircraft – Air Corps haven't a Ju left. And once again: don't take that teleprint too seriously. D'you promise me that?'

What could I say over a telephone line that might go dead at any time? We had already discussed this question once before for several hours and had found no solution, so it was quite pointless to say anything further now. I therefore replied:

'Yes, sir.'

I felt almost ashamed of my attitude when speaking to the general. It seemed to me that I had been an accessory to an act of treachery of which our pilots were the victims. At the same time I realized how diabolical was the dilemma in which the general found himself. I had thrown in the sponge, simply answering 'Yes, sir'. In this answer lay that trust in one's superior – a whole attitude towards life – which had been instilled into us, into our fathers and into their fathers before them. For us soldiers it had hitherto been the only right attitude, indeed the only conceivable one. The obedience practised for centuries by the German soldier had always presupposed an unshakeable trust that the orders he received would be sensible orders and that the high command would search their hearts very carefully before sacrificing whole formations. And the many who were sacrificed died in the certainty that this was so. Increasingly of late I had found this reflected in the mute expressions of my pilots though for some time there had been a distinct note of interrogation. It still holds good, doesn't it, sir? they seemed to be asking me. It

G

surely must have some sense if the high command demands it of us, surely it must!

But supposing that something had gone wrong with part of this old military equation? Who were the 'high command' anyway? Supposing that after 1933 a new factor had entered this hierarchy of obedience, a factor which had suddenly allowed the high command to do what it liked, even something senseless?

Questions, questions! A man would need leisure to reflect on them. He would have to have caught up with his sleep. He would need time, would need someone else to discuss them with. In our business such matters were not discussed. Yet it might have been better if they had been, for in that way our doubts could perhaps have been dispelled.

For the past few minutes I had been standing beside the telephone table with the receiver in my hand. Kegel and Tubby were looking at me thunderstruck. From the earpiece came a quacking voice: 'Are you still speaking? Have you finished? I'm disconnecting you.'

These were no thoughts for the CO of a group at the start of a day's operations. I grabbed my belt and pistol from the back of the chair where they usually hung and buckled the belt round my waist. For a soldier there is something extremely salutary in this gesture: he is taking a grip on himself, discarding all unnecessary thoughts, focusing his mind on immediate things, on essentials.

How I detested those flights to Gerbini! Whenever I stood on that barren expanse under the blazing sun, a landscape pockmarked with bomb craters and covered with wrecked aircraft, the scene always brought home to me the hopelessness of our battle for the island.

'Tubby, let the ops room know that I'm on my way to fetch Captain Straden and Mr Bachmann. We're flying to Gerbini.'

Kegel got into the Kübelwagen with me and we drove between gardens along a narrow, deserted lane which debouched into the main road through a constricted alleyway. Spread out below us in the morning mist, the western tip of the island with the airfield and the white houses of Trapani presented a magnificent spectacle. It was the brief hour before sunrise when a semblance of freshness could be felt coming off the sea, before the scorching heat descended on the countryside from the eternally clear southern sky. Over on the horizon, above Marsala, a row of dark blue smudges floated above the mist – flak bursts. The idyll was deceptive and the war went on. It was five o'clock in the morning and the day was going to go on for ever.

As we drove up to the operations room I gave Kegel the necessary instructions regarding the preparations for the move.

'All ground personnel,' I told him, 'other than those needed for the final servicing of the aircraft, should be despatched to Messina. Check our loading lists and make arrangements to destroy the equipment we can't take with us.'

When we arrived, Kegel and I jumped out of the Kübelwagen and climbed the few steps into the hut. Straden was already walking towards me.

'The general wants to speak to you,' he said.

He was continuing to avoid my eyes. I had the impression that the Reichsmarschall's insults were still sticking in his throat. But it was a case of swallow or choke.

While I perched on the folding chair and waited to be connected, my eyes travelled over the plain.

The direction finders near Marsala had reported the approach of heavy bombers. There would, however, be no point in sending up our few available aircraft against them since our intention was to leave for Gerbini in a few minutes' time. The attack might be directed against our airfield, but equally the target could be Palermo harbour. The Allies' intention was to cut off our supplies so as to lighten their task on the island. To achieve that end they would have to attack the Straits of Messina as well as Palermo harbour. Probably they would attack both at once – they certainly possessed sufficient equipment to do so.

The firing of warning shots by the flak was followed by the immediate cessation of all activity on the airfield below. In front of the hut a number of airmen were gesticulating and pointing towards Chinisia. And then I, too, saw a long stream of bombers approaching from the west. Suddenly the white strip of runway, which usually gleamed in the sun, was veiled in an enormous cloud of dust. The bomb carpet must have been very wide for the whole length of the airfield was obscured. Only then did we hear the rumble of explosions. As I shouted into the handset, vainly trying to get my connection, the first black clouds of petrol smoke from burning aircraft began to rise up out of the gloom.

The sight of Chinisia's blasted airfield reminded me of my visit to the Italian fighter wing stationed there, and at the same time I realized that I had almost completely forgotten about the existence of the Italian fighter arm. During the gruesome finale on this island it was a case of every man for himself. The heavy attacks had begun before we had had time to establish signals communications with each other or to co-ordinate our tactics – steps we would have taken as a matter of course had conditions been anything like normal. This meant that each air force had begun fighting its own war. And, in circumstances where relations between the Italian and German high commands were far from good, not only were the arrangements for controlling the units of the two nations entirely separate but the orders they received were also different, so that any co-ordination in the operational field was out of the question. Indeed, that had been the main defect of the joint command ever since the start of the Mediterranean campaign: the two controlling organizations had been so much concerned with prestige that each had taken all possible steps to prevent its own units being placed under the other's command. Thus, although the battle was a common one, the assignments and orders were invariably different.

A bomb carpet is a terrible weapon when used against an airfield and is extremely demoralizing for the airfield personnel, even though they may have a measure of protection while squatting in bunkers or slit trenches. Particularly effective were the smaller bombs which the enemy released by the thousand. They made only shallow craters and the fragments, projected outwards at high velocity and close to the ground, shredded the outer skins of our aircraft as though they were made of paper.

How would the Italian fighter wing be feeling now, unaccustomed as they were to such attacks and knowing that their superiors had moved them to Sicily only with reluctance? A few days previously I had gone to make my number with the commander of the Italian group. On landing I had noted the surprisingly good condition of the airfield. Having taxied up the long runway, I was directed to a pen surrounded by a protective rampart of white tuff. Macchi fighters, still in the desert camouflage of the North African campaign, occupied the neighbouring pens.

In front of the flying-control building I was approached by an officer who introduced himself as Major Visconti, the commander of the fighter unit. He said that his CO had his operations room and his quarters on Mount Erice, if I should wish to visit him there.

The man walking beside me had a virile and extremely likeable face. His small white cap with its short peak was pulled down well over his forehead almost as far as his bushy, prominent eyebrows. Beneath the aquiline nose was a black, curling moustache. There was no hint of timidity as he looked at me with his expressive, surprisingly blue eyes. His name was familiar, for I had heard much about him. He had been known to the veterans of my group since the days in North Africa and they spoke of him as a gallant and outstanding fighter pilot.

He began talking about their wretched communications, his main command channel being a field telephone which, however, seldom enabled him to communicate with his CO. Moreover, he had no contact with the German direction finders near Marsala and when he saw the German fighters take off to attack, having been alerted in good time, he could only look on enviously, for he had learnt that without guidance from the ground any success was a matter of chance. Nobody, he told me, warned him of the approach of the enemy and in the air he received no orders whatsoever.

I could sympathize with his position. If we ourselves felt misunderstood by our high command, what must he feel? Wondering how I could help him, I felt something like pride when I compared his own hopeless situation with ours. At least we had had the technical means to wage a successful battle – indeed we still had them! And it was a poor sort of CO who sat back, high up on a mountainside, watching part of his group lying idle on a first-rate airfield until such time as it should be knocked out by an accurate massed bombing attack! As I shook Visconti's hand and turned towards my aircraft, I resolved to call on his CO as soon as our daily operations allowed.

The present attack on Chinisia airfield reminded me of the resolution – and the prediction – I had made then. I was surprised that the Allies had not attacked this admirable airfield before. Had they, perhaps, ceased to take the Italians seriously? Had they ever taken them seriously?

It was a line of thought I did not wish to pursue, for it somehow seemed uncomradely towards Visconti with whom I felt a bond. At all events I intended to seek out his peculiar CO up on Mount Erice.

Then the preparations for take-off, the take-off itself and the task of leading my small formation into the air claimed the whole of my attention. Again and again the demands of the moment prevented us from reflecting and this was just as well. For one way or the other, anyone who gave himself over to brooding was lost: either he would be killed through lack of concentration and resolution at the crucial moment of the battle or else, faltering even before he had made contact with the enemy, he would turn back, not once but again and again, until finally he would have to be posted away, his days as a fighter pilot at an end.

We circuited Gerbini airfield, searching for the landing strip which had been marked out for us with small, barely identifiable flags. At last, having formed a picture of the layout, I decided to land. In the fields much of the yellow stubble had been burnt. The plain, a notably fertile one, was patterned hideously with bomb craters and the black scars of fires. Descending towards them I felt an almost overpowering reluctance to land. As the machine came to a standstill opposite the hut, the propeller continued to give a few fitful jerks accompanied by loud bangs. It was much too hot for the engines when one had to taxi at walking pace. I had had some trouble in finding my dispersal pen and the mechanics had guided me half way round the airfield before I arrived at the hut and the place reserved for me. In the chaos of bomb craters and skeletons of aircraft among the burnt olive trees it was difficult to keep one's bearings, much more so than it had seemed when coming in to land.

Straden, Bachmann and Zahn had parked their 109s close by. Even at this hour of the morning they were already exhausted and they dragged their feet as they walked towards the hut. Outside it was a bench made of a few stone slabs and a balk of timber, and on this they sat down without further ado.

I walked past them in silence and went into the hut where I began trying to make contact with the Fighter Leader, Air Corps or indeed any other higher formation. Eventually Sergeant Korn came in – how on earth had he got here? – and announced that no purpose would be served by contacting any of the headquarters since orders had already arrived for us to 'refuel, take off and fly cover over the Straits of Messina'.

Armed with this cut-and-dried information I joined the men on the bench who, with legs outstretched, were dozing in the scanty shade. Resting my head against the hot wall, I, too, closed my eyes. From all sides came the familiar noises of an advanced landing ground: the click of the fuel hand-pumps, the shouts of the mechanics, the rising howl of an engine being run up on test. I heard it all and as I listened I consciously registered the passing of every minute.

In this place we were utterly exposed. It had only to occur to the enemy to come here; he need only pass this way by chance, and it would be the end of us. Nervously we awaited the completion of refuelling, well aware that we would be lucky if we managed to get into the air unscathed.

When the dull rumbling crumps of a distant bombing raid

assailed our ears we leapt instantly into the slit trenches. As though at the touch of a spectral hand all signs of life disappeared from the surface of the field. The flak to the south began firing heavily and then fell silent again. This time the attack was being directed against another part of the huge plain, not against us. It was only when the distant drone of aircraft engines had diminished in volume to the level which persisted, almost without intermission, throughout each day, that we emerged suspiciously and very cautiously from our trenches. An Me 109 was taxiing across the airfield in a cloud of dust and someone in the group operations room reported that Colonel Larsen had just landed.

He threaded his way between the bomb craters and parked his machine close to the hut. As Larsen was climbing out, my chief mechanic, Schwarz, told me that my engine needed a change of plugs. This meant that the aircraft would be out of action for an hour.

'Straden, get through to No 1 and tell them that Godert is to lead the group. Will you take over HQ Flight, please.'

'Right, sir.'

While I was still greeting Larsen engines began springing to life round the edge of the airfield and the remnants of the group started to move. A few minutes later they were in the air, their task the protection of the Straits of Messina. Larsen removed his life-jacket and handed it to the mechanic who was to refuel his machine. As we walked slowly towards the hut I caught myself scanning our surroundings, instinctively registering the location of the nearest slit trench. I steered him towards a spot where some empty ammunition boxes had been piled up to form a kind of seat beside a deep trench. Probably some of the airmen had had a game of skat here the previous evening.

'I'm sorry about that signal. You may be certain that we did everything we could to stop it.'

Reluctantly I looked my old friend straight in the eye. His present appointment being what it was, even he was probably not wholly immune to the prevailing doubletalk.

'Franzl,' I said, 'I'm utterly sick of hearing that. You're all apologizing to us – you yourself, the general, Air Corps – now I'm only waiting for the field marshal! Perhaps you'll start complimenting us again if you find that it makes us fight better and go more cheerfully to our doom. First you send us that shameful signal and a bit later you're slapping us jovially on the back saying: "Don't take it so seriously, ha ha ha," or else "Chins up! It'll soon be forgotten." At the same time you know as well as I do that every teleprinter section, every HQ between us and the Reichsmarschall has taken note of our disgrace without your being able to explain to them that the whole thing is not to be taken too seriously. I can't help it, Franzl, but the whole performance strikes me as utterly vile. It's just slaughtering our reputation as soldiers.'

He returned my gaze and answered calmly: 'Of course you're right – the thing's impossible and we're all in the same boat. I agree that as an example of leadership it couldn't be worse. But what are we to do? The Luftwaffe is in an atrocious situation. The Reichsmarschall has been under fire ever since the Fortresses began penetrating east of Berlin. The Führer blames him for the failure of the air arm and he gets out of it by saying over and over again, "It's not me, it's the fighter pilots!" I've found out for myself that it's no longer possible to converse rationally with the Reichsmarschall in the way officers ought to converse. Believe me, I often have grave doubts . . .'

He broke off without divulging the nature of those doubts. I had them, too, but these were things that could not be said by people in our situation. For to do so would have precipitated a conflict of conscience unendurable to a fighting soldier. So we both remained silent for a while, each of us perfectly aware of what the other was thinking. At last I said:

'I haven't announced the contents of the signal although all the pilots know about it, of course. I've pigeon-holed it.'

'No one's going to ask about that . . .'

'How much longer d'you give us in Sicily?'

Larsen lit a cigarette, expelling the smoke with a hiss.

'The spearhead of the British Eighth Army is now about twenty-five miles south of here,' he said. 'The American Seventh has advanced from Gela presumably with the intention of linking up with the British here on the plain of Catania. What that signifies for you in western Sicily and for the defence of the island as a whole is pretty obvious.'

'You mean evacuation – an orderly withdrawal if possible?'

'What else?' replied Larsen. His voice was expressionless but his look spoke volumes as he continued: 'And who has greater experience of that than you?'

'What do you think this withdrawal is going to be like? In Tunisia the order arrived much too late. But in our service, paradoxically enough, it's not called an order but permission, as though the high command kept nursing a secret hope that there might be some intrepid individuals who would prefer to fight to the last gasp in a series of Thermopylaes rather than take advantage of their magnanimous offer. But here there's nothing left to salvage. This time I've made up my mind to get every single man over to the mainland, even if it means burning or blowing up most of the equipment. We're slowly reaching a stage when everyone is going to be needed. In any case, the really skilled, responsible ground crews will become fewer and fewer if these bomb carpets continue to drop on us.'

'You may be right there,' he said thoughtfully. 'Aircraft and other equipment can be replaced; experienced mechanics can't. If you can get your people across the Straits of Messina safe and sound, we'll be able to re-equip the group. Did you know that we are now turning out a thousand fighters a month and can possibly go even higher? Admittedly our losses are also very heavy. We're losing hundreds at the training stage alone.'

At that moment two fighters flew unsteadily across the airfield, and then the group, their operation concluded, came in to land, the pilots following each other down in rapid succession. Immediately all was again dust and din and apparent chaos.

'Captain Straden has baled out quite close by,' called Sergeant Korn through the window of the hut; he had to shout as loud as he could to make himself heard above the noise. 'We need a Storch!'

He settled down to some brief but concentrated telephoning and shortly after was able to announce: 'No 2 are sending their Storch, sir. They know where he baled out.'

Bachmann then reported and told me about the battle. Apparently they had climbed on a westerly course so as to be up-sun when they pounced on the Fortresses. But they had still been climbing over grid square 'Martha' when they had seen Boeings beneath them heading north. Instantly Godert had commenced the attack, which had proceeded almost in textbook fashion. At the same moment, however, a squadron of Spitfires had dived on them and split them up. Keeping in close formation, Straden and HQ Flight had pressed on and, under intense fire, had managed to get within range of the rear section of bombers. Suddenly his machine had started climbing away and he reported that he had been hit and wounded. He had then turned round and gone into a steep glide in the direction of Gerbini. Almost immediately, however, he had jettisoned his hood, half-rolled and baled out. Bachmann had seen his parachute open.

The Storch, with Straden on board, landed a few yards from the hut. Carefully the stretcher was lowered out of the aircraft and the MO attached to No 1 Wing of the 53rd Fighter Group at once began slitting the wounded man's blood-drenched trouser leg as far as the hip.

'Another one come to grief,' I said to Larsen as we walked up and down close by. 'No 1 say they have lost three. The group keeps on losing more and more pilots. It's going to be the finish here, Franzl.'

He seemed to be working out a picture in his mind of the operation on which we were engaged. As the Inspector, South, he had, of course, little influence on tactical decisions in this theatre, but his words nevertheless carried some weight in the councils of the men round the General of Fighters. Maybe this first-hand impression would facilitate the decision to break off the unequal struggle on the island.

I had seen dead and dying men. In four years of war, four years of almost uninterrupted operations, an eternity, I had seen them crash and bleed and burn: some mere boys, fledglings who had been instantly struck down by what is called fate; others, older men, veterans whose experience exceeded that of all the rest yet whose hour had suddenly struck. Admittedly Straden was 'only' wounded but I was not going to see him for a long time, perhaps never again, and so the scene of the pilots standing round the Storch while the doctor attended to Straden became indelibly branded on my mind.

This was now one of the last bases on the island. The sun shone pitilessly down on the yellow plain about which groups of men like ourselves were hectically engaged in putting the few available aircraft into the air against the enemy, a process that inevitably resulted in fewer aircraft still. While the mechanics, with speed born of practice, refuelled the aircraft and rattled ammunition belts over the engine cowlings, the pilots, wilting and expressionless, stood or squatted beneath the dusty olive trees. Barely a word was exchanged. Every man knew that he and his companions were at the end of their tether.

There was nothing now to recall the dashing, stylish fighter pilot with his yellow scarf and his imaginatively modified uniform. Our outward appearance accurately reflected the pass to which we had come: crumpled, filthy, oil-stained trousers, ancient, greasy life-jackets, emaciated and in many cases unshaven faces. Everything was a dusty brown – earth, clothes, faces, aeroplanes. There are the hardships of victory, hardships which in Russia and North Africa we cheerfully shrugged off and which, on occasion, we had not even noticed, so elated had we been by our sense of superiority. And there are the hardships of defeat, the hardships of dirt and dishonour which feed on morale, impair the fighting spirit and only serve to engender fresh defeats. This, we had been taught, was the hour of the born military commander, the hour when he would jerk his men out of their state of depression, give them a purpose, inspire them with new élan and lead them boldly to death or glory against the foe. But to all of us here, engaged in the routine task of fighting in the heat and dirt, that concept was a highly dubious one. It was a relic of the First World War, if not of the days of cavalry charges, and was utterly useless in the situation in which we now found ourselves. The war in the air is a technological war which cannot be won by a technologically inferior fighting force, however high its morale or dauntless its resolution. This was a point our field marshals had failed to grasp and it was also the reason why the Reichsmarschall could think only in terms of bravery and cowardice and why, to his mind, a fighter arm which had lost its superiority could be nothing other than cowardly.

Larsen's voice suddenly intruded on my thoughts. 'We've got to move you over to the mainland while there's still a nucleus round which to rebuild the group. In North Africa it was left until much too late. Obviously a group is more than just a conglomeration of aeroplanes and equipment plus a given number of men.'

'Who d'you think you're telling that to?' I answered bitterly. 'Tell it to the general, although he should be perfectly well aware of it. He was still a group commander himself only two years ago.'

'You mustn't be unfair to him. I'm positive he's perfectly aware of all these things. After all he belongs to the same generation as we do and his experience in action has been exactly the same as ours. But what can he do . . .?'

I shrugged my shoulders and turned towards the wounded man again. Perhaps Larsen was right. There was no solution and we had to carry on. We had invested our military leaders and the commands that issued from them with a kind of sanctity and, while we had still been winning, we had thought that splendid. Now, in time of defeat, we had no alternative but to await their orders and carry them out, even if those orders should be wrong and even if we knew them to be wrong.

After climbing out of his aircraft Bachmann had sat down under an olive tree. His eyes never strayed from the back of the doctor who was still kneeling down attending to his patient. As he gazed fixedly at the scene, he kept restlessly stroking his chin with his sunburnt hand. His attitude, it seemed to me, was that of an old man and I found myself observing his person in minute detail: the worn-down tropical shoes with their leather toe caps and canvas uppers, the greasy, shiny dye pouch attached by its snap hook to the life-jacket, the battered, shabby gloves whose only purpose was to prevent one's hands, which were invariably damp with sweat, from slipping off the stick and the other controls.

Then the doctor rose to his feet. The wounded man's leg was now heavily bandaged and he lay with his eyes closed. He had been conscious throughout but had not uttered a word. Probably he was suffering from the effects of shock.

'His right calf has been chewed up by an explosive bullet,' the doctor said. He spoke quietly so as not to be overheard by the patient. 'It's impossible to say immediately whether or not the leg can be saved. We'll have to get him to hospital at once.' He paused for a moment before continuing: 'On the mainland if possible. I've given him morphia and anti-tetanus injections.'

'We'll have to wait until dusk before we risk a Storch,' I said, 'but if we alert Vibo Valentia airfield, they can arrange to send him on without delay.'

'Telephone, sir!' Sergeant Korn called from the hut.

It was Temme, the commander of the Focke-Wulf fighter-bombers. His people had been holding out here for days, flying mission after mission – to negligible effect, since they could administer no more than pinpricks.

'An order has just come in from Air Corps,' he said. 'It reads: "Proceed to alternative landing grounds near Trapani forthwith together with HQ and Nos 1 and 2 Wings 77th Fighter Group. No 3/77th will return to Sardinia." '

'Thank you. I'll get moving as soon as my aircraft have been refuelled and rearmed. That's to say in a few minutes. I think the airfield near Salemi is the better of the two and I suggest you make for that one.'

'Fine,' replied the fighter-bomber commander evenly. 'But

first I'll have a go at the shipping off Gela so as to give the whole thing some point.'

The airfield near Salemi was the one with the farmhouse that had so annoyed the Kittyhawks. Without doubt the enemy had taken it to be a strong point, but he could, for that matter, seek us out anywhere. The airstrip near Corleone was little more than a last resort, to be used if we had to evacuate Trapani yet continue to remain in the western portion of the island.

'We'll be taking off for the advanced landing ground near Salemi,' I shouted to Korn. 'I'd like to know soon how many aircraft are ready.'

Some of us would leave now and the aircraft still being serviced would have to follow on later. This meant that we would be flying in groups too small to constitute viable fighting formations. On our way to the west we intended to carry out ground attacks against the beach-heads. I had not seen Abben, who led my No 3 Wing, since our arrival in Gerbini. He had reported the wing's presence by telephone and had spoken of engagements over Etna and now he was getting ready to return to Sardinia. His preparations were going ahead with the same speed as ours, for we all wished to depart as quickly as we could from our exposed position before the enemy unloaded his next bomb carpet on us.

Larsen came up to say good-bye. 'I'm going to Catania,' he said. 'I'll be telling the general how things stand with you. If only the Führer would give us permission to evacuate the island.'

The Führer, I thought absently. Yes, of course, the Führer! But at that moment the enemy seemed more important. Would the enemy, I wondered, permit us to evacuate the island?

This time, as my aircraft left the ground to carry me back to Trapani, the sense of relief that had grown stronger with every departure from Gerbini was totally absent. It might well be the last time, for the end was very near. Even if the bombing were suddenly to cease, it would be weeks before we could mount an effective attack since we lacked everything necessary to the conduct of a fighter unit's operations – skilled personnel, spares, ammunition, even petrol – and obviously we could only take off from those advanced landing grounds to which the little that was available had been transported at the cost of tremendous effort. What we had witnessed in this theatre was, to use the words Temme had quoted, 'the destruction of one air arm by another in order to ensure the unhampered action of the latter's airpower and the safe deployment of its ground forces'. Without doubt the operation on which I was now embarking would show the Americans that we were not completely finished – it would cost the enemy a few lives and bring destruction to some of his equipment – but by comparison with the tons of bombs he had dropped on Sicily it would be of little significance.

There were only nine Messerschmitts behind me. The remainder would take off from Gerbini as soon as they had been serviced and would rejoin us on the advanced landing ground. We were not in any sense a large formation; indeed the few aeroplanes at our disposal would be useless against the enemy bombers and their bristling array of weapons. We might, perhaps, be able to shoot down a few fighters in a dogfight but both in quantity and in quality those aircraft were our superiors.

The sky to the west had turned a steely grey and thunderclouds had started to build up over the island's central massif. With the map spread out on my knee I applied myself to skirting the wall of cloud without losing my bearings. Near Enna, which could be readily identified by the extensive remains of the Hohenstaufen *castello*, I turned south in order to reach the Bay of Gela. Visibility was poor and the cloud so low that I throttled back as I flew down the long valley. I knew that the Americans were moving up through this valley in their northward thrust and that if I wished to reach the coast I should have to reckon with their attentions. At first I kept well away from the road, flying close to the slopes which disappeared into the mist overhead. All at once I was surrounded by strings of tracer. They looked like fireworks as they climbed towards me, inaudible above the sound of my engine. It was a pretty display but at any moment it could prove lethal. This so bewildered me that I applied full boost and raced down the valley in a series of violent evasive manœuvres.

A sudden torrent of rain struck the windscreen like a blow and for a few seconds I could see nothing whatever. Then the curtain of cloud parted abruptly to reveal Gela's white beach where, not long before, I had met the Italian sentry patrol. I turned to starboard so as to avoid the beach and the inevitable anti-aircraft fire from the destroyers and landing craft. I was now a few hundred feet above the road that runs parallel to the coast, flying through a continuous hail of tracer with the others behind me well closed up as though threaded on a string. By introducing an element of surprise we could use our firepower to maximum effect before the troops on the ground managed to jump for cover or the gunners take aim.

Lorries and tanks were lined up along the road as though on parade, and as I dived, with the 'pop-pop-pop' of my cannon drowning the noise of the engine, my mouth was dry and the old bitter taste was back on my tongue. I had only a few seconds firing time left and my speed built up rapidly as I pressed home the attack. The illuminated cross-wires stood out against the dark ground, and the silhouettes of vehicles flowed rapidly across them. With violent kicks on the rudder bar, I tried to line up the illuminated ring and its cross-wires with the road and the transport. A large tank loomed up rapidly in my sights and my cannon shells smacked onto its armour-plate, ricocheting in all directions. Soldiers leapt for the verges and melted into the ground before my eyes.

Then the 'g' force was pressing me hard against my parachute as I went into a climbing right-hand turn and continued my headlong progress along the coast road. Leaning my head right back I looked over the armour-plate and through the sloping plexiglass window down on to the road which was flowing away behind me as though in a greatly speeded-up film. There were burning vehicles, cannon shells bursting on the road and jeeps bumping over the ground in a wild dash for the open country. It was an absorbing sight which gave one a deceptive sense of superiority. I banked to the left and, still looking back, saw one of our aircraft going down low – far too low! – until it struck one of the vehicles in the convoy and immediately exploded in a welter of metal and a column of flame as high as a house.

This was what we termed a 'fire on impact', which could be caused either by anti-aircraft fire or by inadvertent contact with the ground. Such a death, spectacular and gruesome, was seen but fleetingly, with half an eye. One heard the droning of one's engine and, in the headphones, the staccato sounds of battle. But, as in a silent film, the tremendous explosion seemed to make no noise at all. So it had been when Sergeant Meyer had cut a swathe through a wood near Novgorod; when Second Lieutenant Behrens had rolled along like a fireball in the middle of a convoy of Russian army lorries; when Flight Sergeant Stumpf had lost a wing while flattening out and had crashed on the steppe among the enemy tanks.

All at once there were no more streams of tracer rising ahead of me. The pale ribbon of road below was deserted. The front had been left behind. I wondered who the unlucky one had been for I didn't know who had taken off with me apart from Bachmann and Zahn. These two were flying close by in battle formation but the others had left Gerbini in the order that their aircraft had been serviced and found airworthy.

Agrigento was on our left. I made a wide detour round the town and harbour so as to avoid stirring up the anti-aircraft guns and began to climb. The sun was shining on my face and the wall of cloud to the east gleamed brilliantly white. My intention, provided that we did not encounter the enemy in the meanwhile, was to fly in a large semicircle so that I could observe Chinisia, Trapani and the two advanced landing grounds from above.

'Odysseus One to Erice, how are you receiving me?'

'Receiving you beautifully Odysseus One. We've just picked up a formation of Marauders with fighter escort approaching Trapani. Report your position and height. Over.'

'Odysseus One to Erice, understood. Position Castelvetrano. 16,000. Over.'

Once again those idiotic bombers were 'approaching Trapani' so as to deliver yet another load on to the same expanse of rubble. But fundamentally the Allies were right in doing so for we were still attacking them even though it was with the last remnants of our effective strength. And by now they had no illusions about our toughness.

By my reckoning we should make contact in ten minutes. What sort of a bunch, I wondered, was I leading? I twisted round and tried to make out the numbers painted on the aircraft accompanying me. There were eight in all, my entire fighting force, and I had no idea who was piloting them, apart from Bachmann and Zahn, of course. These two were flying close beside me to right and left, their machines rock-steady in the calm air. I had somehow suspected that the enemy would be reported. A sense of foreboding had told me that this battle was inevitable and that, with no reserves of strength, I was nearing the end of my tether.

The Erice controller kept reporting the latest position of the bomber formation. If there had been more of us and if we had been a little fresher, this teamwork between air and ground could have been entirely pleasurable, but as things were now it was nothing more than the prelude to an unequal struggle.

'Erice to Odysseus One, pantechnicons now immediately north of airfield, height 10,000. You'd better get a move on!'

'Message received.'

By now we could see the dirty smudges of the flak bursts and, in front of them, the bombers flying in close formation. They were coming in over the mountain from the north and at any moment would be opening their bomb doors. My altimeter was showing 13,000 feet. 'You'd better get a move on!' he had told me. That I was most assuredly doing, hastening towards another clash with our old acquaintances from North Africa. Where were the fighters? As yet I had seen none. The flak's shooting was brilliant. Their shells were bursting accurately among the Marauders, forcing them to make repeated changes of course.

One of the big aircraft dipped a wing and a for a few seconds accompanied the formation in a side-slip – a wholly unnatural manœuvre. Suddenly it touched another aeroplane in the section and immediately the two machines locked together and hurtled downwards in a tangle of metal. Surprisingly, two parachutes appeared above them, floating calmly in the air.

And then I saw the fighters immediately ahead of me on the same course. They were Thunderbolts with big radial engines, ambling along well above the flak bursts.

Almost subconsciously I moved the lever into position above the button on the control column, thus setting my weapons at 'fire'. Provided I was certain that I was going to shoot I invariably did this well beforehand. And once again the bitter taste was in my mouth.

As soon as I engaged them with my cannon the fighters broke formation. I had taken them by surprise. The section leader half-rolled and broke away in a spectacular dive. However, I hadn't hit him yet; the black smoke emerging from his exhaust stubs simply meant that he was on full boost. As the ground came racing towards me I managed to keep in position, firing at short intervals. Where my section could be I didn't know; doubtless they were locked in battle elsewhere. We were very low now, hopping over trees and houses as we neared the coast, and then suddenly we were over the sea, only a few feet above the surface of the water. I was racing in the direction of Pantelleria with little reserve of fuel but once again the fever of the chase had me in its grip. I was faster than he was and I continued to close.

If he had turned his head he would have looked straight along my engine cowling. I had expended all my cannon ammunition. But I didn't intend to fire my machine guns just yet, because it was very easy to miscalculate when engaging fighters. The American could in his turn force me into a dogfight. I hadn't enough fuel for that but he was not to know it. Hence he was seeking safety in escape, putting his trust in his powerful engine.

All of a sudden, acting instinctively, and independent of any conscious decision, I pulled the throttle back and began a wide turn towards the land. I returned the firing lever to the 'safe' position, screwed the knob behind the sights to the left to extinguish the illuminated cross-wires, and opened the radiator flaps.

A few minutes later I saw the airfield. My mind had been so empty that I had gained height and navigated almost automatically. I had to make two circuits before I identified the narrow landing strip between the bomb craters and committed myself to a landing. Just as I was touching down, the engine began to misfire violently and then suddenly cut. I had got back on my last drops of petrol. The airfield looked dead and deserted as though it had already been abandoned by the group. All at once I knew that the end had come – irrevocably.

I had spent the afternoon with Kegel making arrangements for the transfer of the remnants of the group left in Trapani. Our assets were pitiful. The few stores were now exhausted and we had received no supplies of petrol or ammunition since the previous day. What we still possessed would have to be husbanded so that we would have enough for our serviceable machines when they took off on their last journey to the mainland. As regards the overland journey to Messina, prospects were reasonably favourable since it was likely that the northern coast road would remain clear of the enemy right up to the end.

At sunset we drove as usual up the mountain. When we reached the place where the road turned off to Erice village, I motioned Kegel to stop. He looked at me in surprise.

'We'd better take one more look at Trapani; it may be our last. And then we'll go and pass the time of day with the Italian group commander.'

He drove up the dusty road that zig-zagged to the summit, and halted in front of the Porta Trapani.

At this point the road described a wide sweep just below the craggy mountain top. A wall of massive rocks formed a parapet where, at this hour, large numbers of people had forgathered to enjoy the magnificent panorama. As it were from the dress circle of this splendid amphitheatre the spectators could observe the tragic events taking place upon the stage beneath them. They were not directly involved and, because the small, rocky eyrie that was their place of refuge had no strategic importance, they were relatively safe. Nevertheless the process they were witnessing was a historic one. The ruins of the bombed airfield symbolized not only the end of the German occupation, but also the piecemeal destruction of their homeland. The Allies had taken obvious pains to confine their attacks to military targets and it was not until the recent raids on Messina that they had departed from this principle. Here in Trapani the only occasions on which their bombs had devastated the villages or the parts of the town adjoining the airfield had been when our defending fighters or the heavy fire from the flak had spoilt their aim. And that, of course, had been happening frequently of late.

Many of Trapani's citizens had taken refuge in the small mountain parish. The houses were overflowing with grown-ups and with children of all sizes. Now in the cool of the evening they had come out to take the air and the narrow roads were animated. People were standing in groups, talking and gesticulating, but it was not as it had used to be. They had grown more or less accustomed to the war in the air and had quickly returned to their usual occupations in spite of the continuous threat of raids. Now, however, there was a growing tenseness about their conversations and their faces plainly betrayed their disquiet. They sensed that a change was in the offing, a transition to a new state of affairs. And the days ahead in which all this was to happen were full of menace. The fate of their houses and villages, indeed of the whole island, was reaching a point of crisis. Was their town to become a battlefield? Would the victors be humane? Would peace and quiet at last return? Questions and rumour were rife among these volatile people who were always prepared to believe the unbelievable if it was put to them convincingly enough. As we walked down the crowded alleyway, the conversations died down. Some gave us hostile glances; others turned their backs, but for the most part the faces expressed a stolid fatalism.

The house where the Italian group commander had his head-quarters was situated at the edge of the small park which contained the remains of the mountain *castello*. Inside, the air was refreshingly cool for the thick walls of the entrance hall did not permit the heat to penetrate. The colourful tiles on the floor and the valuable tapestries gave one the impression of entering a castle. Through the glass doors at the far end of the hall there was a magnificent view of the bay spread out at the foot of the mountain.

The colonel received us in the drawing-room. He was a man to whom the weight of his massive body was obviously a burden. When, I wondered, had this pilot last laid hands on a control column? He wheezed and panted for air while inundating us with a stream of compliments and meaningless courtesies. Without giving us time to answer he clapped his hands in oriental fashion and ordered coffee from the mess waiter who appeared in the doorway. Then he steered me towards the window and, flinging out his arms, cried enthusiastically: 'Isn't that a magnificent view?'

I could agree with him there. As we sat down at the low table, I began to feel some sympathy for this man. He kept giving me imploring glances as though hoping that things would take a turn for the better as a result of my visit. He informed me that he had just been speaking to his army corps in Corleone – to the general himself, whom he had told about the gallantry of the fighter pilots in the face of the enemy's superior strength. But he had also complained that he and his group were being neglected, for no one informed him about the situation or gave him any warning of the enemy's approach. His telephone – here he pointed at an ancient Italian field telephone with its wooden box standing on a map-covered table – was the only link with his army corps, indeed with any of his superiors. His radio set, intended to keep him in touch with his air force superiors, was old and virtually useless. It took an entire day to have a radio message confirmed so that his information was always a day old. Major Visconti, he continued – 'an excellent man, a *really* excellent man' – had urged him to ask us for assistance. Visconti was in despair through perpetually seeing the German fighter units take off in good time or else evacuate their airfields before the arrival of the bombers.

What means did we use, the *colonello* wanted to know, to detect the approach of the enemy? He spoke in a way that suggested we were in possession of supernatural secrets. He went on to ask whether we would be prepared to include the Chinisia wing in our communications net.

Then he began furiously winding the handle of his telephone to demonstrate how this one link with his superiors worked. He was lucky, for it really didn't work; the line had obviously been cut again. After a few minutes of fruitless effort he raised despairing eyes to heaven and resignedly dropped the receiver.

I promised him my immediate help and proposed that Visconti's operations room should be linked with my own so that his wing could receive timely reports not only from our monitoring section on Mount Erice but also from the direction finders near Marsala.

This arrangement should, of course, have been made weeks before but we had been too busy rebuilding the group after the defeat in Tunisia to pay heed to our Italian allies. For their part the Italians may possibly have been too proud to ask for any kind of co-operation. It struck me that they were all still somehow living in the First World War. My encounter with the colonel confirmed my impression that the Italian commanders had failed entirely to understand the technological aspects of this war, indeed could not understand them because they had grown too old and were no longer capable either mentally or physically.

I tried to explain to him that although we could arrange for these things to be done, it would be to little purpose since the enemy was already on the island and our airfields had been virtually destroyed. Hence there was little or no question of planned operations in the air. I was on the point of telling him that we were getting ready to leave the island and that the two of us, the captain and myself, had spent the entire afternoon preparing to evacuate the most important part of my group, its people. But something prevented me telling him the truth. If he was still in touch with his army corps – and in this respect he was better off than I was – someone would inform him whether he might leave his post or whether, in the knowledge that he had done his duty, he should surrender to the Americans.

However, he seemed to have little taste for realistic forecasts about the immediate future. He quickly switched to matters of a purely conversational nature, becoming all of a sudden relaxed and almost cheerful – a change which, in view of the situation, seemed to me almost uncanny. Soon afterwards we took our leave of the colonel who again expressed his effusive thanks.

As we walked up the road to the fort in the gathering dusk, we talked about our depressing experience and about poor old Visconti.

'I expect the colonel will want a bit of a rest now,' I said. 'He seemed quite done in, and it can't have been easy for him to ask favours of us Germans. But we've got to stop regarding ourselves as superior. We're not all that marvellous now. Better to help Visconti at once before it's too late.'

Tall aerials rose above the tower of the *castello*. Our monitoring section had installed its equipment in tents beside the tower and there they listened in to the enemy's radio messages both in speech and morse. Through being in direct contact with these specialists and their evaluations, my group was informed in good time of the matters that most concerned them. Sergeant Henrich, who was in charge of the monitoring section, had been born in Canada and English was his mother tongue. We were bound by close ties of mutual confidence.

'What are our pals up to now?' I asked.

'There's so much traffic, sir, there's hardly time to cope with it all. And it's building up all the time. Looks as though more and more units are pouring into this area. Just listen to the racket! English, American, Canadian – fighter-bombers from Pantelleria, Spitfires from Malta! They're all on the air.'

'Able three this is Baker one . . .' It came through loud and clear. In the background I could hear another Englishman calmly testing his set. 'One, two, three, four, how do you read me?'

'Our old Marauder friends are about again, sir,' he said. 'Remember the lot who were so inconsiderate that time at La Fauconrie?'

It was not an exploit of which I cared to be reminded. At that time, having just taken over command of the group, I had been at pains to earn their respect as quickly as possible. The event in question I regarded as a set-back to these efforts.

We had just returned from a mission – my second in Africa – and I was far from satisfied either with myself or with the way things had gone. My new group's flying methods were unlike those to which I had become accustomed in Russia. It was not that they were in any way timid or cowardly, but they failed to respond when, having quickly detected a favourable position, I tried to make them take advantage of it. They first sniffed the air in all directions, knowing from experience that Spitfires were usually where one least expected them to be. I had bungled the attack, lost control of the group and was thoroughly disgruntled when I returned to the airfield.

As I was about to climb into the operations vehicle at the edge of the landing ground the duty officer informed me that Henrich wished to speak to me. The sergeant told me that the usual Marauders had left Tebessa and were on their way to bomb La Fauconrie – or so he had gathered from their R/T exchanges. Without more ado I got into the Kübelwagen saying: 'I've no intention of staying here and playing the hero. I'm going over to the olive grove.' And with that I drove off.

The grove was a shady plantation of palms and olive trees in which Group HQ had pitched its tents. There, too, was the caravan inherited from my predecessor in which Straden, Bachmann and I used to sleep. And the grove also contained a grand piano – standing unceremoniously in the sand – upon which Lieutenant Merkel used to entertain us every evening.

It was two miles or more from the airfield and I was in no hurry. The throb of approaching aircraft engines brought me to a halt a short distance from the caravan. At the same moment I heard the whistle of falling bombs and only just had time to leap for an irrigation ditch barely deep enough to protect me. From that position I enjoyed the doubtful pleasure of 'playing the hero' amid a downpour of small high-explosive bombs.

When at last I was able to get up, I found the Kübel standing where I had left it. The tires had burst but the engine was still running. Our tents, however, presented a pitiful sight. The fragments had ripped through the canvas, through our camp-beds and packs, and water was spurting out of punctured containers. Miraculously enough the caravan had remained undamaged, but the piano's career as a musical instrument was over, its strings a knotted tangle of twisted wire.

When I returned to the operations vehicle beside the airfield I was received with broad grins and unconcealed glee.

'There's nothing to laugh about!' I exclaimed. 'Just you try being bombed when you're flat on your face in a shallow ditch that barely protects your backside!'

'Immediately after you'd started back for the grove, sir, Henrich rang through. We wrote down what he'd monitored.'

The operations room duty officer handed me a piece of paper which read: 'This is lead, this is lead, we are going to aim at the small wood north of the field, it probably houses the staff.'

As we drove down the mountain slope along the narrow, white-gravelled road that led to the villa, darkness began to fall. It was the hour of deceptive calm when the day attacks were over and the night raids had not yet begun. War or no war, it was the best time of day in Sicily, though the atmosphere at sunrise could sometimes be even more lovely.

Bachmann was standing outside the operations room. He informed me that Godert and Zöhler had already landed and would be arriving in a few minutes' time.

The group had lost four pilots that day, including the second lieutenant who had crashed during our attack on the enemy column near Gela. No 3 Wing had left for Sardinia, as ordered.

The Kübelwagen arrived with Godert and his squadron commander, Zöhler. They screwed up their eyes as they came into the brightly lit hut, where they immediately began to dictate their combat report.

While Kegel, Tarnow and I were discussing the final details of the move, Bachmann went over to join Godert and Zöhler, in his hand a bulbous bottle of dark, heavy Marsala. After a while he turned to me asking:

'Like a go, sir?'

I nodded, accepted the proffered bottle and took a long pull. It was this kind of small gesture that eased the tension from which we all suffered and which we could shake off only for short intervals.

'A pre-dinner aperitif,' said Godert, watching me drink.

Bachmann gave a mirthless laugh.

'I have a feeling it'll be our last dinner in this particular hotel!' he said and, as an idea suddenly struck him, continued, 'Why not celebrate by eating in the villa instead of sitting in that gloomy old grotto?'

'What about the Wellingtons?' objected Zöhler.

'To hell with that. The place is still standing. Why should it be hit tonight of all nights?' Turning to me, he said, 'Suppose we invite the two prisoners, sir? Considering they're lucky to be alive at all, they might care to celebrate as well.'

'Very well,' I said. 'Ask them. It might be amusing. Anyway, I've got a feeling we'll soon be changing places with them. It'll give Tubby a chance to show what he can do. In any case he won't be able to take his hoard of titbits away with him. We'll have a party for once.'

Bachmann was already enthusiastically winding the telephone to arrange for the festive meal. In spite of all the frightfulness these men had experienced in this war, their youthful high spirits were so effervescent that they kept on breaking through.

I asked about the prisoners.

'We're not sure whether they're English or Canadian. At the moment they're being interrogated through an interpreter. But they're keeping their mouths shut.'

When, an hour later, I entered my room down at the villa, I found Tubby had put a bowlful of water ready for me.

'Supply's been cut off again,' he said.

As it happened, the electricity and water supply had been kept going for most of the time during the past weeks of bombardment in a way that was little short of miraculous.

On going through to the dining-room, I found that Tubby had indeed performed wonders. Between the balcony and the wall with the oval mirror he had set up a long table. It was covered with a white tablecloth (a sheet, of course), and was festively laid with plates, cutlery and glasses. There were two candlesticks containing slim candles whose light was reflected back from the oval mirror, and the centre of the table was decorated with bougainvillea in tumblers.

When I entered, those already seated rose to their feet, thus beginning our 'dinner' in truly ceremonial fashion. Standing round the table were Godert and Zöhler, Dr. Sperrling, von Köster, Kegel and Zahn.

At the same moment the other door opened and Bachmann, speaking his schoolboy English, politely ushered in the two prisoners.

Germans and British, we stood there staring across at each other. Maybe they were thinking – quite erroneously of course – that we had stood up in their honour.

The Canadian was slim, almost lanky, with a good physique and an open expression. His flight lieutenant's uniform, consisting of bleached khaki drill trousers and a shirt with rolled-up sleeves, was reasonably clean. The English sergeant was small and thickset by comparison, with a freckled face and close-cropped reddish hair. His uniform shorts were much too baggy for our taste, and he wore stockings up to the knee. We had placed them next to one another, but each behaved as though the other did not exist. We could not make out whether this was due to their difference in rank or to the fact that one was Canadian and the other English. As they sat down, they eyed us suspiciously. Heaven knows what stories they'd been told about us Huns; now perhaps they were discovering to their surprise that the enemy was made of just the same stuff as any other human being.

The menu Tubby had devised was a substantial one. His excellence lay not so much in culinary refinements as in the variety he provided. The pièce de résistance consisted of two large dishes of scrambled egg mixed with Italian tinned meat of the variety known as 'old man' [*Alter Mann*] from the letters AM (*Administrazione Militare*) stamped on the tins. Besides this there were dishes and plates piled with tunnyfish, tinned sardines and anchovies, liver sausage, tinned ham, Italian saveloys and tomatoes.

We enjoyed our food in spite of our exhaustion and we talked little as we ate. The prisoners answered our questions politely but laconically and retreated into their shells the moment any military topic was raised. They too were enjoying the unexpected banquet.

A great deal was drunk that night. No sooner was anyone's glass empty than Tubby filled it again.

'Drink it now and we won't have to pour it away when we leave,' he said, himself suiting action to word. Suddenly Bachman remarked:

'We've lost the Storch, sir.'

I wondered how long he'd been brooding over the bad news before plucking up courage to break it to me.

'Sergeant Schulz wrote it off. He was on duty in the ops room when he suddenly caught sight of these two floating down by parachute. The Storch was on the small airstrip so he dashed down and took off to collect the prisoners. One of them, the flight lieutenant, had landed on the side of Erice. Schulz thought he'd found a suitable field but it turned out to be too steep. He lost his horizon, stalled and crashed. So that was that.'

What was there to say? Once I'd have exclaimed 'Amateur!' or 'Rabbit!' or 'Some people never learn . . .' But now it didn't really seem to matter. So much was being lost; what was one Storch more or less? But Bachmann didn't share that opinion.

'We could certainly have used it,' he said.

'But supposing no one gives us the order to move?'

'Then we shan't need a Storch!'

'And we shan't be turned into infantry on the eastern front either!'

It was a bitter remark of the kind they had been making since the arrival of the notorious teleprint. Everyone was aware of its contents although nothing had been said officially.

But no one took up the cue. Apart from the fact that there was no point in venting our anger yet again, the presence of the prisoners precluded such talk. They sat there behaving very correctly, and eating rather to conceal their embarrassment than because they were hungry.

When at last everyone had finished, Tubby cleared away the remains while we went on drinking and smoking. We were all tired after a day of futile battles in which, while achieving virtually nothing, we had nevertheless lost four pilots. Everyone was secretly waiting for the order that would deliver us, if it was not already too late, and determine our fate.

I forgot how the subject of Stalingrad suddenly cropped up. Perhaps because someone had said 'Sicily is the Stalingrad of the south', or words to that effect. At any rate I soon found myself talking about Stalingrad. The conversation died down and the company, including the two prisoners, began listening attentively, although it was impossible to tell whether the latter could understand.

'So long as it was possible to land,' I told them, 'and the range of our Messerschmitts permitting, I kept on shuttling to and fro between our advanced airfields and the Volga pocket. Putting down on a minute patch of steppe was always a great strain and these makeshift airstrips were often under fire from the Russian guns and multiple rocket launchers – the Stalin organs. One of our nightmares was having to jump for cover, leaving our aircraft to be shot at by the enemy and set ablaze. The infantry were used to their earthbound role: they had their companies and platoons; they had learnt how to fight this sort of battle, and land warfare was their element. We pilots, however, were helpless when deprived of our aircraft and left exposed on the ground. Our combat value was negligible; we were incapable of assessing the hazards correctly; we were over-respectful of each oncoming shell – in short, we did everything wrong. Hence, whenever possible, I avoided visiting those small airstrips within range of the Russian artillery.

'Our custom was to keep low when flying towards Stalingrad up the roads – or rather, tracks – across the steppe along which our troops were advancing, and the infantry would go wild with joy and wave frantically whenever they saw us. It was summertime then and the leading tanks were sending up great clouds of dust high into the clear air.

'Later on we began to support the battle for the city, escorting the Stukas and the He-111 bombers. Never before had we found the hunting as good as it was then, for the Russians were throwing in every fighter they possessed so as to protect their troops against the dreaded Stukas. We marked up victory after victory on our rudder units and felt extremely pleased with ourselves. We didn't know yet what we had let ourselves in for.

'Before long there was a change in the pattern of our operations. Instead of bombers and Stukas we now escorted the transport aircraft which were already having to fly long distances over enemy territory to reach their destination. The army, having been surrounded, had established airfields in the pocket for the reception of supplies. On the eastern front it was by no means unusual for a large formation to be temporarily encircled by the enemy and no one seemed unduly concerned. To those of us, however, who could observe the development of the situation as a whole, and had to calculate daily on our maps the number of miles to be flown, the worrying aspect was the ever increasing distance between the front itself and the Stalingrad pocket. More and more of our time was spent escorting the old Ju transports, a job we found deeply depressing. It was almost worse than the demise of the Jus here in the Mediterranean, just before we capitulated in Tunis. The heavily laden Junkers couldn't climb higher than 10,000 feet – the ideal height for the medium anti-aircraft guns of which the Russians had whole brigades. Any deviation from course was precluded primarily by the short range of our fighters but also by the widening gap between the Junkers' departure points and the Pitomnik airstrip west of Stalingrad. Hence they had to fly along a veritable avenue of anti-aircraft fire for the whole time they were over enemy territory. We were able, of course, to keep the Russian fighters at bay but we could do nothing to protect our charges against the ground defences.

'When the first snowflakes began to fall we moved south, to the Kalmuk Steppe, to assist in the attempt to break through to Stalingrad. It was a very long way now to Pitomnik and we could no longer fly escort so that the Junkers and Heinkels and Dorniers had to make their own roundabout way under cover of night. Each time I flew over the dried-out ravines near Stalingrad I could see the grey forms of German soldiers, crowded together in their thousands in those death-traps.

'Many others beside myself saw disaster looming ever closer, especially when winter came and the army was exposed without protection to the icy blizzards. It was plain to see that ammunition and supplies were running low, but had not the Reichsmarschall proclaimed: "The Luftwaffe, my Führer, will assume responsibility for supplies to the Sixth Army at Stalingrad"?

'A pilot can watch a battle in every phase of its development as though on a sand-table. Each morning when he makes his first flight over the terrain he observes the changes that have taken place at the front and can estimate what the ground forces can or cannot do, and what the prospects are for attack or defence. He acquires a practised eye from his years of experience on different fronts. We were more aware than the people on the ground of the tremendous distances involved, perhaps because to us they represented real measurements which we had to calculate daily. All at once we realized that we had been swallowed up in the limitless expanse of this steppe. We would arrive somewhere in that expanse at a place without a name, a place where our Junkers

H

had set down our mechanics and from where they had taken off again to return with barrels of fuel. Thereafter it became an advanced landing ground and it acquired a name: Gigant, for example, or Gumrak, or something wholly unpronounceable.

'By now it was impossible for the Junkers to land in the pocket, so rations were being dropped from the air. When the bags contained crispbread in white cardboard boxes they weighed practically nothing, and once there was even a supply of Christmas confectionery – this a present from the home front.

'Shortly before Christmas a powerful spearhead consisting of infantry and armour began to move up along either side of the railway across the Kalmuk Steppe by way of Kotelnikovo and Zimovniki in an attempt to reach the encircled army. We felt highly optimistic about the outcome and were in the air from dawn to dusk. Rarely have I been engaged in an operation in which I was so emotionally involved. We were in constant radio communication with the Sixth Army and listened to the reports they sent out to assist the relief operation. These often proved a great help, for the Russian air force was concentrating all its efforts on this vital point and caused heavy casualties among the beleaguered men whenever it managed to carry out ground attacks or release its bombs.

'A typical message would be: "Grain-silo signals section calling – swarms of fighters and bombers over Pitomnik." And in the evening we would hear: "Till tomorrow morning then. Please come back again."

'On 16 December the Red Army broke through the Italian and Rumanian positions on the Don. The 6th Panzer Division – the spearhead of the relief operation – was pulled out. The attack ground to a halt and Operation Winter Storm, of which we had had such high hopes, had come to nothing. Towards evening on that day, flying northwards along the railway line, I fell in with a long column of white-painted tanks on the outsides of which were clusters of soldiers in white parkas. I went down low in order to identify myself and suddenly met with a savage hail of machine-gun fire. To my horror I realized that they were Russian tanks and that they were moving south at high speed in the direction of our airfield on the steppe.

'I attacked twice, exhausted my ammunition and radioed for help. We did what we could, but I can hardly suppose we made much impression on those T-34 tanks.

'While we were attacking we could hear in our headphones the voice of the signaller in the grain silo, repeating at short intervals and almost in a whisper: "Grain silo Stalingrad calling. Are you receiving me? Please come!"

'But no one answered him any more. That same night we made a hasty move to an advanced landing ground in the south.'

Throughout the dinner the little Englishman had sat stiffly in his chair. He had drunk no alcohol. Every now and again, in an attempt to dispel the awkwardness, someone would ask him a question in broken English, to which he would answer politely, 'Yes, sir,' or 'No, sir.' His Canadian companion had at first confined himself to occasional sips, saying 'cheers' whenever someone raised his glass to him. But later he began drinking in earnest while Tubby, without batting an eyelid, kept refilling his glass. A small tumbler of brandy had been placed in front of him and this he drank at one gulp when I raised my glass to him to drink his health.

Godert reached out an unsteady hand for a bottle of red wine but Zöhler placed it out of his reach.

'You're drinking more than you can carry. You'd better ask Tubby for a strong coffee.'

'I'm cold stone sober,' Gobert murmured sadly, as his right elbow swept a glass off the table leaving a large pool of red wine which gradually began to seep into the tablecloth.

'Bachmann, the prisoners had better go back now,' I said. I bade them farewell with a nod which they returned unsmilingly.

'Come on, boys,' said Bachmann, leading the two men to the door where they stopped for a moment to wish us goodnight.

The room was full of cigarette smoke. We sat on the cane sofas and chairs, our shirts open at the neck and our sleeves rolled up, wiping the sweat from our faces with the backs of our hands. Every now and then a bottle glugged as glasses were replenished. Through the closed shutters came the drone of the Wellingtons' engines and, at irregular intervals, the thud of an explosion.

No one paid any attention to their random bombing. The probability that they would hit the villa was so remote as to be absurd. We had become extraordinarily indifferent to everything, taking hardly any interest, for example, in what was happening at home. Here, events followed upon each other so quickly that nobody had time to think about them, and then again one day might seem as long as a year. Who could dare think of tomorrow and plan ahead? We had become used to the futile rhythm of the war, and lived only for the next flight, the afternoon's operation or, at the very most, for the following morning. What the day after that might bring was, to us, a matter of complete indifference, for the time between now and then seemed an eternity.

We had all got so accustomed to Freiberg and his astringent manner that his absence continued to cast a gloom over us. We could not help wondering if he were still alive, whether he had had a period of freedom after coming down by parachute or whether he had fallen straight into American hands. We speculated about it endlessly but I, for one, felt little hope. On evenings of this kind, Bachmann and Straden had been inseparable. They had invariably had a great deal to say to each other during their whispered conversations and for this reason had contributed little to the general talk. It had been Freiberg who had set the tone. Now that Straden, too, was gone, wounded and evacuated, Bachmann had withdrawn into a corner where he sat silently, with eyes downcast. It almost looked as though he was trying to put a physical distance between himself and the rest of us and wanted to be left alone, at least for this one evening.

Zöhler was virtually monopolizing the conversation. His tone was sarcastic and bitter and Godert, sitting beside him, punctuated his companion's savage remarks with emphatic nods. He looked ill, his eyelids reddened by drink or, perhaps, tiredness. Intermittently Zöhler would burst out laughing like a maniac.

'We're despised, my lads! Doesn't that split your sides? Despised by all the other fighter boys. Godert's despised – d'you hear that Godert? They despise you. And Freiberg as well if he's still alive. If he's dead, of course, he's a hero, a despised hero. The only good fighter pilot is a dead fighter pilot . . .'

Suddenly and unexpectedly Bachmann flared up.

'Shut up!' he snapped. 'You'll get nowhere talking like that. Reduction to the ranks and a transfer to the eastern front as ordinary infantry might be the best we can expect – if they leave us together, that is.'

'You haven't a clue,' Zöhler answered harshly. 'You don't know what they do to cowards. They post you to a punishment battalion among others of your own kind – men summarily convicted, deserters, defeatists. They even send real criminals to these outfits so that they can get some use out of them. And it's always the really poisonous sectors they shove you into. The only difference, actually, is that instead of resting your bottom on a pilot's seat you're lying in the muck with your blunderbuss at your side . . .'

It was time to put an end to this talk. In deliberately loud and formal tones I said:

'What are tomorrow's orders, Captain Kegel?'

Kegel, understanding at once, stood up and replied briskly:

'We've been trying for hours to contact the Fighter Leader or Air Corps by radio and telephone. But so far without success, sir. No doubt we'll have to fly a dawn reconnaissance tomorrow morning, probably to Cape Bon, Pantelleria, Malta and over the beach-heads . . .'

He was going on to discuss the details of what we could and might do the following day, when I motioned to him to stop. I got up and went across to the door leading to my room. As I closed it behind me I saw that Bachmann and Godert had fallen asleep.

'The morale of the civilian population was very low because of Allied air bombardments and the restricted food supply – the rationing system had broken down, and black market operations were widespread. The people wanted only an end to the war.'

UNITED STATES ARMY IN WORLD WAR II
SICILY AND THE SURRENDER OF ITALY

'Teleprint from the Fighter Leader to the Commanding Officer, 77th Fighter Group: "The western portion of Sicily will be evacuated. 77th Fighter Group will fly all serviceable aircraft to the mainland forthwith. Ground personnel will be despatched to Milazzo by way of the north coast without delay. The Führer's orders that no soldier may leave the island are still in force." '

WAR DIARY, 77TH FIGHTER GROUP

13 July 1943

I was woken by movements in the next room. Tubby was laying the breakfast table. Bright daylight filtered in through the slats of the shutters. It was five o'clock.

I reached for the telephone receiver and turned the handle.

'Get me the ops room please.'

'Operations room speaking, Captain Kegel.'

'Is there anything fresh to report? How many aircraft can we put in the air?'

'We haven't had any orders yet, either from Corps or from the Fighter Leader. It's been impossible to establish radio contact and we're never in telephone communication for more than a few minutes at a time. And we still don't know yet how many serviceable machines we have.'

Our few remaining aeroplanes were dispersed over four air-fields, Trapani, Sciacca and the two advanced landing grounds. Prospects were bleak since we had no more spares. We could not send up aircraft against the enemy if their radios were faulty, their brakes useless or their armament badly harmonized. Such were the technical laws of aerial warfare by which we were governed. The reconnaissance patrols would soon be back from Tunisia, Pantelleria and Malta. At present the Allied bombing attacks were being directed exclusively against the eastern part of the island. According to the radio monitoring service, bomber formations were already approaching the Straits of Messina.

'I'll be at the ops room in half an hour.'

'Very well, sir.'

The French windows leading onto the balcony were wide open and the morning sun cast a brilliant rectangle of light across

H*

the breakfast table and onto the wall beyond with its big looking-glass. Tubby had laid the table sparingly. On the bare wood, thick Wehrmacht-pattern china cups stood saucerless, beside each one a knife. Evidently he had packed up everything else for the move, though he could have had no idea how he was going to transport it. The leaves of the bougainvillea in the tumblers were drooping. At the sight of them I recalled our 'dinner' of the previous night.

Bachmann rose as I entered. He was wearing freshly-washed tropical uniform and behind his chair stood a bulging pilot's holdall of blue canvas equipped with a pair of straps so that it could be carried on his back.

Tubby poured out the coffee and busied himself about the table in order to listen to what we were saying, afraid that we might leave him here alone or even forget him. As I listlessly sipped my black coffee my eye happened to light on the *Adler im Süden*, Air Fleet's forces' newspaper, which Bachmann had brought back from Gerbini.

It was the 10th July edition and its front page, crumpled and coffee stained, carried headlines about 'the heroic defensive battle' and the resolve 'to drive the enemy back into the sea'.

How disgusting, I thought, that they should disseminate catch-phrases like that, when everyone knew that none of it was true.

We drove to the operations room without meeting a soul. As though aware that their sufferings were nearly over and that we would have to pull out, the Sicilians were keeping indoors. Hence absolute peace reigned in the countryside through which we drove, the only discordant notes being the rattling of our Kübelwagen and the noise of its engine.

From the white gable end of a house at the entrance to the village enormous letters proclaimed: '*Noi tireremo diritto.*'

By now the pilots on the dawn reconnaissance patrols had returned. They reported a great deal of seaborne traffic between Tunisia and Pantelleria – presumably supply vessels. Fighters had taken off from Pantelleria as they had flown over the island.

The airfield had been packed with single-engine machines – Thunderbolts. So secure did the enemy feel there that they had not even made use of the rock shelters previously built by the Italians.

No I had reconnoitred the sea area as far as Malta. According to their report, cruisers and destroyers were making their way to the scene of the landings. Off Gela itself small craft were shuttling busily between the larger vessels, some of which were lying at anchor in a great semicircle round the beach-head while others were steaming to and fro.

Just as I was trying for the umpteenth time to estimate the number of Mes we could put into the air, Bachmann came out of the hut with the message pad in his hand.

'This has just come in via Corleone, sir,' he said, and in a loud voice – loud enough, in fact, for everyone to hear – he began to read: ' "The western portion of Sicily will be evacuated. 77th Fighter Group will fly all serviceable aircraft to the mainland forthwith. Ground personnel will be despatched to Milazzo by way of the north coast without delay. The Führer's orders that no soldier may leave the island are still in force. Fighter Leader, Sicily." '

So it had been decided. Perhaps this order was the result of Larsen's unobtrusive work behind the scenes. It amounted in fact to an admission by the high command that yet another battle had been lost. But oddly enough its effect was not in the least demoralizing. On the contrary, the future once again seemed to hold out some prospect – of a new beginning, perhaps, or maybe even of victory. Such is the effect on soldiers of an unequivocal order.

'What's the time?'

'Eight-thirty.'

'Kegel, pass the order on to No I in Sciacca; they'll have to look sharp if they're going to get to Milazzo in time. And you'd better start destroying the equipment.'

As if intending to close this particular chapter, the Marauders appeared from the north over Mount Erice. Henrich reported that he had picked up their R/T wavelength and, even as he was speaking, the flak went into action.

But the bombers' aim was bad. Their entire load went to plough up the olive grove at the end of the airfield, tearing the roofs off one or two cottages. Then the flak stopped firing and the men went about their business again as though nothing had happened.

We wondered how far the Americans had got. The Fighter Leader's message had come to us via several relay stations since we were no longer in regular communication with the east. We would have to hurry if our transport was not to be cut off. Should the Americans have pushed on northwards as far as the coast road, it would mean the end of the group.

I wondered what to do next, and decided there was nothing for me to do except relax in my deck-chair under the awning outside the hut and wait until the work of destruction was complete and everything had been burnt, blown up or smashed to smithereens. It was absolutely pointless to attempt any further sorties.

I would watch them take off one after the other to fly to the mainland and then I would be free, relieved of responsibility – for a few days I'd be out of contact, out of action, out of service and out of the running.

Once again bombers would lay waste this already scarred landscape, bringing home to the Sicilians the fact that our last hour had come. The tall, hatchet-faced Germans with their self-confident demeanour who behaved as though they owned the whole island along with its mixture of races, its colourful, animated and, by comparison, pygmy-sized inhabitants – those Germans would now be forced to retreat.

The crunching of tires on gravel shook me out of my meditation. Personnel carriers and trucks had drawn up on the narrow strip of level ground and, under Kegel's instructions, airmen were collecting and loading the radio equipment and the most essential items from the operations room. Rolls of cable and telephones were heaped up outside the entrance to the tunnel leading to the half-finished cave in the cliff that was to have been our bomb-proof shelter. For days the pneumatic hammers, drills and picks had lain idle. Each time there was a bombing attack we would hurry across the mounds of yellow rock rubble into the cool protection of the dark tunnel, each time finding there the same workmen in their dusty, sombre clothes huddled silently in a corner, sheltering like ourselves from the bombing.

They would accept the proffered cigarette with a *'grazie'* and a little bow, generally tucking it away under their sweat-stained caps. Latterly they had stopped talking when we entered, but the expression in their eyes was not one of triumph at our defeat. Rather, it betrayed the knowledge that the end had come, that we were about to withdraw.

Today they were standing in the scorching sun on the scree outside the cave, attentively watching our destructive activities. They moved away a little when Kegel put a match to the mountain of paper – teleprints and reports, correspondence with the Fighter Leader, with Corps, with Air Fleet and so forth – that had been piled up near the cave. Great tongues of flame shot up into clear morning air, every now and again carrying with them some important document whose charred remains would land high above on the rock face before gliding down into the valley like a child's paper aeroplane.

The workmen waited in stoical silence, their eyes fastened on the hut. They had placed their water jugs, wrapped in damp rags, in the shadow of the cliff next to baskets containing cheese and tomatoes. 'They're surely not going to set fire to the hut?' their expressions seemed to say. 'And we can use every scrap of that wire,' or again, 'Push off and be quick about it – we've got time enough, we'll be staying here . . .'

'What shall we do about the hut?' Kegel asked.

'Nothing,' I said. 'Leave it for the workmen.'

Bachmann came back from the villa, brakes squealing as he pulled up in front of the operations room. With him he brought my travelling kit – the shabby brown leather suitcase and my sleeping-bag.

He told me that Tubby had been most reluctant to board the truck and leave behind all the treasures he had hoarded.

'I found him in the garden, surrounded by empty wine and brandy crates, filling in a trench he had dug. He'd been making a cache because, he said, "There's no knowing we won't come back again." '

The girl, Teresa, had sat inscrutable in front of the grotto observing the hectic coming and going. The doors and shutters of the neighbouring houses had remained closed as if their owners were purposely ignoring our departure – or rather our retreat.

Everything was very quiet and from the yellow sky the sun beat down mercilessly. Not a breath of wind came to stir the sticky, suffocating air. Every now and then we could hear the airmen shouting instructions to each other on the airfield below. Suddenly I became aware of the scene that was being enacted round the far side of the perimeter.

As if at a word of command, great tongues of flame leapt up in quick succession between the rows of olive trees. Above them dirty grey smoke rose in clouds which did not disperse but remained hanging there like huge balloons. Then I heard shouting and yelling. The work of destruction had begun. More trucks drew up on the level ground in front of the hut; their tail-boards fell open with a crash and soldiers jumped down onto the coarse gravel. Loudly urging each other on, they began to drag up rolls of wire and pieces of radio equipment.

An hour or so later I was woken by the operations clerk.

'The officer commanding the flak wishes to speak to you, sir.'

A captain in tropical uniform was standing in front of the hut. As I walked towards him he saluted with a hostile air. Hanging round his neck he wore a large pair of binoculars and at his hip, making his belt sag, an 08 pistol in a gleaming black leather holster.

'What kind of nonsense is going on down there, sir?' he asked. 'Did you give the order for all that senseless smashing and burning?'

'Yes, I did.'

'But surely you can't answer for what your chaps down there are doing?'

'I'm the best judge of that!' I replied coolly.

He was obviously finding it difficult to control himself.

'Look here, sir, my men are over in the emplacements standing by their guns. During the past few days we've had heavy casualties and as for sleep, we hardly know what it is. Now they're seeing your people pile up valuable equipment and pour petrol over it. They're seeing engines smashed to pieces and crates full of spares and tools destroyed, not to speak of tents and rations. It's utterly beyond us. We've got to stay here and fight while you push off.'

'Push off, you say? Do you propose to hold western Sicily with your battery?'

Suddenly the captain's expression changed.

'I don't propose to,' he said evenly, 'but if those are my orders it's what I'll have to do.'

Seeing him standing there in front of me, his demeanour faultless in spite of his intense annoyance, I recalled that, all through the period of incessant bombing, the eighty-eight millimetre flak stationed round the airfield had performed magnificently. Under the scorching rays of the sun, and even during the night, the gunners had had to manhandle their heavy shells and they could not, like us, take refuge in the trenches when the bombs were falling and the roaring carpet unrolled towards us destroying everything in its path.

'I can quite understand that you should be annoyed and upset,' I said without acerbity. 'I never ordered rations to be destroyed and I'll see it's stopped at once. If it hadn't been for you people they'd have finished us off in a couple of days. But what can we do except destroy everything we can't take with us? I hardly suppose you want some aircraft engines or a complete workshop?'

Still glowering, he shook his head. 'It'll play hell with discipline. All this burning and busting things up will end in panic and a general exodus.'

'You needn't worry,' I said bitterly. 'It's an exodus all right.

The western part of Sicily's to be evacuated, as no doubt you'll be told shortly.'

'But why does all this valuable stuff have to be destroyed?'

'I'll tell you why. Because I want to get every man across to the mainland. Because there's no room in the trucks for tools, engines and bumf. We can get more engines if we manage to cross the Straits of Messina, but we can't get new fitters, riggers or radio operators!'

Again he shook his head, looked angrily at me and replied:

'I don't understand . . . You're leaving us alone here – well and good, it's what you've been ordered to do. But before doing so you put up a display of unparalleled vandalism. Then you'll climb into your fast aeroplanes and an hour later you'll be safe in some peaceful backwater.'

He was giving vent to all the pent-up rage of the non-flier at what he believes to be the incredible privileges enjoyed by the 'cavalry of the air', the men who simply fly away leaving him to do the dirty work on the ground.

Ever since there has been an air arm it has been thus. The fighter pilots of the First World War were, in fact, recruited from exclusive cavalry regiments. In France they lived in fine châteaux and drank champagne as other men drink water. We, in 1940, had happily followed suit. We, too, had lived in châteaux, drunk champagne and, in contravention of all military dress regulations, had given free rein to our individual tastes, wearing floppy fur-lined boots and marvellous leather jackets taken from the enemy so as to mark ourselves off from the earthbound military.

The Reichsmarschall, himself conspicuous by reason of the extravagance and variety of his fancies, had detected this weakness of ours. In his impotence, he ruthlessly insulted those for whose desperate situation he alone was responsible: had he not contemptuously described the fighter pilots in France as the 'Silk Pyjama Squadrons'?

Possibly our affectation in this respect did go too far – rakish moustaches, say, or things like our yellow scarves, Freiberg's sandals and white stockings or, perhaps, a captured light brown belt with its natty 6.35 mm revolver. Maybe the non-fliers saw us in a rather different light. At 30,000 feet, up in the icy air, ours was an almost limitless battlefield, invisible to the naked eye. They saw us only when, clad in our unmilitary garments, we were on the ground relaxing in the intervals between patrols. But it never occurred to them that our next mission might involve an all-out attack such as every veteran had experienced hundreds of times.

The captain saluted, got into his car and drove away. He looked bitter and angry.

Below on the runway the first 109s were taxiing into the wind before taking off to fly to the mainland. I would supervise the work of destruction myself and make sure that the troops did not get too much out of hand.

The road that led down to the town was completely deserted. Outside the entrance to the airfield the bombing had made the lane impassable. I reached the perimeter track round the almost circular airfield by threading my way through gardens and the courtyards of ruined farms. The hangars and the administrative and flying control buildings lay in ruins, in front of them the charred skeleton of a burnt-out aircraft, a tangled mass of useless metal.

I turned south off the perimeter track and drove along a rutted sandy lane through several olive groves, before reaching a large open space where the workshops had once stood.

Even before I got there I could hear shouting as the men egged each other on round the voracious fire, symbol of senseless destruction. A black cloud of smoke rose high above the trees, where it fanned out like the top of a pine.

I drew up beside a gap in the cactus hedge, got out of the car and had just begun to wade through the soft sand when I was brought to a sudden halt by the sight that met my eyes. Where the workshop tent had once stood there blazed an incandescent bonfire of vast dimensions. The men from my group were circling nimbly round the pile whose flames they were feeding with the contents of the trucks that had been unloaded or tipped out at the edge of the field. The fresh fuel, as they hurled it into the fire, described a high arc and, on landing, sent out a shower of sparks over a wide area, while the flames roared like greedy animals.

There was something orgiastic about this dance round the fire. The troops were seizing hold of anything they could lay their hands on and yelling as they hurled it into the flames. Crates, chairs, tents, camp-beds, telephones, tools – everything, in fact, that serves to keep a group HQ and a fighter wing fit for action and to maintain it in battle. In one corner of the field they were piling up a huge heap of engines and metal components.

'Here, mate – a bit higher. When it's finished, we'll pour petrol over this lot!' yelled an NCO who was setting about the engines with a sledge hammer as though berserk. They were working at a tremendous pace for they knew that only when they had finished would they be able to leave for Messina and thus perhaps avoid being captured. But if the Lightnings and Kittyhawks discovered the convoy, it might well be the last trip many of these men would make.

'Watch out! Ammo!'

One of the men had swung round a wooden box and sent it hurtling with all his might into the flames.

'You're out of your mind!' I shouted.

But my voice was drowned by the din. And suddenly bullets were whizzing and whistling in all directions like fireworks. Looking about me I saw that everyone was lying flat on their stomachs or had taken cover behind earth ramparts.

I told an officer to see that things were done in more orderly fashion. Yet had it, I asked myself, really been any different three months before in Tunisia? And was it in fact possible to carry out such senseless destruction in disciplined and orderly fashion?

The crackling of the flames and the 'vrrp' and 'fft' of the exploding ammunition seemed to fill the troops with inordinate glee.

Not far away, behind the next cactus hedge, it was clear that other wreckers were at work, for I could see another cloud of smoke rising up. Just as the exploding ammunition had begun to spend itself another truck drove in through the narrow gap, loaded with equipment and gear of all kinds. Crates and boxes, hammers, pulleys, batteries, shovels, steel helmets, tires and ropes were hastily thrown to the back of the lorry and tipped on to the ground or else sent flying in a high arc into the fire. All was hurry and bustle. There was no time to be lost!

Then I became aware of the observers hidden behind the agave hedges – the occupants of the nearby farms. Every now and then a figure would creep out from among the cactus bushes, dart forward a yard or two and grab a rope, a tarpaulin or a box before scurrying back to safety with his loot.

I could hear Captain Kegel's hoarse voice roaring out orders. Becoming aware of my presence, he said:

'Nearly finished, sir. Another two truckloads. But the Eyties are pinching stuff like jackdaws.'

His arms were covered with soot to the elbows and his tropical shirt was soaked with sweat. Indeed, the heat close to the fire was unendurable.

'Can I start sending the trucks that aren't needed any more to Milazzo?'

'Of course. Start right away. They'll be safer if they get off individually.'

When I got back to the operations room I found Bachmann, Zöhler and Tarnow sitting in deck-chairs under the awning. The baggage they were going to take with them stood ready at their side and across Bachmann's knees was spread a map of Sicily and southern Italy.

Tubby, in full marching order, was sitting on the steps of the hut. As soon as he saw me he began unwrapping packages of bread, cheese and ham which he set out on tin plates on a stool. Nearby stood the big radio truck, its doors open, waiting for the order to leave. Tubby kept a wary eye on it, since he was to leave with the signallers as soon as their services could be dispensed with.

'Better get moving,' I said, turning to Bachmann and Zöhler.

243

'Take off now and report to our rear base at Foggia. In two or three days' time we'll know where we'll be operating from over there.'

I heard Bachmann mutter something. It could have been: 'I'd like to fly with you, sir,' or 'Why aren't you coming with us?'

But they both got up, shouldered their rucksacks and, burdened as they were, attempted an indifferent salute before trudging across to their Kübelwagen.

The heavy noonday hours passed slowly. Down on the airfield the fires had been put out. Every now and then aircraft took off, singly or in pairs.

The Marauders had not put in another appearance since early morning, as though they knew that our end was near and that we no longer presented a worthwhile target. The 109s had left and the transport was on its way to Milazzo. I now gave orders for the departure of the radio vehicle whereupon Tubby jumped nimbly onto the running-board and disappeared through the door.

A Kübel, with two somnolent mechanics inside it, stood ready to take me down to the airfield as soon as I made up my mind to start. My mission here was over. The burden of responsibility had suddenly been lifted from me. I had been given permission to destroy the group, to smash it until it was unrecognizable – but not before infinitely more had been asked of us than we could possibly perform. And, because everything had been against us, shame and anger overwhelmed me, effectively banishing all sense of liberation.

How I loathed it all! The Flying Fortresses and their almost arrogant contempt for our ineffectual attacks, the high command with its slights and humiliations, the heat of the Sicilian summer and the perpetual sunshine . . .

If I was to reach the mainland before sunset, it was high time I started for the airfield. The shadows had grown longer and in the late sunlight, as every afternoon in Sicily, the colours were beginning to glow.

My Me was standing immediately beside the runway. The small leather suitcase and sleeping-bag had been stuffed into the tiny baggage space behind the armour-plating. There was nothing to keep me now. The other pilots, as so recently in Tunisia, had taken off carrying ground crew in their fuselages. 'The poor man's Lufthansa' they called it. In my own Me 109 this space was taken up with war diaries and the officers' records. Bachmann had only just succeeded in wresting the ammunition box containing those documents from the grasp of a man who was about to consign it to the flames.

Something seemed to be holding me back, as though the mission with which we had been entrusted – and which we had 'failed' to carry out – was still not quite complete.

The silence was broken by the 'whop' of ammunition exploding in the fires on the airfield. Beyond the nearest hedge, the muzzles of the eighty-eight millimetre flak pointed vigilantly skywards from among the olive trees as though there were still something to be protected here. The telephones had been dismantled or destroyed. Sergeant Henrich and his monitoring section had long since abandoned their fairytale surroundings in the tower of the ancient fort and were now on their way to Milazzo.

The workmen had taken possession of the erstwhile operations room. Looking up towards Erice, I saw that the hut was in process of disintegration. First the roof disappeared, then the sides, then the ends.

The airmen in the Kübelwagen were looking at me out of the corners of their eyes as if asking themselves, 'When the hell is he going to take off?' I walked over to the Me and slowly, one by one, I began my preparations. Life-jacket. Pass harness between legs and tighten up. Strap flare cartridges to calves. Fold map to show route. (Not that a map was really necessary for a flight to Calabria. In this case navigation was absurdly simple.)

The airmen climbed silently onto the Me's wing and opened the plexiglass hood. As the parachute strap clicked home into the closure on my chest, the whine of the inertia starter began to grow louder. Everything was proceeding according to plan. The last take-off from Sicily was going to be no different from any other.

245

The engine was running smoothly. In accordance with a system to be found nowhere in the manuals, my eyes travelled over the instrument panel while at regular intervals I looked to right and left and scanned the air space behind and above me. A pilot flying alone had to be doubly careful. Once again, there were the accustomed smells – oil, coolant, dope and petrol – the reek peculiar to the Messerschmitt which came from the hot engine, the hot oil in the lines and the glycol in the cooling system. Every aircraft has a different smell.

The workmen outside the cave on Mount Erice looked up as I banked my Me to bring it round the cliff face. They stood there motionless. For a brief second I caught sight of our villa and then there was nothing but sea in front of me. I made a long detour northwards to fly round Palermo Bay. Above the town there was a haze out of which Mount Pelagrino rose, reflecting back the evening light.

The sun was directly behind me. At 13,000 feet I gently eased back the throttle and brought the engine cowling level with the dark rim of the horizon.

Where the mountains went sheer down into the water I could see, between my right wing tip and the revolving propeller, the pale ribbon of the coast road. High above it soared the snow-capped summit of Etna, easily recognizable through the triangular side window next to the thick blue-tinted armoured glass in front of the sights.

Along that coast road between Palermo and Messina my group, or rather the human component of my group, was making its way. Travelling separately in small convoys were tiny parties of men who had been despatched with orders to assemble where they could. How they would get across the straits was still not clear. There was said to be a shuttle service of Siebel ferries and pontoon craft but the Allies were making murderous attacks on the Straits of Messina. The area was flanked by a correspondingly large concentration of heavy flak. In my headphones little or nothing was to be heard of the din that usually accompanies aerial combat. Now, just before sunset, all was quiet. Only a whispering and crackling, then for a few seconds, the loud roar of transmitters being switched on and off, followed by a silence that was complete.

When I had flown to Trapani in the spring – at the beginning of April – the hillsides had been bright green and the mountain tops shrouded in rain clouds. I was then on my way to Africa and, as today, I was flying alone. The final phase of the war in Tunisia had begun and the Allies were pushing northwards through the Mareth line.

And today I, as the last of my group, was flying to the mainland and the evacuation of the island had begun. The mountain slopes were bare and scorched by the summer sun, yet only three months had gone by since that first flight. The extent to which the 'fortress of Europe' had shrunk was frightening.

Below me to the right lay Cefalù. I decided to fly northwards over the Lipari group of islands, giving a wide berth to the Straits of Messina. Even if by this time of day the fighters and Flying Fortresses were already on their way home, I would still be running the gauntlet of our flak and I had no desire to do that. The mountain tops were deep blue and above them the summit of Etna glowed like a torch. I set course for the southern tip of Calabria between the straits and Stromboli, over which a black cloud hovered.

The Straits of Messina, a bright strip of water framed between blue hills, reflected the evening sunlight. Slowly the outline of my wing moved over the glittering water until, for a moment, it formed a link between island and mainland. It was then that I became aware of innumerable little dark smudges dotting the sky to form a magnificently shaped dome over the straits. The heavy flak was putting up a vigorous defensive barrage against the Flying Fortresses.

The circular grass expanse of Vibo Valentia airfield was visible from afar, being the only levelled expanse of grass among the olive groves and thickly overgrown slopes of the ridge that runs down right into the toe of the Italian mainland at Reggio.

I brought my Me in at minimum speed towards the landing

marker which had been laid out where the airfield ended and the hillside began. Just before I touched down, the tops of the tall poplars went rushing past on either side of my wing tips.

Though the airfield had often been bombed it was little damaged by comparison with our landing grounds in Sicily. The hangars, however, which were situated to the east beside the road to Reggio, were in ruins. Bomb blast had pushed in the doors and torn the roofs to shreds. Although the many craters had been filled in and smoothed over, my aeroplane bounced on landing and I had to work hard at the rudder bar to prevent it ground-looping before coming to rest.

Only a few minutes later Colonel Larsen's car drew up beside me. As the officer responsible for fighter control here, he was to give me instructions about my group's future operations.

We sat in the grass beside my aircraft while Larsen tersely described the situation in Sicily. It was easy to see that the end was near. The total evacuation of the island had now been ordered and, in spite of the tremendous efforts made by the Allies to disrupt it, the withdrawal appeared to be taking place in orderly fashion.

There had been continuous bombing attacks in an attempt to bring the ferry service between island and mainland to a stand-still, but the flak had been putting up a massive barrage, forcing the bombers to take evasive action and interfering with their aim.

The field marshal had given orders that I was to assemble the group on the mainland and prepare for the air defence of Calabria and Apulia. We were, however, to avoid the larger airfields which were well known to the enemy. Possible alternatives were the stretches of arable land near Crotone, the Calabrian coastal strip near Catanzaro, or the relatively treeless plain of Basilicata. The choice of advanced landing grounds was left to me.

Good, I thought. New orders, new duties, new hopes! But for today I was on my own, without a group and without responsibility. I had only myself to think about. I didn't, however, want to stay where I was. Larsen agreed.

'All right, carry on to Apulia then, but hurry so that you can find somewhere to land before nightfall . . .'

Before I began my wide sweep round the town and port of Taranto, I saw the seemingly endless white sandy beach of Basilicata glide away under my fuselage. In the blue dusk the white surf was sparkling with phosphorescence. The airfield at Manduria was a long, narrow strip of land between vineyards and olive groves.

The lamps had already been lit in the adjoining cottages when I touched down on the springy turf.

With a German captain, I stood waiting for a car in front of the tent which combined the functions of flying control and administration.

'It's been pretty quiet here,' he said. 'Sometimes we see the heavies going over, but they haven't dropped anything on us yet. Night before last the British attacked Gelsenkirchen. The town's still in flames and there were heavy casualties among the civilian population. My people live in Gelsenkirchen.'

And since I made no answer, he continued:

'A few minutes ago we were listening to a broadcast from home and heard they'd raided Danzig last night. Just think, sir! Danzig!'

Night had fallen fast. I breathed in the scent of the pines and eucalyptus trees that grew behind the tent and listened with delight to the noisy chorus of crickets. The sky was dark purple and the trees stood out against it like paper cutouts.

Although the words 'Gelsenkirchen' and 'Danzig' were still ringing in my ears, I could do nothing to avert the overwhelming feeling of happiness that suddenly came over me. I was going into the town to spend the night in a clean, quiet hotel room. A Topolino ('Sorry, that's all we've got') was to take me to Lecce. I'd be all on my own. No one would come to seek me out – for who could have orders or instructions for me today? Tired though I was, I'd have a meal in a restaurant and drink a bottle of wine and look at the other diners, the people living carefree lives here, as though it were peacetime.

The Topolino came bouncing across the grass and drew up beside me.

'I'd like to be fetched at eight tomorrow. I'm flying to Foggia. Would you see that my machine's refuelled please.'

'Very well, sir. Goodnight.'

There was a lot of traffic on the road to the town. The fertile vineyards through which it ran extended right to the outskirts of Lecce. In the outlying part of the town, people were sitting outside their houses to enjoy the cool of the evening. Soldiers and their girls jumped for the side of the road when they heard our car coming.

The Hotel Grande Italia was in the Piazza Sant'd'Oronzo. Architecturally it harmonized with the rest of the town, being one of those large, stone-built palazzi called 'Grande Hotel', 'Hotel Roma' or 'Albergo Napoli' such as are to be found in any town worthy of the name. The porter carried up my modest baggage to the first floor where I was given a room with a window and balcony giving onto the piazza. The curtains were drawn because of the blackout. Placing my suitcase and sleeping-bag on the stand beside the bed, I put out the light and, drawing back the curtains, looked out of the window. The square was bathed in the twilight of a summer night. The great baroque façades of the houses round it seemed to glow as if giving off the sunlight they had soaked up during the day. They were the colour of pink marshmallows.

I lay down on the bed with my face towards the window so that I could see the starry sky. My tiredness was weighing me down. If I had closed my eyes for only a few seconds I should have fallen fast asleep. But I wanted to make the most of the evening. I wanted to take stock of the fact that I was alive, that I would be alive on the morrow and that I had the right to live. I wanted to sit at a table laid for dinner, with wine glasses and a napkin and cutlery. And I wanted to eat well, to sprinkle cheese over the *pasta* with a spoon, and I wanted to feel in my hand a dark bottle of red wine with its brightly coloured label and the seal stamped into the glass. I wanted to do all this slowly and deliberately, and with enjoyment. And round me there must be people. I saw them in my mind's eye – vivacious Apulians who, in their own way, chose to ignore the circumstances of the war and the fact that little more than a hundred miles away a lost battle was nearing its end. I imagined them arguing with spirit and propounding their theories, thus intimating that in their view it was high time all this business was over.

Unfortunately my appearance was far from perfect. At the last moment Tubby had just managed to wash a shirt for me, but my trousers were stained and crumpled. Not that anyone would take any notice of that. I got up and, going down the broad staircase, entered the little restaurant which threw just sufficient light onto the tables in the arcades outside for people to be able to eat at them. In Lecce no one worried too much about the blackout.

The tables, which were covered with red and white checked cloths, were surrounded by oleander bushes in full bloom. The arcades were occupied mainly by soldiers, but there were also a few local people whose animated conversation, mingled with cheerful exclamations and the laughter of women, filled the little square with the pleasant sound of their musical tongue.

I chose *past'asciutta* and delicious smoked ham and melon, accompanied by a heavy red *salice*. The bread was snowy white and its crust crackled when I bit into it.

Inside the restaurant a bar ran along the whole length of one wall. The wall itself consisted of a large sheet of mirror fitted with shelves on which stood a vast array of bottles with coloured labels. I was joined at my table by an Italian paratroop captain and his girlfriend. He sported a rakish little moustache and, even after he had sat down, he still kept on the red beret which he wore tipped jauntily over one eyebrow. He gesticulated constantly as he talked to emphasize what he was saying – and he never stopped talking.

Where could the others have landed? Perhaps in Bari, the air-field where nearly all the reserve aircraft for our group were held on arrival from the Reich. Or maybe in Foggia, where we maintained a small base camp for personnel and equipment. Then again they might have landed at Brindisi, Gioia del Colle or Taranto.

Bachmann, I felt sure, would put up at some luxurious hotel in Foggia and eat in one of the numerous restaurants which, as in peacetime, provided culinary delicacies for all tastes. Foggia was still deep in the base country – but for how long? Reinhold would be in Bari having 'language lessons' with his girlfriend. I wondered if they had in fact managed to arrange a meeting. The cab drivers there used to ask with a wink, '*Settanta-cinque?*' if their fares were German. Seventy-five was the number of a house accommodating girls of easy virtue. I felt pretty sure that there'd be some riotous parties there tonight.

If the British night bombers were now flying as far as Danzig, the Americans would not rest content until they had sent their huge armadas there by day. The Reichsmarschall would be furious and lay the blame on the fighters. The unfortunate survivors would roam about among the smoking rubble searching for their children and relations. Then, sick at heart and exhausted, they would return wearily to the endless routine of their factories and offices.

The battle in the plain west of Catania must have reached Gerbini by now. Tonight parachute troops were to be dropped to hold up the Allied advance so as to allow as many men as possible to cross the Straits of Messina.

In Foggia we wouldn't find any peace either. The heavies would begin their onslaught on the mainland as soon as Sicily had fallen.

Nothing was left of the strange attraction that drew us almost compulsively to aerial combat, first over the English Channel and then in Russia. The chivalry associated with the duel in the air, the readiness to accept challenge again and again had given way to a sense of vulnerability, and the pleasure we had once taken in fighting a sporting battle against equal odds had long since become a thing of the past.

A man with virtually no chance of survival grows disillusioned and bitter and is not inclined to mince his words. But our sarcasm had assumed forms incomprehensible to anyone who was not so vulnerable. In their isolation as nothing more than 'engines of destruction' (and failures at that!) the pilots became proud, almost arrogant, regarding as their equals only other airmen, or else parachutists or U-boat men.

They seldom referred now to the 'final victory' and to the days that would follow. They were repelled, too, by the pathos of newspaper articles about the front. The pomposity of journalistic propaganda elicited their scathing comments. They no longer had faith in anything whatsoever. Could this be incipient defeatism I wondered?

We suddenly became aware of the throb of a bomber's engine high overhead. The noise brought a momentary lull in the conversation round the tables but, as soon as it had died away in the distance, the little square once more became alive with the sound of voices. The red wine was heavy, and I felt numb with exhaustion. I rose and left the restaurant to go upstairs to my room. From the mirror the face of a stranger looked back at me, yellow and drawn.

When I put out the light the darkness seemed so intense that I felt a kind of panic rising up in me, but the linen sheets were deliciously cool and smelt of soap. Gradually I was invaded by an immense feeling of security.

Early the next day I'd fly to Bari to find out whether enough new machines had arrived there from the factories. In Foggia, Bachmann would have made the necessary preparations for our search for an airfield. We badly needed a new Fieseler Storch. I myself didn't favour the vast yellow corn fields near Crotone, since they were situated in an extensive malarial area. Moreover it would be unbearably hot there, and the dust raised when we took off would betray our position.

In the wooded, mountainous district of Sila, east of Cosenza, which rose to an altitude of more than three thousand feet, there were said to be large stretches of uncultivated pasture land which we might be able to convert into advanced landing grounds. The woods would provide good cover for our Mes.

It was to be hoped that there would be enough 'gunboats' among the aircraft in Bari – the kind, that is, which in addition to the 20 mm cannon firing through the propeller boss had two more mounted in pods under the wings.

It was lucky that the group still had a few vehicles in Foggia. We would drive to the depots and draw tents, tools and lifting tackle, new engines and all the thousand and one things to replace those that had been destroyed only this morning.

Once again we would not be given any time to recover. Perhaps a couple of days in Foggia, to make up our sleep and bathe in Manfredonia Bay.

We would have to practise our formation attacks against the Fortresses. We would have to keep close together, wing tip to wing tip, approaching head-on until 'the bomber's silhouette was exactly in the sights . . .'

Twenty-five Years Later

More than twenty-five years have gone by since the Allied landing in Sicily. The painful wounds inflicted in the days when bombs rained down on fighting soldiers and civilian population alike are now healed. For the Allies the landing meant that a door had been forced open, but for us Germans it was no more than a stage – and perhaps the decisive one – on the way to defeat, a road along which other milestones had been Stalingrad and Tunis.

Why, since then, should I have felt the wish to describe in detail this short episode of a war that lasted five and a half years? It was an episode that occupied barely twelve pages of my group's war diary, an episode dwarfed by the great battles and defeats of the war.

The events of those days engraved themselves deeply in my memory although the war left no time for lingering or retrospection. Compared with what ensued, the operations in Sicily dwindle into insignificance. My group accompanied the army in its retreat up the Italian peninsula, made a jump across to France for a few days to 'repel the invasion', was transferred to Rumania to hold back the Russian advance and then moved to the Reich, its final engagement being the defence of Berlin. The odyssey was to terminate in capture by the Russians.

The unit retained its identity but the wing and squadron commanders and pilots were either killed in action or 'replaced' – men like Straden, Zöhler, Godert, Bachmann and many others.

It was never my intention to write war memoirs, nor did I ever wish to make an original contribution to the documentation and history of the war. In the years after May 1945, first as a pottery painter and then as a junior advertising executive, I led the far from heroic and in many ways humdrum existence of an ordinary employee. Instead of flying streamlined fighters I was now handling calculating machines or dictating business letters. But the memories that constantly assailed me were not those of great air battles and victorious advances. Rather my mind would dwell on the days we spent in Sicily. It may have been the exceptional nature of the events that took place there which had left such an impression on me – exceptional because we were assigned a task which was incapable of execution. It was then I had realized that a turning point had come and that we were on the road to final defeat.

In my mind's eye I clearly see the faces of the young men for whom I was responsible. I see them as they were when they reported for the first time 'at the front', self-confident and psychologically prepared for the battle (of which they had only a hazy conception) by slogans such as 'the final victory will be ours', or 'the German soldier does not cede a foot of ground'.

They soon lost the superficial veneer acquired through ideological indoctrination in the Hitler Youth. The jargon of the Third Reich disappeared from their vocabulary and they became human beings who, out of self-preservation, drew ever closer to one another.

Once the newcomers had known what it was to lie in a slit trench during an air raid and to fly a sortie against the Flying Fortresses, they quickly adapted themselves to the flippant style of the old hands, those who, with scathing irony, made light of everything (though inherently they had become mature and serious-minded men who now lived only from one day to the next). During those days I can remember few cases in which our communal life was upset by anyone's insufferable behaviour, or lack of adaptability.

The Luftwaffe that entered the war was an incomplete weapon and, when that war had to be conducted against great powers on several fronts, the high command and its instrument were very far from adequate to the task that confronted them.

The first manual of aerial warfare (LdV 16) was produced under the first Chief of Air Staff. It was concerned mainly with air attack, air defence being relegated to second place.

Thus in 1939 the military conceptions that governed the Luftwaffe failed to take into account the possibilities and limitations of our own forces. Air warfare as an 'independent' factor – the destruction of the enemy's vital centres, aptly named 'strategic air warfare' by the Allies – was never consequentially planned by the Luftwaffe General Staff. Air offensives were instead to be conducted by means of medium-range bomber forces whose size and composition would enable them at best temporarily to disrupt the enemy potential but not to destroy it.

'Ural-Bomber' was the name given to the project for a big bomber which, however, never came into production. There can be no doubt that the economic resources of the Third Reich would never have permitted the construction of an air arm adequate for the conduct of both air defence and strategic air warfare with big bombers.

At the outbreak of war, the defence of the Reich had been grossly neglected. The intention – an over-optimistic one – was that active air defence should devolve almost exclusively on the anti-aircraft artillery. There was no overall organization for the conduct of defensive warfare since air raids on the Reich were not anticipated.

When the British began their night raids – shortly to be followed by American daylight attacks – it was too late to repair these omissions.

Whereas Göring, like Richthofen before him, had himself been a serving pilot and hence must have been aware that air warfare had come to be an independent factor in war, many Luftwaffe generals and high-ranking officers were of military or naval origin and very few of them succeeded in understanding the different laws governing air warfare. They did their best by qualifying as pilots or observers, but since few of them had 'grown up' with this new weapon, their notions of air warfare derived from the narrower conceptions of land warfare.

I

Moreover, during the course of the war the high command grew increasingly out of touch with the fighting component of the air arm. The former's inability, despite the almost revolutionary advances in the field of aeronautics, to concentrate on development and production in a desperate defensive situation in which we were assailed from all sides did not remain concealed from the combat units.

To the junior officer the high command's mistakes and wrong decisions became obvious at about the time the Battle of Britain was drawing to a close. That battle had inflicted on the fighter arm – then only five years old – losses in men and material which, relatively speaking, could not be made good. The extension of the air war and the beginning of the Allied bombing offensive against the Reich eliminated any possibility there might have been of conducting with material superiority either an offensive war in the air or an effective aerial defence. The reaction increasingly took the form, not of careful calculation and organization, but of improvisation and over-precipitate action with insufficient means. The great technological advances in the field of jet propulsion and rocket techniques could not change the course of events.

The high command began to compensate for its mistakes and omissions with a 'psychological war effort'. The demands on the courage and endurance of the fighting forces were stepped up to the point of ruthlessness. The self-immolation of the German soldier was expected to succeed where equipment had failed.

At the very point when a realistic assessment of military prospects would have readily revealed the inevitability of defeat, calculation and foresight were cast to the winds in favour of that pathetic unknown quantity, sacrifice and heroism, which has played so disastrous a role in German military history.

A quarter of a century of political development has since taken place. During that time we Germans have achieved a position in the world which could hardly have been prognosticated in 1945. This is said without any kind of chauvinistic pride.

Germany is still divided. Its western section, though enjoying only limited freedom of action, is nevertheless a sovereign state and a free one which is worthy of being defended. Economically the Federal Republic is a power; militarily she is a valuable and esteemed ally. We possess a modern air arm whose fighting forces have been placed wholly at the disposal of NATO.

This means that we are under the obligation, so far as aviation and air armaments are concerned, to plan independently and to develop or produce those technological weapons and materials which we need and can afford. For the same thing still applies today to every fighting force: good soldiers, excellent morale and heroism in action can never make up for lack of expertise. To fail to provide an air arm with adequate technological equipment and to persist in that failure is as irresponsible now as it was in the Second World War. All countries are under an obligation to prevent this happening and such, indeed, is the constant preoccupation of the German Air Force.

If this erstwhile group commander were to be asked today what principles, in view of his experience during six years of war and twenty-five of peace, he would adopt as immutable and indispensable axioms for his present office, his reply would take the form of five theses, of which the first two require no comment:

1. At our stage of civilization war can only be regarded with abhorrence. The use of force between nations provides no solution to their problems. Defence measures will remain necessary, however, so long as there is a threat of violence.

2. In the sphere of defence measures, the development everywhere is towards vast, supranational formations. For a country like the German Federal Republic, if she is not to remain perpetually at risk as a neutral, integration into the Western alliance is the only possible course, a course which also helps to reduce the danger of narrowly nationalistic action.

3. Armaments, particularly air armaments, represent an

advanced technology. Only countries with sufficient technological and industrial potential can develop and produce weapons systems that are up to date and of high quality and, having produced them, keep them properly maintained and equipped. Co-operation and division of labour at supranational level make it easier for a country to shoulder this burden.

The deterrent value of modern fighting forces is wholly determined by the extent to which they participate in technological progress. They quickly become obsolescent and of small political influence if they are not constantly developing. Hence they involve considerable investment which not only requires a large share of public funds but ties it down over a long period.

Experience has shown that theoretical military security requirements, which derive solely from the threat of attack, often exceed the limits of possibility. But what is possible is determined on the one hand by the financial resources of the state (as also its human resources) and, on the other, by the economic and technological ability to produce modern defensive weapons or, if these are produced abroad, to master them and control them in accordance with modern management techniques.

Now where state funds are concerned, there are definite limits on the amounts that can be allotted to defence. If the essence of political leadership consists in the 'co-ordination of the aims of state', the art of legislature (which includes the allocation of funds), consists in balancing the aim of defence against other political aims in such a way as to satisfy the demand for security on the one hand and, on the other, to maintain the stability of the national economy. An equally decisive factor is the efficiency of defence technology.

Independent and efficient armaments production demands a corresponding capacity for research and development, a reserve of scientists and engineers – in other words, all that the Americans describe as 'know-how'. But even where there is no domestic production, the mastering of imported systems demands considerable expenditure and much experience in the sphere of 'systems management'. This must be taken into account when examining the feasibility of military requirements. Here again a realistic assessment of a country's limitations will lead to the decision that only a given proportion of the theoretical demand can be fulfilled. And here too, as any responsible soldier would at once admit, the demands of security must be so tailored to the capacity of the whole as not to impair that whole. By 'whole' in this instance we mean the general civilizing endeavour of science, research and technology for the welfare of the people who live in the state.

As is evident from the example of the space nations, the maintenance of a modern air force bears a certain relation to this civilizing sphere of activity or, at least, reflects it to a considerable degree. The same is equally true of a state with insufficient resources to undertake its own exploration of space.

A country's air force and its aviation are only two of the criteria by which its technological standing is measured. And today a country's technological standing determines
– its weight and authority *vis-à-vis* other nations,
– the effectiveness of its own defence,
– the efficiency of its economy,
– the welfare and well-being of its citizens within the ordered structure of the state,
determines, in short, what we call the 'future'.

4. Defence technology demands material and, above all, intellectual effort. It is not enough simply to possess weapons systems. A nation must be capable of maintaining them in the highest state of readiness by the application of technological management techniques; it must be able to develop them and make provision for their replacement. This in turn requires new forms of thought and leadership in the field of defence technology. Air forces are major technological concerns, in which tactics and technology go hand in hand.

The tactical application of combat procedures is coming to be increasingly determined by the imperatives of technological processes. Inevitably this restricts the scope of individual military decisions. It is becoming increasingly difficult to reach correct decisions in matters of planning and armaments because the importance of experience recedes as forecasting becomes more accurate. Traditional military methods of appreciating a situation are rapidly giving way to accurate forecasting which in turn increasingly demands precise calculations based on vast quantities of data. This necessarily entails some degree of centralization in planning and command.

In the civilian and military fields these manifestations are sometimes regarded with disfavour because of the constraint they are held to impose. Again, it would seem that, in the sphere of the armed forces, the Second Industrial Revolution has not been generally understood. And the above-mentioned technological constraint is a source of particular disquiet. There is a tendency to look upon it as a form of thraldom to factors that are barely comprehensible. But this is due to the failure to realize that a full appreciation of the technological factors would to a large extent eliminate the element of constraint. It is only when a military commander has understood the scientific and technological factors that he becomes, in the true sense of the word, the master of his weapons rather than their servant. He has gained freedom of decision because he is able to recognize alternatives where others see only constraint.

The main consequences as far as the control of the Air Force is concerned are as follows: Our technological planning must extend far into the future. This planning postulates appropriate forecasting with regard to both the potential enemy's and one's own technological capacity. This is possible only in concert with allies, the aviation industry and science. We need a command structure capable of measuring up to the inescapable demands of technology. 'Systems management' is not just an empty phrase; our practice here must accord with its principles.

We need a command technology. Technology calls for technological leadership. Electronic command systems are bringing data processing into the operations room. We must learn how to handle them properly.

This gives rise to new methods of command. In complex circumstances correct predictions can only be made with the aid of operations research.

At the same time the nature of command is changing. It is becoming less *authoritarian* and more *co-operative*. Nevertheless a military order must still retain its ascendancy. Once it has been issued the only restrictions that can apply to it are those of the Soldier's Law. To the soldier one of the most convincing features of the present constitutional state is the fact that his duties and rights are now laid down by law. It is sometimes forgotten that this has never happened before in the history of the German armed forces.

5. While the armed forces have a claim to a certain proportion of the country's labour force, they are also under an obligation to provide the young citizen with a training which will be of benefit to him on his return to civilian employment. The Air Force offers an exceptional opportunity in this respect. It should form part of the open industrial society which constitutes the human way of life in this, the latter part of the twentieth century.

Technological methods and the men who control them are the two main components from which an air force derives its efficiency and combat effectiveness. Leaving out of account the larger issues of the 1939–45 war, an inquiry into the causes of the defeat of the German Army and Air Force reveals that the crucial mistakes of the then high command lay in their mismanagement both of technology and of men. It is the purpose of the present book to demonstrate this from the viewpoint of the fighting soldier.

Apart from certain subsidiary problems which constantly recur, the development and control of technological methods in the form of weapons and equipment systems have shown satisfactory progress. In this sphere we have had to catch up with the lessons already learned by other air forces in their continuous process of evolution.

A problem that still remains is how to integrate individuals into the general organization of the Air Force. The structure of our corps of officers and NCOs does not accord with the demands of modern technology.

Co-operation between the upper technological strata and the military high command is still not close enough. The combat effectiveness of an air force depends on a proper relation between expenditure on training and the useful employment of its officers during their period of service.

Our concept of the officer no longer corresponds to the rapid progress of technological development which is the particular characteristic of the Air Force. Nor does it correspond to the sociological structure of an open industrial society based on the division of labour and on individual performance. Hence it also fails to correspond to the individual who, being employed in the technological sphere of the Air Force, is part and parcel of that society. Indeed, there can be no doubt whatever that the traditional image of the officer is out of keeping with a society in the throes of the Second Industrial Revolution and already in process of becoming a society based on the tertiary industries. Changes, some revolutionary and some evolutionary, are being wrought in this form of society by automation, cybernetics and electronic data processing; in other words, the human intellect is being complemented, replaced or reinforced by technological devices.

The new type of officer or NCO should be one who, after a limited period of practical training and activity in the Air Force, returns to the community whence he came. We have found from investigation that other countries have largely succeeded in integrating their armed forces into the civilian sector of society, namely into civilian educational and employment structures.

From the beginning, the reformers and builders of the Bundeswehr have taken for granted the demand for real (not just 'social') integration. The intention is that the Bundeswehr, unlike the Reichswehr (often described in retrospect as a 'state within a state'), should be fully integrated, as an army of both conscripts *and* volunteers, into society and the state.

This aspect is closely related to the internal control of technologically equipped combat forces. Such control comprises, amongst other things, up-to-date man-management – and here 'up-to-date' can only mean 'commensurate with our technological age'.

When the commanders of a technologically equipped combat force put forward their requirements in accordance with the logical conclusions they have drawn from the growing implications of technology, they are sometimes reproached with unduly emphasizing the rational-technological aspect to the detriment of the individual with all his needs, emotions and weaknesses. This point of view is as superficial as it is false. In fact the opposite is true: for as long as there have to be armies they will, at our present stage of civilization and whether we like it or not, have to be technological armies. Now soldiers in technological armies cannot exist unless they derive constant satisfaction from their profession. Such satisfaction is only attainable if:
– they are provided with good technological means of defence;
– their training, employment, pay and status is commensurate with the technological level of those means of defence.

A country and its way of life will not be defended, in case of need, by automatons but by thinking and feeling individuals who must be both willing and prepared to undertake that defence. Humanity clearly demands that they should be given the best that training and technology can provide.

Such was not the case in the episode described in the *Diary of a Fighter Commander*.

By the time those events took place, the leaders of the Reich had abandoned every standard of responsible action, even as regards their own soldiers.

It is the responsibility of every one of us to ensure that no such thing ever happens again.

Sources

Alexander, Field Marshal Sir Harold. 'The Surrender of Sicily'. *London Gazette*, February 1948.

Churchill, Winston S. *Closing the Ring*. The Second World War, vol 5. London: Cassell, 1952.

Deichmann, General d Fl a D Paul. *Die Luftschlacht im westlichen Mittelmeer, vom Verlust Tunesiens bis zur Landung in Sizilien*. Studie. Neustadt, January 1948.

Europe: Torch to Pointblank, August 1942 to December 1943. Army Air Forces in World War II, vol 2. The University of Chicago Press, 1949.

Feuchter, Georg W. *Geschichte des Luftkrieges, Entwicklung und Zukunft*. Bonn: Athenaeum Verlag, 1954.

Garland, Lieutenant Colonel Albert N. 'Sicily and the Surrender of Italy'. *The Mediterranean Theater of Operations*. United States Army in World War II. Washington, 1965.

Kriegstagebuch des Geschwaderstabes des Jagdgeschwaders 77, Feldpost Nr L-39410 – Lg Pa München, Begonnen: 12.6.43 – Abgeschlossen: 3.11.43.

Kriegstagebuch des Hauptmanns Armin Köhler, Jagdgeschwader 77.

Kriegstagebuch des Oberkommandos der Wehrmacht.

Kurowski, Franz. *Das Tor zur Festung Europa*. Die Wehrmacht im Kampf, vol 41. Neckargemünd: Kurt Vowinckel Verlag, 1966.

Morison, Samuel Eliot. *Sicily–Palermo–Anzio*. History of the United States Naval Operations in World War II, vol 9. Washington: Little, Brown, Atlantic Monthly Press Book, 1954.

Völker, Karl-Heinz. *Geschichte der deutschen Luftwaffe*. Stuttgart: Deutsche Verlags-Anstalt, 1967.